Study Guide

Business Communication
Process & Product

FIFTH EDITION

Prepared by

James M. Dubinsky
Director, Professional Writing Program
Virginia Polytechnic Institute and State University

Mary Ellen Guffey
Emerita Professor of Business
Los Angeles Pierce College
Woodland Hills, California

THOMSON
＊ ™
SOUTH-WESTERN

Australia · Canada · Mexico · Singapore · Spain · United Kingdom · United States

THOMSON
™
SOUTH-WESTERN

Study Guide for Business Communication: Process & Product, 5th Edition
James M. Dubinsky and Mary Ellen Guffey

VP/Editorial Director:
Jack W. Calhoun

Acquisitions Editor:
Keith Chasse

Developmental Editor:
Mary Draper

Sr. Marketing Manager:
Larry Qualls

Sr. Production Editor:
Deanna Quinn

Technology Project Editor:
Kelly Reid

Manufacturing Coordinator:
Diane Lohman

Production House:
WordCrafters Editorial Services, Inc.

Cover Designer:
Imbue Design/Kim Torbeck, Cincinnati

Cover Illustration:
Brian Jensen

Printer:
Darby Printing Company

For more information about our
products, contact us at:
Thomson Learning Academic
Resource Center
1-800-423-0563

Thomson Higher Education
5191 Natorp Boulevard
Mason, OH 45040
USA

Asia (including India)
Thomson Learning
5 Shenton Way
#01-01 UIC Building
Singapore 068808

Australia/New Zealand
Thomson Learning Australia
102 Dodds Street
Southbank, Victoria 3006
Australia

Canada
Thomson Nelson
1120 Birchmount Road
Toronto, Ontario
M1K 5G4
Canada

Latin America
Thomson Learning
Seneca, 53
Colonia Polanco
11560 Mexico
D.F.Mexico

UK/Europe/Middle East/Africa
Thomson Learning
High Holborn House
50/51 Bedford Row
London WC1R 4LR
United Kingdom

Spain (including Portugal)
Thomson Paraninfo
Calle Magallanes, 25
28015 Madrid, Spain

Preface

We designed this Study Guide to help you master chapter concepts and to expand your communication skills. Like *Business Communication: Process and Product, 5e,* it contains many visual elements to enhance its readability and interest.

Each Study Guide chapter contains similar elements to help you master course content, practice key principles, and expand your communication skills.

- **Review of key concepts.** A variety of questions (including true-false, fill-in, multiple-choice, and matching) outline key chapter concepts. These questions include page references in the textbook so that you can easily confirm answers and review your responses.

- **Career Track Spelling.** Because in any career you will be judged by your communication skills—including your ability to spell—you have an opportunity to hone those skills in regular exercises. Chapter 1 reviews useful spelling guidelines, and each subsequent chapter includes a self-checked exercise. The complete list of spelling words, from which most of the words are taken, appears in Appendix A.

- **Career Track Vocabulary.** A wide vocabulary enables you to express your ideas clearly. To expand your word power, each chapter includes challenging vocabulary words, along with 5 or 6 confusing words for you to master. Appendix A contains the complete list and definitions of confusing words.

- **Competent Language Usage Essentials (C.L.U.E.).** Each chapter concentrates on a few guidelines that review English grammar, punctuation, and usage. Particular attention is given to troublesome concepts that often cause business communicators to stumble. C.L.U.E. review exercises and Super C.L.U.E. (cumulative) reviews help you master these guidelines.

We have also included features that should help you develop specific skills.

- **Career track application and critical thinking questions.** In chapters that teach letter-, memo-, and report-writing, you have the opportunity to respond to a realistic assignment that applies your learning. Critical thinking questions help you analyze the assignment and organize your response. After preparing a document, you can turn to the solutions in Appendix B and compare your response with the key to see how you stack up. Naturally, you'll want to complete your application exercise before examining the key.

- **Employment Interview Kit.** In this edition of the Study Guide, you'll find an Employment Interview Kit to supplement Chapter 16, Employment Communication. The kit includes tips for fighting fear and for sending positive nonverbal messages. Most important are the lists of commonly asked interview questions (and some answers!), as well as questions for you to ask. Use this kit to help you ace your next interview!

Learning is a process. Begin by reading and studying the textbook chapter. Then complete the exercises in the Study Guide that supplement and reinforce the concepts presented in that chapter. We believe that your efforts will be rewarded with enhanced skills that will pay big dividends for you and your career.

Jim Dubinsky and Mary Ellen Guffey

Contents

UNIT THREE • BUSINESS CORRESPONDENCE

UNIT FOUR • REPORTS AND PROPOSALS

UNIT FIVE • PRESENTATIONS

Employment Interview Kit   187

Appendix A   199

Appendix B: Solutions   202

Chapter 1

Communicating at Work

CHAPTER REVIEW

Indicate whether the following statements are true or false by using T *or* F.

_____ 1. The most successful players in the new world of work will be those with highly developed communication skills, including the abilities to listen, write, read, and speak effectively. (Obj. 1, p. 4)

_____ 2. Global competition and team-based projects are having little effect on the workplace. (Obj. 1, p. 4)

_____ 3. As a skilled business communicator, you must develop a tool kit of new communication skills to use new resources such as text messaging and wireless networking effectively. (Obj. 1, p. 6)

_____ 4. Because communication's central objective is the transmission of meaning, the process is successful only when the sender knows exactly what to transmit. (Obj. 2, p.11)

_____ 5. Feedback helps receivers evaluate messages. (Obj. 2, p. 13)

_____ 6. Recognizing that the communication process is sensitive and susceptible to breakdown is a major step toward achieving successful transmission of information. (Obj. 3, p. 14)

_____ 7. The three basic functions of business communication are to inform, to persuade, and to promote goodwill. (Obj. 4, p. 15)

_____ 8. To improve the flow of information, many companies have restricted open communication and produced policies that limit communication channels. (Obj. 5, p. 21)

_____ 9. Obstacles to the horizontal flow of communication include prejudice, ego involvement, and turf wars. (Obj. 5, p. 23)

_____ 10. Many businesses know that they face less litigation, less resentment, and less government regulation if they are ethical. (Obj. 6, p. 24)

Multiple Choice

Choose the best answer.

11. Successful communication in the new global marketplace requires developing new skills and attitudes such as cultural knowledge and sensitivity,
    a. quick reaction time, and flexibility.
    b. patience, and knowledge of two languages.
    c. flexibility, and patience.
    d. flexibility, and good decision-making ability. (Obj. 1, p. 5)

12. To conduct meetings with associates around the world, companies use technologies such as
    a. e-mail and text messaging.
    b. text messaging and teleconferencing.
    c. teleconferencing and e-mail.
    d. teleconferencing and videoconferencing. (Obj. 1, p. 6)

13. As a knowledge worker, you can expect to
    a. work with upper-level managers only.
    b. work with words, figures, and data.
    c. benefit from physical labor, raw materials, and capital.
    d. work at home and telecommute. (Obj. 1, p. 9)

14. Physical distractions that can disrupt oral communication include
    a. faulty acoustics, noisy surroundings, and poor cell phone connections.
    b. faulty acoustics, thick walls, and noisy surroundings.
    c. noisy surroundings, poor cell phone connections, and poor listening skills.
    d. faulty acoustics, poor listening skills, and poor cell phone connections. (Obj. 3, p. 14)

Short Answer

15. Name four obstacles to interpersonal communication. (Obj. 3, pp. 13–14)

16. List three technologies that have speeded up the flow of communication. (Obj. 4, p. 17)

17. List five steps in the communication process. (Obj. 2, p. 11)

18. List five ways to improve the upward flow of information. (Obj. 5, p. 22)

19. List three disadvantages of oral communication. (Obj. 4, p. 18)

20. What five questions can you ask yourself when you are facing an ethical dilemma? (Obj. 6, pp. 28–29)

Matching

Identify the meaning of each of the following key terms by selecting a term from Column B to match its definition in Column A. Use each term only once; the first answer is provided for you! Some of the terms are common words, but their meanings may be special in this context.

Column A

b 21. Transmission of information and meaning

_____ 22. Converting an idea into words or gestures

_____ 23. Miscommunication resulting when individuals have different meanings for words

_____ 24. Translating a message from symbols into meaning

_____ 25. Verbal or nonverbal response flowing back to sender

_____ 26. Combination of your experiences, education, culture, expectations, attitudes, and personality through which messages are filtered

_____ 27. Honesty, integrity, fairness, and concern for others

_____ 28. Medium that physically transmits a message (letter, telephone, fax, etc.)

_____ 29. Anyone who works with technology

_____ 30. Informal communication channel within organizations

Column B

a. information worker

b. communication

c. encoding

d. grapevine

e. principles of ethical behavior

f. filtering

g. decoding

h. channel

i. frame of reference

j. feedback

k. bypassing

l. horizontal communication

Now that you've reviewed the chapter concepts, check your responses at the end of this guide. For items that you missed, reread the relevant material in the chapter to be sure you understand the basic concepts.

CAREER TRACK SPELLING

In any professional or business career, you will be judged by your communication skills, including your spelling. In one study, business managers revealed that they had significantly less confidence in employees who could not spell. One executive explained, "Poor spelling . . . can be a reflection of poor basic habits, training, intelligence, and diligence."

In this section, you will work on strengthening your spelling skills. Although spell-check programs solve many spelling problems at the computer, such software cannot be with you every moment of your life. When you are away from a computer, you must be capable of spelling words correctly. Even at the computer such programs do not detect all errors. The wrong word spelled correctly (such as *their, for,* and *there*) will not be detected by a spell-check program.

Spelling Pretest

Here's a brief spelling pretest to help you assess your present skills. Write the correct spelling for each word, and then check your answers at the end of the guide.

31.	calandar	_____	35.	endispensable	_____
32.	concensis	_____	36.	knowlegjible	_____
33.	defandent	_____	37.	pirmenant	_____
34.	eksagerate	_____	38.	rekemendation	_____

Three Approaches to Improving Spelling

If your spelling pretest results were disappointing, you are certainly not alone. Most people are not born with innate spelling skills. Luckily, spelling is a skill that can be developed, just as skills in adding, subtracting, and typing can be developed. Most of us, though, need to practice to improve. Here are three techniques that have met with varying degrees of success:

- **Rules or guidelines.** The spelling of English words is consistent enough to justify the formulation of a few spelling rules, perhaps more appropriately called guidelines, since the generalizations in questions are not invariably applicable. In other words, such guidelines are helpful but do not always hold true.

- **Mnemonics.** Another approach to improving one's ability to spell involves the use of mnemonics or memory devices. For example, the word *principle* might be associated with the word *rule*, to form in the mind of the speller a link between meaning and the spelling of *principle*. To spell *capitol*, one might think of the *dome* of the capitol building and focus on the *o*'s in both words. The use of mnemonics can be an effective device for the improvement of spelling only if the speller makes a real effort to develop the necessary memory hooks.

- **Rote learning.** A third approach to the improvement of spelling centers on memorization. The speller studies the word until it can be readily reproduced in the mind's eye.

The 1-2-3 Spelling Plan

Proficiency in spelling, of course, is not attained without concentrated effort. Here's a plan to follow in studying a list of spelling words:

- Is a spelling guideline applicable? If so, select the appropriate guideline, and study the word in relation to that guideline.

- If no guideline applies, can a memory device be created to help you recall the word?

- If neither a guideline nor a memory device will work, the word must be memorized. Look at the word carefully. Pronounce it. Write it or repeat it until you can visualize all of its letters in your mind's eye.

Spelling Guides

Guide 1: Write *i* before *e* except after *c* and when it sounds like *a*, as in *neighbor* and *weigh*.

i before *e*		Except after *c*	Sounds like *a*
achieve	grief	ceiling	beige
belief	ingredient	conceive	eight
believe	mischief	deceive	freight
convenient	piece	perceive	reign

Exceptions: caffeine, either, height, neither, seize

Guide 2: For most words ending in an *e*, the final *e* is dropped when the word is joined to a suffix beginning with a vowel (such as *ing*, *able*, or *al*). The final *e* is retained when a suffix beginning with a consonant (such as *ment*, *less*, *ly*, or *ful*) is joined to such a word.

Final *e* dropped	Final *e* retained
believe, believing	arrange, arrangement
care, caring	require, requirement
hope, hoping	hope, hopeless
desire, desirable	like, likely
move, movable	definite, definitely

Exceptions: acknowledgment, argument, judgment, ninth, truly, wholly

Guide 3: When *able* or *ous* is added to words ending in *ce* or *ge*, the final *e* is retained if the *c* or *g* is pronounced softly (as in *change* or *peace*).

advantage, advantageous	change, changeable
courage, courageous	service, serviceable
outrage, outrageous	manage, manageable

Guide 4: Words ending in a *y* that is preceded by a consonant normally change the *y* to *i* before all suffixes except those beginning with an *i*.

y preceded by consonant; change *y* to *i*	*y* preceded by vowel; do not change *y* to *i*
accompany, accompaniment	annoy, annoying, annoyance
company, companies	attorney, attorneys
industry, industrious	
secretary, secretaries	**Do not change *y* to *i* when adding *ing***
carry, carriage	accompany, accompanying
try, tried	apply, applying
empty, emptiness	study, studying

Guide 5: If one-syllable words or two-syllable words accented on the second syllable end in a single consonant preceded by a single vowel, the final consonant is doubled before the addition of a suffix beginning with a vowel.

One-syllable words	Two-syllable words
can, canned	acquit, acquitting, acquittal
drop, dropped	admit, admitted, admitting
get, getting	commit, committed, committing
plan, planned	occur, occurrence, occurred
slip, slipped	prefer, preferring (BUT *preference* has no double *r* because the accent shifts to the first syllable)

Guide 6: In adding prefixes or suffixes, retain all the letters in the root word. For example, when the prefix *mis* is added to the word *spell*, a double letter results (*misspell*). Don't be tempted to drop it.

Prefix	+	Root word		Root word	+	Suffix
dis		satisfied = dissatisfied		accidental		ly = accidentally
ir		relevant = irrelevant		incidental		ly = incidentally
il		literate = illiterate		clean		ness = cleanness
un		necessary = unnecessary		even		ness = evenness

On the other hand, do not supply additional letters when adding prefixes to root words.

Prefix	+	Root word
dis		appoint = disappoint
dis		satisfied = dissatisfied
mis		take = mistake

Guide 7: Pronounce words carefully so that all their syllables can be heard. Note the following words and letters that are sometimes omitted.

February	quantity	government
congratulation	representative	surprise

Spelling Challenge

Every study guide chapter will include a spelling challenge. Many of the words come from the list of 160 frequently misspelled words in Appendix A. The pretest words were from this same list. Make it your goal to master those words (and more) by the end of this course.

In the following groups identify misspelled words and write correct versions in the spaces provided. More than one misspelled word may appear in a group. Write C if all are correct.

_____	39.	grateful	usage	yield	paide
_____	40.	attornies	likely	manageable	valuable
_____	41.	unnecessary	suprise	fiscal	represenative
_____	42.	accidently	writting	preference	applying
_____	43.	achieve	decieve	definitly	courageous
_____	44.	congradulation	seize	incredable	hopeless
_____	45.	convenient	changeable	industrous	applying
_____	46.	companys	procedure	irelevant	occurrence
_____	47.	permanent	occured	goverment	requirement
_____	48.	biege	servicable	weakday	valleys

Now check your answers with the solutions at the end of the guide. If you're like most business writers, some words cause you more trouble than others. A good way to conquer your own spelling monsters is to make a special list of them and practice frequently.

My Spelling Monsters

List each troublesome word. Be sure to spell it correctly. Then write it four or more times. Review this page often to help you vanquish these spelling demons.

_____

_____

_____

_____

_____

CAREER TRACK VOCABULARY

Expressing ideas clearly requires an extensive and precise vocabulary. To help you expand your career vocabulary, every study guide chapter presents carefully selected words. Some of these words will become part of your reading vocabulary; others will become part of your speaking and writing vocabulary.

Use your dictionary to define the words in Column A. Then select the best definition in Column B to match each word in Column A.

		Column A		Column B
_____	49.	abut	a.	pardon, vindicate
_____	50.	accrue	b.	pacify, calm
_____	51.	acquit	c.	clever, skillful
_____	52.	adroit	d.	touch, adjoin
_____	53.	allay	e.	deposition, written avowal
_____	54.	affidavit	f.	accumulate, amass

Choose the best meaning for the following underlined words.

_____ 55. Good business <u>acumen</u>, a superior product, and efficient service all contribute to an entrepreneur's success.

    a. partners   b. accountants   c. knowledge

_____ 56. Despite appearing <u>affable</u>, the manager had a reputation for outbursts of anger whenever the production line slowed.

    a. unfriendly   b. pleasant   c. acrimonious

_____ 57. Tabloid headlines <u>allude</u> to sensational news, but their stories are more bizarre than newsworthy.

    a. refer   b. inflate   c. repudiate

_____ 58. Working conditions will <u>ameliorate</u> when we move from these cramped quarters into a suite of offices.

    a. brighten   b. decline   c. improve

_____ 59. In a clever <u>analogy</u>, the Canadian prime minister said that living next to the United States was like sleeping with an elephant: when it rolls over you know it.

    a. distinction   b. comparison   c. divergence

_____ 60. His will specified that each of his grandchildren would receive an <u>annuity</u>.

    a. bond   b. stock certificate   c. annual payment

_____ 61. The customer service department explained that the delay in shipping was an <u>anomaly</u> caused by the recent hurricanes.

    a. exception   b. surprise   c. interlude

_____ 62. Voter <u>apathy</u> caused a low turnout at the polls.

    a. anger   b. indifference   c. despair

Confusing Words

Because words like accede and exceed sound or look alike, they create much confusion. In each chapter you will review a small group of these confusing words. The complete list is located in Appendix A of this study guide. Study the confusing words below, and then insert your choices in the following exercise.

accede:	to agree or consent	*advice:*	suggestion, opinion
exceed:	over a limit	*advise:*	to counsel or recommend

adverse: unfavorable, antagonistic
averse: unwilling, opposed to

63. Because of _____ economic circumstances, profits are slipping.

64. By taking her supervisor's _____, Ms. Kent was quickly integrated into the company.

65. If the union will _____ to the demands of management, production may resume.

66. Although she was generally _____ to buying anything on credit, she had to borrow to purchase a home.

67. The banker sought to _____ the Smiths not to worry about the short-term rise in interest rates.

68. These last two transactions will cause you to _____ your credit account limit.

Look back over the 20 vocabulary words in this chapter. Select five new words that you would like to own. To "own" a word, you must be able to use it correctly in a sentence. Double-check the meanings of your selections in a dictionary. Then write a sentence for each of your words.

_____

_____

_____

_____

_____

_____

Chapter 2

Communicating in Small Groups and Teams

CHAPTER REVIEW

Indicate whether the following statements are true or false by using T *or* F.

_____ 1. Experience on teams is one of the key skills recruiters look for in job candidates. (Obj. 1, p. 42)

_____ 2. While teams are not a panacea for workplace problems, they function as the primary performance unit in most models of future organizations. (Obj. 1, p. 42)

_____ 3. During the storming phase of team development, a good leader should avoid setting limits, controlling the chaos, or offering suggestions. (Obj. 2, p. 45)

_____ 4. Team members play many different roles when they work together in groups. These roles can be grouped together into three categories: task roles, relationship roles, and functional roles. (Obj. 2, p. 46)

_____ 5. Two common response patterns for dealing with conflict are *compromise* and *accommodation/smoothing*. (Obj. 2, p. 48)

_____ 6. Effective teams avoid groupthink by striving for commonality among members, choosing those who agree on key issues. (Obj. 2, p. 49)

_____ 7. The most creative teams have males and females, as well as people who differ in age, training, social background, and experience. (Obj. 3, p. 50)

_____ 8. Team projects work best when members establish ground rules and follow guidelines related to preparing, planning, collecting information for, organizing, rehearsing, and evaluating projects. (Obj. 4, p. 53)

_____ 9. A meeting consists of two or more individuals who gather to pool information, solicit feedback, clarify policy, and solve problems. (Obj. 5, p. 55)

_____ 10. Collaboration tools include screen sharing, instant messaging, and hot-desking. (Obj. 6, p. 61)

Fill in the Blank

Use the listed words to complete the following sentences. You may use a word only once.

Team Skills

consensus	ground rules	individuals	norming
deadlines	group	interdependently	task
dysfunctional	groupthink	joining	team
goals	independently	leadership	unresolved

11. A team is a group of individuals who interact over time to achieve a purpose. A _____ is a collection of three or more individuals who think of themselves as a unit but who may work independently. (Obj. 1, p. 43)

12. Some organizations are creating _virtual teams,_ which are defined as groups of people who work _____ with a shared purpose across space, time, and organizational boundaries using technology. (Obj. 1, p. 43)

13. If you play the role of attacker or joker, you are disrupting the group and slowing its progress by serving in a _____ group role. (Obj. 2, p. 47)

14. Most teams struggle through disruptive, although ultimately constructive, team-building stages. These stages include forming, storming, _____, and performing. (Obj. 2, pp. 44–46)

15. Most teams experience some conflict. However, _____ conflict can destroy productivity and seriously undermine morale. (Obj. 2, p. 48)

16. When teams fall victim to _____, they tend to make faulty decisions because they are overly eager to agree with one another. (Obj. 2, p. 49)

17. The way teams reach decisions affects their morale and commitment. In American culture the majority usually rules. But other methods work well. One method for reaching decisions that produces creative, high-quality discussion and generally elicits commitment by all members is called _____. (Obj. 2, p. 49)

18. The most successful teams are generally small and have a diverse makeup. They agree on their purpose and procedures. They are able to confront conflict, collaborate rather than compete, use good communication techniques, and accept ethical responsibilities. They also share _____ and demonstrate good manners. (Obj. 3, pp. 50–51)

19. Team projects can be harmonious and productive when members establish _____ related to preparing, planning, collecting information for, organizing, rehearsing, and evaluating their activities. (Obj. 4, p. 53)

20. In planning a group document or presentation, you should establish the purpose, decide on the final format, discuss the audience, and develop a work plan. If time is short, work backward from the due date and then set _____. (Obj. 4, p. 54)

Meetings and Collaboration Technologies

action items	dysfunctional	media	team
agenda	face-to-face	motivation	understanding
background	few days	problem solving	unrestricted
collaboration technology	ideas	sales transactions	week

21. In spite of employee reluctance and terrific advances in communication technology, _____ meetings are here to stay. (Obj. 5, p. 55)

22. No meeting should be called unless the topic is important, can't wait, or requires an exchange of _____. (Obj. 5, p. 56)

23. The number of meeting participants is best determined by the purpose of the meeting. For the purpose of intensive _____, a group of five or fewer is the ideal size. (Obj. 5, p. 57)

24. At least two days in advance of a meeting, a list of topics to be discussed should be distributed. It should include the date and place of the meeting, the start time and end time, and a brief description of each topic and its time allotment. This list is called a(n) _____. (Obj. 5, p. 57)

25. Meetings should start on time and begin with a three- to five-minute introduction that includes the goal and length of the meeting, some _____ about the topics or problems, possible solutions and constraints, a tentative agenda, and ground rules to be followed. (Obj. 5, pp. 57–58)

26. At meetings some members may play the roles of blocker, attacker, joker, and withdrawer. To manage this _____ behavior, team leaders should establish rules, seat members strategically, and use a number of other techniques to encourage harmonious participation. (Obj. 5, pp. 59–60)

27. At the end of a meeting, the leader should summarize what was decided, name who is going to do what, and establish deadlines. No one should leave a meeting without a full _____ of what was accomplished. (Obj. 5, p. 60)

28. If minutes of a meeting were taken, they should be distributed within a _____ after the meeting. (Obj. 5, p. 60).

29. Software designed to facilitate group activities is called _____. This software relates to a number of constantly evolving technologies that help groups exchange information, collaborate in project management, and reach consensus. (Obj. 6, p. 59)

30. The latest technologies use a _____ conferencing approach. Relying heavily on the Web, these technologies facilitate meetings by incorporating PC functionality with media features that enable "real-life" meetings. (Obj. 6, p. 62).

31. Completing a group project often requires _____ sharing of information. Project management software can allow remote team members, suppliers, partners, and others with an interest in the project's successful completion to view the project and modify their own tasks via the Web. (Obj. 5, p. 63)

32. Live data sources, such as _____ and digital dashboards enable team members to create reports with information that can help forecast or explain shifts in business performance. (Obj. 6, p. 64)

Short Answer

33. List five characteristics of self-directed teams. (Obj. 1, p. 43)

34. Name nine kinds of positive group task roles. Which of these roles do you think you have played or would play in a team? (Obj. 2, pp. 46–47)

35. Name five kinds of positive group relationship roles. Which of these roles do you think you have played or would play in a team? (Obj. 2, p. 47)

36. List six ethical responsibilities of group members and leaders. (Obj. 3, p. 52)

Identify the meaning of each of the following key terms by selecting a term from Column B to match its definition in Column A. Use each term only once; the first answer is provided for you! Some of the terms are common words, but their meanings may be special in this context.

Matching

	Column A	**Column B**
f	37. One who defines problems, sets rules, and contributes ideas	a. participation encourager
	38. One who compares the group's ideas with feasibility of real-world implementation	b. consensus
	39. One who distracts the group with excessive humor, inappropriate comments, and disruptive comments	c. accommodation
	40. One who seeks to involve silent members	d. collective efforts to rationalize
	41. A form of decision making that requires all team members to agree	e. groupthink
	42. Conflict response pattern when one person gives in quickly, which results in the conflict being smoothed over	f. initiator
	43. A symptom of groupthink	g. joker
	44. A technology that combines audio, video, and communication devices to enable real-time team collaboration	h. norming
	45. A group of individuals who interact over time to achieve a purpose	i. reality tester
	46. Faulty decision-making processes by team members who are overly eager to agree with each other	j. team
		k. videoconferencing

Now that you've reviewed the chapter concepts, check your responses at the end of this guide. For any items that you missed, reread the relevant material in the chapter to be sure you understand the basic concepts.

CAREER TRACK SPELLING

Underline misspelled words. Write correct forms in the spaces provided. Some sentences may have more than one misspelled word. If a sentence is correct, write C. Then check your answers with those at the end of the guide.

_____	47.	Her absense made it difficult to accommodate all the customers.
_____	48.	You can acheive higher grades if you emphasize your studies.
_____	49.	The error in the letter was noticeable.
_____	50.	On his reccommendation we invested in stocks and bonds.
_____	51.	The director of personal had to write a report about the problem filling key positions.
_____	52.	With suficient training you, too, will be offered many opportunities.
_____	53.	The table in the proposal ommited key data.
_____	54.	As an independent manufacturer, Mark relied on key suppliers.
_____	55.	Lisa must occassionally call freight companies to check deliveries.
_____	56.	Mark's business prospered because of his excellent judgement.

My Spelling Monsters

List each troublesome word. Be sure to spell it correctly. Then write it four or more times. Review this page often to help you vanquish these spelling demons.

_____

_____

_____

_____

_____

CAREER TRACK VOCABULARY

Use your dictionary to define the words in Column A. Then select the best definition in Column B to match each word in Column A.

	Column A		**Column B**
_____	57. appendix	a.	overdue debt
_____	58. arbitrate	b.	examine, review
_____	59. arrears	c.	collection of supplementary material
_____	60. articulate (adj)	d.	hobby, pastime
_____	61. audit (v)	e.	intelligible, well-spoken
_____	62. avocation	f.	judge, settle

Choose the best meaning for the following underlined words.

_____ 63.   Donna Karan's <u>bailiwick</u> is designing clothes, not sewing them.

a. associate   b. field of knowledge   c. deputy

_____ 64.   The division of Yugoslavia into three ethnic states will further <u>balkanize</u> the region.

a. break up   b. benefit   c. isolate

_____ 65.   That attorney sometimes <u>barters</u> her services for car repair and child care.

a. employs   b. contracts   c. trades

_____ 66.   Cautious investors will not let salespeople <u>beguile</u> them into risking their life savings on junk bonds.

a. coerce   b. flatter   c. mislead

_____ 67.   His sentence was overturned, making this case a <u>bellwether</u> for change.

a. leading indicator   b. procedure   c. cauldron

_____ 68.   Because of his <u>benign</u> nature, Edmond is reluctant to fire anyone.

a. kind-hearted   b. wimpy   c. fiendish

_____ 69.   Although a glass partition <u>bisects</u> the office, it preserves the room's bright, spacious ambience.

a. illuminates   b. improves   c. cuts in half

_____ 70.   Most professional football commentators have a <u>blasé</u> attitude about flying, but John Madden, who travels by bus, is not among them.

a. casual   b. fearful   c. belligerent

Confusing Words

affect	to influence	*all ready*	prepared
effect	(n) outcome, result	*already*	by this time
	(v) to bring about, to create		
altar	structure for worship		
alter	to change		

71. He wrote the contract yesterday, and it is _____ for your signature.

72. The women decorated the _____ with flowers.

73. Changing the production schedule had a dramatic _____ on worker morale.

74. Mark and Maria had _____ decided to attend Penn State.

75. The surge of criticism did not _____ the CEO's decision to shut down the local plant.

76. The hurricane in Florida caused us to _____ our plans.

Look back over the vocabulary words in this chapter. Select five or more new words that you would like to own. Remember, to "own" a word, you must be able to use it correctly in a sentence. Double-check the meanings of your selections in a dictionary. Then write a sentence for each of your words.

_____

_____

_____

_____

_____

_____

COMPETENT LANGUAGE USAGE ESSENTIALS (C.L.U.E.)

Sentence Structure

In this chapter and the following ones you will concentrate on the most used—and abused—elements of language. These C.L.U.E. exercises are not meant to teach or review *all* the principles of English grammar and punctuation. Instead, they focus on 50 guidelines that cover the majority of problem areas for most business communicators. You will be examining these guides and applying them in exercises that review and reinforce what you are learning. By looking closely at these frequently used language concepts and by applying the clues and tips, you will develop confidence in expressing yourself correctly in writing and speaking.

Guide 1: Express ideas in complete sentences. You can recognize a complete sentence because it (a) includes a subject (a noun or pronoun that interacts with a verb), (b) includes a verb (a word expressing action or describing a condition), and (c) makes sense (comes to a closure). A complete sentence is an independent clause. Punctuating a fragment as if it were a complete sentence is one of the most serious errors a writer can make. A fragment is a broken-off part of a sentence.

Fragment:	Although the candidate spoke well and seemed to communicate confidently.
Improved:	Although the candidate spoke well and seemed to communicate confidently, the recruiter required a writing sample.
Fragment:	Because most recruiters agree that a one-page résumé, is the right length for a recent graduate.
Improved:	Because most recruiters agree that a one-page résumé is the right length for a recent graduate, you should try to fit yours on a single page.

TIP. Fragments often can be identified by the words that introduce them—words like *after, although, as, because, even, except, for example, if, instead of, since, so, such as, that, which,* and *when*. These words introduce dependent clauses. Make sure such clauses are always connected to independent clauses.

Independent clauses make sense by themselves and can stand alone. Dependent clauses require additional words to be complete.

Independent Clauses	**Dependent Clauses**
Rick graduated in June.	After Rick graduated in June, . . .
Finding a job is tough.	Although finding a job is tough, . . .
Her résumé was flawless.	As her résumé was flawless, . . .

Guide 2: Avoid run-on (fused) sentences. A sentence with two independent clauses must be joined by a coordinating conjunction (*and, or, nor, but*) or by a semicolon (;). Without a conjunction or a semicolon, a run-on sentence results.

Run-on:	Nancy read the classified ads, she also tried a little networking.
Improved:	Nancy read the classified ads, and she also tried a little networking.
	Nancy read the classified ads; she also tried a little networking.

Guide 3: Avoid comma-splice sentences. A comma splice results when a writer joins (splices together) two independent clauses—without using a coordinating conjunction (*and, or, nor, but*) or a semicolon.

Comma Splice:	He wrote to the hiring manager, she wrote to the personnel department.
Improved:	He wrote to the hiring manager, but she wrote to the personnel department.
Improved:	He wrote to the hiring manager; she wrote to the personnel department.
Comma Splice:	James sent a résumé to GE, however he didn't receive a response.
Improved:	James sent a résumé to GE; however, he didn't receive a response.

TIP. In joining independent clauses, beware of using a comma to precede words like *consequently, furthermore, however, therefore, then,* and *thus*. These conjunctive adverbs are preceded by semicolons. They are followed by commas, unless the adverb has only one syllable (*thus, then, hence*).

C.L.U.E. Checkpoint

In the following word groups, identify any fragments with FG, comma splices with CS, and run-ons with RO. Write the identifying initials after each group of words. Then revise the group to rectify its fault. If a sentence is correct, write C.

77. Give workers defined targets to hit get them involved in their jobs.

78. We use toll-free lines and comment cards, however they only supplement our constant customer surveys.

79. The company's president hoping for a holiday rush.

80. The computer technician couldn't understand the frantic customer's problem he asked her to explain it again.

81. You don't ask people what new products they want, you ask them what problems they have.

82. The CEO recognized that you can't control employees, however you can enlist their support.

83. If an experienced operating manager is given the right guidance. He or she can almost invariably do a better job than someone from corporate headquarters.

84. The new theme park's visitors expected to find a clean, well-run resort, however they were disappointed.

85. The team met four times, and each meeting began on time.

86. Managers must set realistic deadlines, then they must go out of their way not to change them.

Chapter 3

Workplace Listening and Nonverbal Communication

CHAPTER REVIEW

Indicate whether the following statements are true or false by using T *or* F.

_____ 1. High-quality communication is a vital ingredient in every successful workplace, and listening is involved in three quarters of high-quality communication in today's world of the Internet, team environments, and global competition. (Obj. 1, p. 75)

_____ 2. Experts say that because executives and workers devote the bulk of their time to listening, they have learned to listen at 75 percent efficiency. (Obj. 1, p. 75)

_____ 3. As an entry-level employee, you will probably be most concerned with listening to your colleagues and team members. (Obj. 1, p.76)

_____ 4. The two most important kinds of listening to use when interacting with colleagues and teammates are critical and discriminative listening. (Obj. 1, p. 76)

_____ 5. Listening takes place in three stages: perception, evaluation, and action. (Obj. 2, p. 78)

_____ 6. Listening to one's fellow workers makes the process easier because friends are more polite and respectful with each other. (Obj. 3, p. 80)

_____ 7. Nonverbal communication includes all unwritten and unspoken messages, both intentional and unintentional. (Obj. 4, p. 84)

_____ 8.   Researchers have found that when verbal and nonverbal messages are contradictory, listeners believe the verbal message. (Obj. 4, p. 85)

_____ 9.   Nonverbal forms of communication include eye contact, facial expression, the space around us, and gestures. (Obj. 5, pp. 86–87)

_____ 10.   In today's increasingly informal culture, the way you look has very little bearing on the judgment people make about you. (Obj. 5, p. 89)

Fill in the Blank

Use the listed words to complete the following sentences. You may use each word only once.

Listening

action	evaluation	opinions	reviewing
assertions	explanations	perception	social
distractions	interrupting	reflecting	worker

11.   Listening skills are important for career success, organizational effectiveness, and _____ satisfaction. (Obj. 1, p. 75)

12.   On the job one of your most important tasks will be listening to instructions, assignments, and _____ about how to do your work. You will be listening to learn and to comprehend. (Obj. 1, p. 76)

13.   Three listening strategies that are useful in team and group interactions are dampening, redirecting, and _____. (Obj. 1, p. 76)

14.   Many organizations are learning that listening to customers results in increased sales and profitability as well as improved customer acquisition and retention. The truth is that consumers just feel better about companies that value their _____. (Obj. 1, p. 77)

15.   Interpretation, the second stage in the listening process, is colored by your cultural, educational, and _____ frames of reference. (Obj. 2, p. 79)

16.   The third stage of the listening process involves _____, the time when you analyze the merit of a message and draw conclusions about it. (Obj. 2, p. 79)

17.   Being able to remember something involves three factors: (1) deciding to remember, (2) structuring the incoming information to form relationships, and (3) _____. (Obj. 2, p. 80)

18.   Workplace listening is hard because information may be disorganized, unclear, and cluttered with extra facts. You can improve your listening effectiveness by controlling external and internal _____. (Obj. 3. p. 80)

19. Facts are truths known to exist. Opinions are statements of personal judgments or preferences. Good listeners must separate facts from opinions. They don't automatically accept _____ as facts. (Obj. 3, p. 81)

20. Men tend to use _____ behavior to control conversations, whereas women generally interrupt to communicate assent, to elaborate on an idea of another group member, or to participate in the topic of conversation. (Obj. 3, p. 82)

Nonverbal Messages

attitudes	distress	permanent	submissiveness
body	eye	six	temporary
business	five	spoken	territory
cues	palm	style	verbal

21. Nonverbal communication helps to convey meaning in at least _____ ways. (Obj. 4, p. 84)

22. Effective communicators must be sure that all of their nonverbal messages reinforce their _____ words and their professional goals. (Obj. 4, p. 85)

23. Good eye contact helps you determine whether a listener is paying attention, showing respect, responding favorably, or feeling _____. (Obj. 5, p. 86)

24. An individual's posture can convey anything from high status to shyness and _____. (Obj. 5, p. 87)

25. Leaning toward a speaker suggests attraction and interest. Erect posture sends a message of confidence, competence, diligence, and strength. Using an upward _____ gesture can help you immediately establish rapport. (Obj. 5, p. 87)

26. How we structure and use time tells observers about our personality and _____. (Obj. 5, p. 87)

27. North Americans generally allow only intimate friends and family to stand closer than about 1½ feet. If people violate their _____, they feel uncomfortable and defensive and may step back to reestablish their space. (Obj. 5, p. 87)

28. Although they seem like conversation, e-mail messages are business documents that create a _____ record and often a bad impression. (Obj. 5, p. 88)

29. Casual dress at work may change the image you project and may even affect your work _____. (Obj. 6, p. 90)

30. When you perceive nonverbal signals that contradict verbal meanings, politely seek additional _____. (Obj. 6, p. 90)

Short Answer

31. List three types of workplace listening. (Obj. 1, pp. 76–77)

32. List six practices of trained listeners that improve customer relations. (Obj. 1, p. 77)

33. List five common mental listening barriers. (Obj. 2, p. 78)

34. List ten recommendations to improve listening effectiveness. (Obj. 3, pp. 80–82)

35. List seven techniques you could employ in improving your nonverbal communication skills in the workplace. Place a check mark next to the five items that you think would be most helpful to you in improving your communication skills. (Obj. 6, p. 90)

Matching

Identify the meaning of each of the following key terms by selecting a term from Column B to match its definition in Column A. Use each term only once; the first answer is provided for you! Some of the terms are common words, but their meanings may be special in this context.

<u>Column A</u>   <u>Column B</u>

__d__ 36. Percentage of time executives spend listening

37. Kind of listening that is necessary when you must understand and remember

38. The kind of questions to identify key factors in a discussion

39. The gender that tends to maintain steady eye contact

40. Percentage of time workers spend listening

41. Reason for asking closed fact-finding questions

42. A function of nonverbal cues

43. The gender that tends to listen for facts

44. Enables message sender to determine whether a receiver is paying attention

45. Technique for improving memory retention

Column B terms:

a. 30 to 45 percent

b. male

c. to identify key factors in a discussion

d. 60 to 70 percent

e. discriminative

f. closed fact-finding

g. female

h. to contradict

i. reviewing

j. 75 percent

k. good eye contact

Now that you've reviewed the chapter concepts, check your responses at the end of this guide. For any items that you missed, reread the relevant material in the chapter to be sure you understand the basic concepts.

CAREER TRACK SPELLING

In the space provided write the correct version of the word in parentheses. If the word is correct, write C. Then check your answers with those at the end of the guide.

46. Several (promenant) attorneys represented the company.

47. For an extra $200 you may purchase an extended 24-month (guarantee) for your computer.

_____   48.   The start-up company came into (exestanse) one year ago.

_____   49.   The supervisor's (excellant) rapport with her employees resulted in a promotion for her.

_____   50.   Economic conditions forced the company into (bankrupsy).

_____   51.   Serving their customers is a (privaledge) for most companies.

_____   52.   Please give this matter your (emediate) attention.

_____   53.   Maintaining a professional appearance will help you (succede).

_____   54.   Formatting throughout the report must be (consestant).

_____   55.   By developing our inventory (controll) procedures, we plan to become less (dependant) on our suppliers.

My Spelling Monsters

List each troublesome word. Be sure to spell it correctly. Then write it four or more times. Review this page often to help you vanquish these spelling demons.

_____

_____

_____

_____

_____

CAREER TRACK VOCABULARY

Use your dictionary to define the words in Column A. Then select the best definition in Column B to match each word in Column A.

	Column A		Column B
_____	56. buoyant	a.	truth
_____	57. burgeoning	b.	light, floating
_____	58. candor	c.	trite expression
_____	59. chronology	d.	cautious, prudent
_____	60. circumspect	e.	growing, enlarging
_____	61. cliché	f.	in order of time

Choose the best meaning for the following underlined words.

_____ 62.   During the development process, the key scientists for the Manhattan Project were
<u>cloistered</u>.

a. secluded   b. neighborly   c. miserable

_____ 63.   Mexico, Canada, and the United States have achieved a free-trade <u>coalition</u>.

a. reunion   b. division   c. alliance

_____ 64.   You can rely on Dr. Jackson to bring council discussions to an end with a few
<u>cogent</u> comments.

a. humorous   b. sound   c. devilish

_____ 65.   Becoming more <u>cognizant</u> of nonverbal cues, particularly when speaking with
nonnative speakers, will improve your ability to communicate effectively.

a. aware   b. sagacious   c. ignorant

_____ 66.   To improve efficiency, we are looking for a copier that sorts and <u>collates</u> sheets.

a. color-codes   b. staples   c. assembles

_____ 67.   The Johnsons used their home equity as <u>collateral</u> for a business loan.

a. deposit   b. security   c. speculation

_____ 68.   A federal judge ruled that the insurance companies were guilty of <u>collusion</u> in the
price-fixing trial.

a. bookmaking   b. conspiracy   c. ingenuity

____   69.   After an unfortunate accident during which three different chemicals were <u>commingled</u>, the supervisor changed the procedures for labeling.

a. mixed   b. returned   c. crushed

Confusing Words

appraise	to estimate		*ascent*	rising, going up
apprise	to inform		*assent*	agreement or consent

assure	to promise
ensure	to make certain
insure	to protect from loss

70.   The nation was shocked to see the *Challenger* explode only 73 seconds into its

_____.

71.   At the checkout stand Sue scanned the register tape to _____ its accuracy.

72.   After the succession of hurricanes in Florida, some people will find it harder to _____ their homes.

73.   The travel agent will _____ you of any changes made in your schedule.

74.   After much negotiation the team members finally gave their _____ to a new schedule.

75.   Carole had a certified gemologist _____ her diamond ring.

76.   Mr. Constable wanted to _____ his employees that the store would not be closed.

Look back over the vocabulary words in this chapter. Select five or more new words that you would like to own. Remember, to "own" a word, you must be able to use it correctly in a sentence. Double-check the meanings of your selections in a dictionary. Then write a sentence for each of your words.

_____

_____

_____

_____

_____

COMPETENT LANGUAGE USAGE ESSENTIALS (C.L.U.E.)

Capitalization

Because capitalization, number usage, and punctuation are so important to business writers, we will present those guidelines *before* discussing grammar guidelines. Therefore, this chapter begins a review of capitalization use.

Guide 39: Capitalize proper nouns and proper adjectives. Capitalize the *specific* names of persons, places, institutions, buildings, religions, holidays, months, organizations, laws, races, languages, and so forth. Don't capitalize common nouns that make *general* references.

Proper Nouns	Common Nouns
Stacy Wilson	the account executive
Everglades National Park	the wilderness park
Towson State University	a university
Sears Tower	the downtown building
Environmental Protection Agency	the federal agency
Persian, Armenian, Hindi	modern foreign languages

Proper Adjectives	
Hispanic markets	Russian dressing
Xerox copy	Japanese executives
Belgian chocolates	Reagan economics

Guide 40: Capitalize only specific academic courses and degrees.

Professor Jane Williams, Ph.D., will teach Accounting 121 next spring.

Lee Walker, who holds bachelor's and master's degrees, teaches business communications and marketing.

Alicia enrolled in classes in marketing, English, and finance.

Guide 41: Capitalize courtesy, professional, religious, government, family, and business titles when they precede names.

Mr. Jameson, Mrs. Alvarez, and Ms. Robinson (courtesy titles)

Professor Andrews, Dr. Lee (professional titles)

Rabbi Cohen, Pastor Williams, Pope John (religious titles)

Senator Tom Harrison, Mayor Jackson (government titles)

Uncle Edward, Mother Teresa, Cousin Vinny (family titles)

Vice President Morris, Budget Director Lopez (business titles)

Do not capitalize such titles when they function as appositives (that is, when they rename or explain previously mentioned nouns or pronouns).

Only one professor, Jonathon Marcus, favored a tuition hike.

Local candidates counted on their president, George Bush, to raise funds.

Do not capitalize titles following names unless they are part of an address.

Mark Yoder, president of Yoder Enterprises, hired all employees.

Paula Beech, director of Human Resources, interviewed all candidates.

Send the package to Amanda Harr, Advertising Manager, Cambridge Publishers, 20 Park Plaza, Boston, MA 02116. (title is part of address)

Generally, do not capitalize a title or office that replaces a person's name.

Only the president, his chief of staff, and one senator made the trip.

The director of marketing and the sales manager will meet at 1 p.m.

Do not capitalize family titles used with possessive pronouns.

my mother, his father, your cousin

C.L.U.E. Checkpoint

Draw three small underlines under any letter that should be capitalized.

Example: The ucla-sponsored survey examined hispanic buying habits.

77. The president of data systems, inc., received his bachelor's degree from pepperdine university.

78. When president bush visited ireland, the crowds lined the streets.

79. At the national ymca convention, students from all parts of the nation exchanged stories about their programs.

80. Attending the conference were vice president atwood and president wilkerson.

81. Our finance class took a field trip to see the new york stock exchange in manhattan.

82. Richard enrolled in management 304, computer science 205, and marketing.

83. Our vacation included shenandoah national park in the blue ridge mountains.

84. Send the xerox copies to kimberly gorman, marketing manager, globex incorporated, 769 valencia street, san francisco, CA 94010, as soon as possible.

85. The pacific design center featured french prints, mexican pottery, and asian fabrics.

86. Until the promotion of her first book, *rise of the meritocracy,* Lucy Stoppard had never traveled outside her native chicago.

Chapter 4

Communicating Across Cultures

CHAPTER REVIEW

Indicate whether the following statements are true or false by using T *or* F.

_____ 1. Learning more about how culture affects behavior helps companies reduce friction and misunderstandings as they expand into global markets and adapt to an intercultural workforce. (Obj. 1, p. 101)

_____ 2. The development of trade agreements has been the most important factor in the rise of the global market. (Obj. 1, p. 102)

_____ 3. Culture teaches people how to behave, and it conditions their reactions. (Obj. 2, p. 105)

_____ 4. Practices in a culture are outward expressions of rules. (Obj. 2, p. 106)

_____ 5. One of the most important dimensions of culture is context, which is the easiest dimension to define. (Obj. 2, p.107)

_____ 6. Being aware of your own culture and how it contrasts with others, as well as recognizing barriers to intercultural accommodation, will help you achieve intercultural proficiency. (Obj. 3, p. 110)

_____ 7. Nonverbal behavior, ambiguous within cultures and problematic between cultures, nevertheless conveys meaning. (Obj. 4, p. 114)

_____ 8.   When using written messages to communicate, consider using humor to bridge cultural differences. (Obj. 5, p. 116)

_____ 9.   Companies active in global markets are creating ethics training programs to address the growing sophistication of ethical codes of conduct. In these programs, ethical trainers teach employees how to solve problems by reconciling legal requirements, company policies, and conflicting cultural norms. (Obj. 6, p. 119)

_____ 10.   Diversity always enhances productivity and propels companies toward success. (Obj. 7, p. 124)

Fill in the Blank

Use the listed words to complete the following sentences. You may use each word only once.

Intercultural Communication

action oriented	empathy	gender	prejudice
adapt	environment	generalizations	prototype
country-specific	ethnocentrism	misunderstandings	self-identity
culture	evasiveness	power	society

11.   In your future career you may find that your employers, fellow workers, or clients are from other countries. Learning about the powerful effect that culture has on behavior will help you reduce friction and _____. (Obj. 1, p. 101)

12.   To be successful in the interdependent global village, American companies are finding it necessary to _____ to other cultures. (Obj. 1, p. 101)

13.   Many multinational companies are now establishing _____ Web sites to sell products, offer customer service, provide technical support, and link directly to suppliers. (Obj. 1, p. 102)

14.   Because it is not fixed and rigid but open to new definitions, _____ is the preferred term for describing the general characteristics of a culture. (Obj. 2, p. 105)

15.   Culture is the basis of our sense of community and the basis of our _____. That is, culture helps us develop who we are and what we believe in. (Obj. 2, p. 106)

16.   A stereotype is an oversimplified behavioral pattern applied uncritically to groups. When a stereotype develops into a rigid attitude and when it is based on erroneous beliefs or preconceptions, it should be called a(n) _____. (Obj. 2, pp. 106–107)

17.   Low-context cultures tend to be logical, analytical, and _____. (Obj. 2, p. 108)

18.   People in different countries have different communication styles. For example, Americans value straightforwardness, are suspicious of _____, and distrust people who have a "hidden agenda." (Obj. 2, p. 109)

19. The belief in the superiority of one's own race is known as _____, a natural attitude in all cultures, and one that causes us to judge others by our own values. (Obj. 3, p. 110)

20. To improve tolerance, which is a desirable attitude in achieving intercultural proficiency, you'll want to practice _____. (Obj. 3, p. 111)

Dimensions of Culture and Intercultural Sensitivity

comprehension	ethnicity	grammar	public
defensive	face	high	tolerance
differ	formal	negative	treaty
diversity	gestures	nonverbal	values

21. People in low-context cultures, such as those in Germany and North America, value candor and directness. But members of high-context cultures, such as those in Mexico and Asia, are often more concerned with preserving social harmony and saving _____. (Obj. 3, p. 106)

22. Deciphering nonverbal communication is difficult for people who are culturally similar, and it is even more troublesome when cultures _____. (Obj. 4, p. 107)

23. To improve oral communication with someone for whom English is a second language, you should speak slowly, enunciate clearly, observe eye messages, encourage feedback, and check frequently for _____. (Obj. 4, p. 109)

24. Because _____ can create very different reactions in different cultures, you must be careful in using and interpreting them. (Obj. 4, p. 114)

25. Verbal skills in another culture can be mastered with hard work, but appropriate _____ behavior, such as eye contact, facial expressions, posture, and gestures, is much harder to learn. (Obj. 4, p. 113)

26. To improve written messages when English is a second language, you should adopt local formats, use short sentences and short paragraphs, avoid ambiguous expressions, strive for clarity, and use correct _____. (Obj. 5, pp. 116–117)

27. In cultures where formality and tradition are important, be very polite. Don't try to be funny in written messages because humor translates poorly and can cause misunderstanding and _____ reactions. (Obj. 5, p. 116)

28. Ethical codes of conduct are _____ documents that can usually be found on company Web sites. (Obj. 6, p. 119)

29. In 1999, many of the world's industrialized countries formally agreed to a new global _____ promoted by the Organization for Economic Cooperation and Development (OECD), which bans the practice of bribery of foreign governmental officials. (Obj. 6, p. 120)

30. Companies that set aside time and resources to cultivate and capitalize on _____ will suffer fewer discrimination lawsuits, fewer union clashes, and less governmental regulatory action. (Obj. 7, p. 122)

Short Answer

31. Name three high-context and three low-context cultures. List four cultural characteristics that distinguish each of these cultures. (Obj. 2, pp. 107–110)

32. List six suggestions that may be helpful for situations in which one or more of the communicators may be using English as a second language. (Obj. 4, pp. 115–116)

33. Name six suggestions for helping business communicators improve intercultural proficiency and communication. (Obj. 5, pp. 117–118)

34. List six tips for improving communication among diverse workplace audiences. (Obj. 7, pp. 124–125)

Matching

Identify the meaning of each of the following key terms by selecting a term from Column B to match its definition in Column A. Use each term only once; the first answer is provided for you! Some of the terms are common words, but their meanings may be special in this context.

	Column A		Column B
__e__	35. A favorable trade agreement that promotes open trade globally	a.	figures
_____	36. Expected size of U.S. population in 2050	b.	descriptiveness
		c.	394 million
_____	37. Country in which harmony with environment is important	d.	China
_____	38. Use when citing numbers in Europe	e.	GATT
_____	39. Region with cultures that correlate time with productivity, efficiency, and money	f.	individualism
		g.	Finland and Denmark
_____	40. Characterized by an attitude of independence and freedom from control	h.	Japan
		i.	linear
_____	41. Country where managers prefer a "consultative" management style	j.	350 million
_____	42. Refers to the use of concrete and specific feedback	k.	North America
		l.	spiral
_____	43. Kind of logic members of low-context cultures value		
_____	44. Countries that are the least corrupt		

Now that you've reviewed the chapter concepts, check your responses at the end of this guide. For any items that you missed, reread the relevant material in the chapter to be sure you understand the basic concepts.

CAREER TRACK SPELLING

For each group below identify misspelled words and write corrected versions in the spaces provided. Write C if all words are correct. Then check your answers with those at the end of the guide.

_____	45.	employe	familiar	undoubtedly	referred
_____	46.	similar	committe	fourth	deductable
_____	47.	yield	excellent	grammer	necessary
_____	48.	control	paid	milage	sufficent
_____	49.	height	fourty	catalog	though
_____	50.	tenant	adiquate	representative	thruout
_____	51.	budjet	noticeable	harrassment	truly
_____	52.	equipped	irelevent	efficint	writing
_____	53.	permanant	facinate	destroy	practical
_____	54.	criticize	itinerary	exaggerate	ninty

My Spelling Monsters

List each troublesome word. Be sure to spell it correctly. Then write it four or more times. Review this page often to help you vanquish these spelling demons.

_____

_____

_____

_____

_____

CAREER TRACK VOCABULARY

Use your dictionary to define the words in Column A. Then select the best definition in Column B to match each word in Column A.

	Column A		**Column B**
_____	55. cohere	a.	stock, merchandise
_____	56. commodity	b.	channel, passageway
_____	57. concede	c.	stick, adhere
_____	58. conduit	d.	seize, take possession of
_____	59. confiscate	e.	admit, acknowledge
_____	60. contraband	f.	smuggled goods

Choose the best meaning for the following underlined words.

_____ 61. Predicting the price of Internet stocks has been, at best, pure <u>conjecture</u> for the past two years.

   a. speculation   b. fact   c. reasoning

_____ 62. Because the stock split is <u>contingent</u> on their approval, we must lobby the shareholders.

   a. certain   b. debatable   c. dependent

_____ 63. The government is probing overseas cartels that <u>contrive</u> to restrict markets.

   a. discriminate   b. diverge   c. plan

_____ 64. As oil prices rise, auto makers are looking at options such as <u>conversion</u> to alternate fuels to power their vehicles.

   a. change in form or use   b. shift in belief   c. unnecessary

_____ 65. Some students take <u>copious</u> notes in class; others rely on the professor's PowerPoint lecture notes that are posted online.

   a. infrequent   b. abundant   c. furtive

_____ 66. The article in the British medical journal raises the issue of the drug giant's <u>culpability</u>.

   a. prejudice   b. suspicion   c. guilt

_____ 67. We invested in the company because it was highly recommended by <u>credible</u> sources.

   a. dubious   b. believable   c. vexing

_____ 68. The <u>correlation</u> between the national election results and the fate of the Washington Redskins finally did not hold in 2004.

   a. incompatibility   b. interrelation   c. difference

Confusing Words

capital   (n) a city in which the official seat of government is located; the wealth of an individual

   (adj) foremost in importance; punishable by death

capitol   building that houses state lawmakers

Capitol   building used by U.S. Congress

cite	to quote or to charge	*cereal*	breakfast food ·
site	a location	*serial*	arranged in sequence
sight	(n) a view		
	(v) to see		

69. With the latest low-carb diet fad, many more varieties of breakfast _____ are available.

70. In a research paper you may _____ authorities to support your argument.

71. The _____ of fireworks exploding on the Fourth of July thrilled the crowd.

72. "This building _____ is unacceptable," said the geologist.

73. U.S. senators and representatives were called into session at the _____ building in Washington.

74. Jane's goal was to publish her work in _____ form.

75. Entrepreneurs must invest considerable _____ to start new businesses.

76. State legislators held weekly budget hearings in the _____ building.

Look back over the vocabulary words in this chapter. Select five or more new words that you would like to own. Remember, to "own" a word, you must be able to use it correctly in a sentence. Double-check the meanings of your selections in a dictionary. Then write a sentence for each of your words.

_____

_____

_____

_____

_____

COMPETENT LANGUAGE USAGE ESSENTIALS (C.L.U.E.)

Capitalization (cont.)

Because capitalization, number usage, and punctuation are so important to business writers, we will present those guidelines *before* discussing grammar guidelines. Therefore, this chapter continues our review of capitalization use.

Guide 42: Capitalize the principal words in the titles of books, magazines, newspapers, articles, movies, plays, songs, poems, Web sites, and reports. Do *not* capitalize articles (*a, an, the*) and prepositions of fewer than four letters (*in, to, by, for*) unless they begin or end the title.

> Book: *Life After College*
> Magazine: *Business Week, U.S. News & World Report*
> Newspaper: *The Wall Street Journal, Boston Globe*
> Article: "Why Complainers Are Good for Business"
> Movies: *A Civil Action, The Insider*
> Song: "What Dreams Are Made Of"
> Web Site: Purdue University *Online Writing Lab*
> Report: "The Search for Intelligent Life in the Universe"

Note that the titles of books, magazines, newspapers, movies, and Web sites are italicized, while the titles of articles and shorter publications are enclosed in quotation marks.

Guide 43: Capitalize *north, south, east, west,* and their derivatives only when they represent specific geographical regions.

from the East Coast	heading east on the highway
living in the South	the house faced south
Midwesterners, Southerners	western New York, southern Ohio

TIP. When the word *the* precedes a compass direction (*the East, the West, the South*), you'll almost always capitalize the direction. *The* signals locations instead of directions.

Guide 44: Capitalize the names of departments, divisions, or committees within your own organization. Outside your organization capitalize only *specific* department, division, or committee names.

Counselors in our Human Resources Department help employees choose benefits.

Four accountants in its Telecommunications Division will be transferred.

Two attorneys serve on our Legal Assistance and Services Committee.

Have you sent an application to their personnel department?

Guide 45: Capitalize product names only when they refer to trademarked items. Don't capitalize the common names following manufacturers' names.

Dell Inspiron laptop computer	Eveready Energizer batteries
Skippy peanut butter	Kingsford charcoal briquettes
Canon copier	Levi 501 jeans

Guide 46: Capitalize most nouns followed by numbers or letters (except page, paragraph, line, and verse references).

Room 340	Flight 28, Gate 4
Apartment C	Form 1040A
Chapter 4	Figure 15

C.L.U.E. Checkpoint

Indicate capitalization with proofreading marks (three small underscores).

77. When the space shuttle columbia burned up on reentry and exploded, many skeptics doubted whether nasa could survive.

78. Ginger Putnam, a systems programmer in our accounting department, drinks diet coke all day.

79. Axelrod's book on queen elizabeth I combines history with twenty-first-century business concepts.

80. In barnes and noble she bought a book called how to buy a house, condo, or co-op.

81. James Dale, president of quaker oats company, discussed gatorade, its popular sports drink.

82. Please complete form 1040 and send it to the internal revenue service before april 15.

83. Our student fees and admissions committee will meet in room 12 on the east side of douglas campus center.

84. The city of new york continues to be the heart of our country's financial operations, even after the tragic events of september 11.

85. Easterners and midwesterners often travel south to florida to spend their winters.

86. Did you see the toshiba computer that vice president rose bought for his trip to europe?

Chapter 5

Writing Process Phase 1: Analyze, Anticipate, Adapt

CHAPTER REVIEW

Indicate whether the following statements are true or false by using T *or* F.

_____ 1. In business writing, much like academic writing, you focus on displaying your knowledge. (Obj. 1, p. 136)

_____ 2. The 3-x-3 writing process helps with issues such as analyzing the purpose of a message, organizing your information, and revising your document to meet readers' needs. (Obj. 1, p. 137)

_____ 3. When scheduling a writing project, you should allocate nearly 45 percent of your time to writing. (Obj. 2, p. 139)

_____ 4. Collaboration in writing is especially important for big tasks, items with long deadlines, and team projects that require a variety of expertise. (Obj. 2, pp. 139–140)

_____ 5. Two important questions to ask at the beginning of a writing project are (1) Why am I sending this message? and (2) What do I hope to achieve? (Obj. 3, p. 142)

_____ 6. When selecting the best communication channel, writers weigh a number of factors such as the importance of a message, the cost of the channel, and the desire to promote goodwill. (Obj. 3, p. 142)

_____   7.   Anticipating the audience for a message helps a communicator determine what language to use and how to shape the message. (Obj. 4, p. 143)

_____   8.   Good writers recognize the limitations of visualizing their audience. Instead, they rely on model documents and templates to help them. (Obj. 4, p. 144)

_____   9.   A business writer should work hard to impress his or her reader by using complex vocabulary words. (Obj. 5, p. 151)

_____   10.   An important consideration when writing for an organization is to avoid using language that might result in legal problems. (Obj. 6, p. 152)

Fill in the Blank

Use the listed words to complete the following sentences. You may use each word only once.

Applying a Writing Process

channel	formality	prewriting	report or proposal
collaborative	impress	profiling	revising
creative	inform	reader oriented	track changes
express	memo or letter	recursive	writing

11.   Business writing is purposeful, economical, and _____. (Obj. 1, p. 136)

12.   The three phases of the writing process are prewriting, writing, and revising. These phases do not follow a linear order; instead they are more nearly _____. (Obj. 2, p. 139)

13.   Because today's workers are increasingly part of teams, you can expect to participate in a _____ writing project on the job. (Obj. 2, p. 139)

14.   In preparing for big projects, team members may not actually function together for each phase of the writing process; they generally work separately in the _____ phase. (Obj. 2, pp. 140–141)

15.   In Microsoft Word the _____ tool allows team members to suggest specific editing changes to other team members. (Obj. 2, p. 140)

16.   As part of the first phase in the writing process, you will analyze your task. You must decide whether your message is meant to persuade or merely to _____. (Obj. 3, p. 142)

17.   In the first phase of the writing process, you will select the best _____ for delivery of your message. You will consider the importance of the message, the amount of feedback required, the necessity for a permanent record, the cost, and the degree of formality desired. (Obj. 3, p. 142)

18.   The best use of a _____ is when you are delivering complex data internally or externally. (Obj. 4, p. 143)

19. An important question to ask when visualizing or _____ your audience is, "What do I know about that person's education, belief, and attitudes?" (Obj. 4, p. 144)

Adapting to the Task and Audience

age	empathy	jargon	race
benefits	familiar	nonverbal	second
blame	first	precise	sender
costs	gender	problems	tone

20. One important aspect of adaptation is _____. Conveyed largely by the words in a message, it reflects how a receiver feels upon reading or hearing a message. (Obj. 5, p. 145)

21. Skilled communicators always stress the _____ to the readers of whatever it is they are trying to get them to do. (Obj. 5, p. 145)

22. Effective communicators develop the "you" view. That is, they emphasize _____-person pronouns, but not in a manipulative or critical manner. (Obj. 5, p. 147)

23. When speaking face to face, communications show sincerity and warmth with _____ signals such as a smile and pleasant voice tone. (Obj. 5, p. 147)

24. The statement *We are certain that our upcoming sale will be of interest to you* is an example of a _____-focused message. (Obj. 5, p. 147)

25. Expressions like "female attorney," "workman," and "executives and their wives" carry _____ bias and should be replaced by neutral expressions. (Obj. 5, pp. 147–148)

26. Certain negative words create ill will because they appear to _____ or accuse readers. (Obj. 5, p. 149)

27. Some communicators show off with big words; they think that inflated language is necessary to impress people. The best communicators, however, try to use _____ words because their goal is to transmit meaning and be understood. (Obj. 5, p. 151)

28. _____ is specialized or technical language that enables insiders to communicate complex ideas briefly. (Obj. 5, p. 151)

Adapting to Legal Responsibilities

adapting	defamation	highlighting	marketing
administration	e-mail	language	promissory

29. As a business communicator, you can protect yourself and avoid litigation by knowing what's legal and by adapting your _____ accordingly. (Obj. 6, p. 152)

30. The information areas that generate the most litigation are investments, safety, _____, and human resources. (Obj. 6, p. 152)

31. Effective safety messages also include _____ techniques, such as headings and bullets. (Obj. 6, p. 153)

32. Companies are warned to avoid _____ phrases in writing job advertisements, application forms, and offer letters. (Obj. 6, p. 154)

Short Answer

33. Name the best use for each of the following communication channels: (Obj. 3, p. 143)

   a. Voice mail message
   b. E-mail
   c. Video- or teleconference
   d. Memo
   e. Letter

34. List five questions that help you profile your primary audience. (Obj. 4, p. 144)

35. List four kinds of bias and provide an example of each. (Obj. 5, pp. 147–149)

Reader Benefits and "You" View

Revise the following statements to emphasize the reader's perspective and the "you" view.

36. So that we may bring our client records up to date and make sure we get our monthly newsletter to you in a timely manner, we require the enclosed card to be completed.

37. Because my credentials are such a good match for the job advertisement, I look forward to your call.

38. Our reputation for fairness and honesty is the reason we publish the actual manufacturer's price along with our retail price.

Language Bias

Revise the following sentences to eliminate language stereotypes.

39. Although Jim is confined to a wheelchair, he travels to all functions easily.

40. A new subscriber may cancel his subscription within two weeks.

41. We filled the position with Juanita Sanchez, a Latina who just graduated from the state university.

Positive Expression

Revise the following sentences to make them more positive.

42. We can't send the MP3 recorder you ordered until March 1.

43. Your jarring complaint about your unpleasant meal is being investigated.

44. Because you apparently did not use our correct address, your letter did not arrive in our New York office until May 5.

Courteous Expression

Revise the following sentences to show greater courtesy.

45. You MUST complete this application and return it IMMEDIATELY if you expect to be enrolled.

46. The copy machine is so easy to use; I cannot understand why anyone would be confused. If you can read, you should see how to load paper.

47. As I'm sure your agent told you, your policy does not cover drivers under the age of 21.

Familiar Words

Revise the following sentences to use familiar words.

48. Please ascertain what the remuneration will be for this position.

49. Pursuant to our meeting, I plan to interrogate Jason about some of the recommendations listed on his report.

CAREER TRACK SPELLING

Spelling Challenge

In the space provided write the correct version of the word in parentheses. If the word is correct, write C. Then check your answers with those at the end of this guide.

_____   50.   Fax messages travel (accross) oceans and continents.

_____   51.   Ms. Jones (omitted) the final section from the proposal.

_____   52.   Bond income is (exemt) from the latest tax laws.

_____   53.   We set up a special file for (miscelanous) items.

_____   54.   Have you (payed) all the bills for this month?

_____   55.   Second-semester classes begin in early (Febuary).

_____   56.   Only (perminant) residents were allowed to enter.

_____   57.   Marissa (recognised) all the signs that the system was failing.

_____   58.   All 500 (envelops) will be sent out by Monday.

_____   59.   The employees were (greatful) for the excellent health benefits.

My Spelling Monsters

List each troublesome word. Be sure to spell it correctly. Then write it four or more times. Review this page often to help you vanquish these spelling demons.

_____

_____

_____

_____

_____

CAREER TRACK VOCABULARY

Use your dictionary to define the words in Column A. Then select the best definition in Column B to match each word in Column A.

	Column A		**Column B**
_____ 60.	contiguous	a.	conditional
_____ 61.	contingent	b.	hidden, invisible
_____ 62.	corroborate	c.	touching, adjacent
_____ 63.	coup de grace	d.	hasty, perfunctory
_____ 64.	covert	e.	confirm, validate
_____ 65.	cursory	f.	death blow

Choose the best meaning for the following underlined words.

_____ 66. In *The Journal of Corporate Law*, Professor Dale <u>denounced</u> the specialist system of the New York Stock Exchange.

    a. praised   b. criticized   c. advocated

_____ 67. The plant manager received a <u>derogatory</u> evaluation after missing the production quota last month.

    a. disparaging   b. excellent   c. well-written

_____ 68. <u>Deterred</u> by heavy traffic and rainy weather, the limousine arrived late for the prime minister.

    a. placated   b. impelled   c. thwarted

____   69.   Trying to decide among the three qualified applicants proved to be a <u>dilemma</u> for the personnel committee.

     a. puzzle   b. certainty   c. expense

____   70.   Any discussion of health care plans is sure to produce sharply <u>disparate</u> views.

     a. disjointed   b. disdainful   c. differing

____   71.   Simply put, the CEO's principle is this: Listen to all the debate before you <u>dissent</u>.

     a. depart   b. disagree   c. consent

____   72.   As a result of its anti-war position, the mutual fund chose to <u>divest</u> $20 million from companies associated with the defense industry.

     a. invest   b. sell off   c. add

____   73.   By surpassing her quota for the fifteenth year in a row, Elaine Jones joined an <u>elite</u> group of salespeople.

     a. golden   b. distinguished   c. tarnished

Confusing Words

coarse	rough	*council*	governing body
course	direction, route	*counsel*	(v) to advise
			(n) advice

complement	that which completes
compliment	to praise or flatter

74.   When the new marketing manager needed _____, she asked a number of different people to obtain a broader perspective on the issue.

75.   The popular vice president makes it a point to _____ all employees personally when their work is exemplary.

76.   Race car drivers followed a winding _____ through the Italian countryside.

77.   To demonstrate his solidarity with the general population, Gandhi chose to wear _____ clothing, which he called "homespun."

78.   Formal gardens surrounding the ornate library _____ its architecture.

79.   Zoning issues make city _____ meetings interminable.

Look back over the vocabulary words in this chapter. Select five or more new words that you would like to own. Remember, to "own" a word, you must be able to use it correctly in a sentence. Double-check the meanings of your selections in a dictionary. Then write a sentence for each of your words.

COMPETENT LANGUAGE USAGE ESSENTIALS (C.L.U.E.)

Number Style

Usage and custom determine whether numbers are to be expressed in the form of a figure (for example, *5*) or in the form of a word (for example, *five*). Numbers expressed as figures are shorter and more easily comprehended, yet numbers used as words are necessary in certain instances. The following guides are observed in expressing numbers that appear in written *sentences*. Numbers that appear in business communications—such as invoices, statements, and purchase orders—are always expressed as figures.

Guide 47: Use word form to express (a) numbers ten and under and (b) numbers beginning sentences. General references to numbers *ten* and under should be expressed in word form. Also use word form for numbers that begin sentences. If the resulting number involves more than two words, however, the sentence should be recast so that the number does not fall at the beginning.

> The jury consisted of *nine* regular members and *one* alternate.
>
> *Eighteen* employees volunteered to tutor students in *three* neighborhood schools.
>
> A total of 117 applicants responded to five classified ads. (Avoid beginning the sentence with a long number such as *one hundred seventeen*.)

Guide 48: Use words to express general references to ages and small fractions. However, you may use figures to express exact ages.

> He started college at *eighteen* and graduated at *twenty-two*. (General reference)
>
> Marissa worried that *one third* of her income went for rent. (Note that fractions are hyphenated only when they function as adjectives, such as *one-third ownership*).
>
> Angela Ross, *45*, and Eric Ross, *47*, were injured. (Exact age)

Guide 49: Use figures to express most references to numbers 11 and over.

More than *175* people from *86* companies attended the two-day workshop.

A four-ounce serving of toffee ice cream contains *300* calories and *19* grams of fat.

Guide 50: Use figures to express money, dates, clock time, decimals, and percents. Use a combination of words and figures to express sums of 1 million and over.

One wrench cost *$2.95*; however, most were between *$10* and *$35*. (Omit the decimals and zeros in even sums of money.)

By *5 p.m.* on *June 2* only a fraction of the residents had not voted. (Notice that *June 2* is not written *June 2nd*, although it may be spoken that way.)

International sales dropped *11.7 percent*, and net income dropped *3.5 percent*. (Always use the word *percent* instead of the % symbol in written material.)

Globex earned *$4.5 million* in the latest fiscal year on revenues of *$235 million*. (Use a combination of words and figures for sums 1 million and over.)

TIP. To ease your memory load, concentrate on the numbers normally expressed in words: numbers *ten* and under, numbers at the beginning of a sentence, and small fractions. Nearly everything else in business is written with figures.

C.L.U.E. Checkpoint

Correct any inappropriate expression of numbers. Mark C if a sentence is correct.

80. 1400 people in 4 different counties have already signed the recall petition.

81. 9 employees have signed up to attend the training session at 1 p.m.

82. On January 15th we will advertise 2 job openings.

83. Marianne bought three gifts; 1 cost $10.00, and the other two cost $15.

84. At the age of 21, Gordon started a business with an investment of ten thousand dollars.

85. Take the second street on the right, then travel 9 miles before turning right at Bonvale Drive. Our office's address is 420 Bonvale; we're the 3rd building on the left.

86. Our sales force of 9 representatives serves 900 accounts in 3 countries.

87. The unemployment rate was five point six percent for the six-month period.

88. Your loan is at 9% for sixty days and is payable on March 12th.

89. Our 3 branch offices, with a total of ninety-six workers, need to add six computers and three printers.

Super C.L.U.E. Review

These cumulative exercises review all the C.L.U.E. guides presented and even contain some spelling and confusing word errors for you to correct. See how many errors you can find and correct.

90. whoppers new Double bacon burger contains eight hundred 10 calories and costs three dollars and forty-nine cents.

91. After Burger King advertised its new creation, an animal rights group began a 2 month protest to end meat and dairy consumption, fishing, hunting, and trapping.

92. The american association for training and development estimates that five percent of the nations employers will annually spend thirty billion dollars on employee training.

93. A rule of thumb for determining office-space needs is one hundred fifty to two hundred square feet per employee, plus fifteen percent for traffic flow.

94. If you propose work related to our twenty-one offices in europe or asia, expect to take center stage occassionaly.

95. The managers latest policy had a positive affect on the production lines performance.

96. Once a week I recieve several notes from president Jones, whose office is in Toronto.

97. Centron oil company, with headquarters in western texas, hopes to accede it's past record of ten thousand gallons in a day.

98. 110 companys formerly located in the world trade center had to relocate.

99. All visitors to Boston should take a walk along the charles river; they should also take the time to visit the museum of fine arts, 1 of the countrys finest.

Chapter 6

Writing Process Phase 2: Research, Organize, Compose

CHAPTER REVIEW

Indicate whether the following statements are true or false by using T *or* F.

_____ 1. Before business communicators can make decisions and convey them in written messages or presentations, they must gather information and organize it. (Obj. 1, p. 164)

_____ 2. Long reports and complex business problems generally require informal research methods. (Obj. 1, pp. 164–165)

_____ 3. Brainstorming is a proven method of gathering data. (Obj. 1, p. 166)

_____ 4. Clustering is a method of organizing a jumble of ideas to show relationships. (Obj. 1, p. 167)

_____ 5. The hardest part of creating an outline is learning to number the items. (Obj. 2, p. 169)

_____ 6. Two major organizational patterns for business messages are the direct pattern and the indirect pattern. (Obj. 3, p. 171)

_____ 7. The direct pattern is the most effective pattern for unreceptive audiences. (Obj. 3, p. 172)

_____ 8. According to the American Press Institute (API), long sentences of 20 words or more improve reader comprehension. (Obj. 4, p. 175)

_____ 9. The pivoting paragraph plan is most effective when comparing and contrasting ideas. (Obj. 5, p. 179)

_____ 10. Transitions enable a reader to anticipate what's coming, reduce uncertainty, and speed up comprehension. (Obj. 5, p. 181)

Multiple Choice

Choose the best answer.

_____ 11. Formal research methods include _all but which_ of the following?
  a. Developing a cluster diagram
  b. Experimenting scientifically
  c. Accessing electronically
  d. Investigating primary sources (Obj. 1, pp. 164–165)

_____ 12. Most businesspeople begin their research by doing which of the following?
  a. Accessing information electronically via the Internet, databases, or CDs
  b. Searching for information manually in libraries
  c. Putting together focus groups
  d. Using controlled variables to conduct a scientific study (Obj. 1, p. 164)

_____ 13. Writers of well-organized messages
  a. always begin with alphanumeric outlines showing ten or more major ideas.
  b. break all subpoints into major components.
  c. strive for overlapping categories so that readers can see relationships.
  d. group similar ideas together. (Obj. 2, p. 167)

_____ 14. Each major category in an outline should be divided into at least
  a. three subcategories.
  b. four subcategories.
  c. five subcategories.
  d. two subcategories. (Obj. 2, p. 170)

_____ 15. An outline that presents details, explanations, and evidence after the main idea follows the
  a. indirect organizational pattern.
  b. direct organizational pattern.
  c. geographical organizational pattern.
  d. informational organizational pattern. (Obj. 3, p. 171)

_____ 16. Dianna is writing a memo to her staff about new benefit options, and she is sure they'll be pleased with the news. Dianna should use the
  a. direct pattern.
  b. indirect pattern.
  c. chronological pattern.
  d. informational pattern. (Obj. 3, pp. 171–172)

_____   17.   The indirect organizational pattern does *all but which* of the following?
a. Saves the reader's time
b. Ensures a fair hearing
c. Minimizes negative reaction
d. Respects the feelings of the audience (Obj. 3, p. 172)

_____   18.   Computers help create more effective written messages, oral presentations, and Web pages in *all but which* of the following ways?
a. Fighting writer's block
b. Improving correctness and precision
c. Controlling sentence length
d. Adding graphics for emphasis (Obj. 4, p. 174)

_____   19.   *Frontloading* means
a. presenting the recommendations at the end of the message where they will receive more emphasis.
b. giving the details at the beginning of the message.
c. supporting ideas with details.
d. presenting the main idea at the beginning of the message. (Obj. 3, p. 172)

_____   20.   Clauses that begin with words such as *if, when, because,* and *as* are usually
a. independent.
b. direct.
c. indirect.
d. dependent. (Obj. 4, p. 175)

_____   21.   To emphasize important ideas, writers should do *all but which* of the following?
a. Use vivid words
b. Label the main idea
c. Place the important idea in a complex sentence
d. Place the important idea first or last in the sentence (Obj. 4, p. 176)

_____   22.   To direct attention away from people and to focus on the action instead, use
a. dependent clauses.
b. passive voice.
c. active voice.
d. independent clauses. (Obj. 4, p. 177)

_____   23.   Stacy wants to emphasize the new features of a product she is selling. What should she do?
a. Use vivid words to describe the features.
b. Put the most important information in the middle of her sentences.
c. Use the passive voice to describe the features.
d. Put the most important information in a dependent clause. (Obj. 4, p.176)

_____ 24.   Paragraphs are generally easier to read when they contain
  a. eight or fewer printed lines.
  b. eight or fewer printed sentences.
  c. five or fewer printed sentences.
  d. at least five printed lines. (Obj. 5, p. 183)

_____ 25.   Which of the following is *not* a useful technique for linking ideas in a paragraph?
  a. Dovetailing sentences
  b. Pivoting sentences
  c. Sustaining the key idea
  d. Using pronouns (Obj. 5, pp. 180–181)

_____ 26.   Which of the following is *not* a transitional expression that shows time or order?
  a. *earlier*
  b. *meanwhile*
  c. *previously*
  d. *still* (Obj. 5, p. 182)

Sentence Elements

Indicate whether the following word groups are independent clauseswith IC, dependent clauses with DC, or phrases with P. In clauses underline subjects once and verbs twice. (Obj. 4)

_____ 27.   you should approach a job interview with self-confidence and a clear understanding of the company

_____ 28.   when the personnel manager reviewed the two résumés

_____ 29.   if a candidate is well prepared and has done his or her homework

_____ 30.   to sit down in an interview before being asked to do so

_____ 31.   naturally, employers are concerned with employee turnover

Sentence Length

Revise, improve, and shorten the following sentences. Use appropriate transitional expressions. (Obj. 4)

32.   Questions about career advancement present a delicate problem because you need this information to make an informed career choice, but you risk alienating an employer who does not want to hire an unrealistically ambitious college graduate for the average entry-level position, so some recruiters warn against asking straight out how soon you can be considered for a promotion.

33. After long negotiations with the artist, the museum persuaded her to show her early drawings, along with three sculptures, two paintings, and several sketches, and this show will be her first on this continent, making the museum the only one in the country, to include the major art museums in New York and Los Angeles, to have the works from all of her periods over the past 40 years in one show.

Active and Passive Voice

Business writing is more forceful if it uses active-voice verbs. In the following sentences convert passive-voice verbs to active-voice verbs. Add subjects if necessary. (Obj. 4)

Passive: The accounting report was not turned in on time [by Melissa].
Active: Melissa did not turn in the accounting report on time.

34. Your vacation request must be submitted by this Friday.

35. Initial figures for the bid were submitted before the June 1 deadline. [Tip: Who submitted the figures?]

36. The survey was designed to capture the emotional reactions of women under 50.

When you wish to emphasize an action or if you must be tactful, passive-voice verbs may be appropriate. Revise the following sentences so that they are in the passive voice. Notice how the doer of the action may go unmentioned.

Active: Mr. Eaton made three significant errors in the Globex audit.
Passive: Three significant errors were made in the Globex audit.

37. The Office of Management and Budget submitted the report to Congress late last night.

38. The government first issued a warning about the use of this pesticide 15 months ago.

39. Because the CEO was ill, the vice president gave the keynote address.

Misplaced Modifiers

Remedy any dangling or misplaced modifiers in the following sentences. Add subjects as needed, but retain the introductory phrases. Mark C if correct. (Obj. 4)

40. As assistant editor, your duties will include interviewing executives.

41. Doctors discovered his ankle had been fractured in five places during surgery.

42. To apply for a job, a résumé must be submitted.

43. To be successful in responding to employee problems, good listening skills are essential.

44. Ignoring the warning on the screen, the computer was turned off.

Transitional Expressions

Add transitional expressions to improve the flow of ideas (coherence) of the following sentence groups. (Obj. 5)

45. We tailor our service efforts specifically to individual customer needs. We have seen the volume at our plants grow. Our profitability has increased. We expect even better results in the future.

46. No business can anticipate every customer's needs. We keep our hotel management staff on duty 24 hours a day. Customers always have someone of authority available.

47. Your responsibility is to listen to customers. Your responsibility is to understand what they are saying. Your responsibility is to make them feel that their concerns are your most important concerns. Your responsibility is to take care of their concerns to their satisfaction.

CAREER TRACK SPELLING

Spelling Challenge

Underline misspelled words. Write correct forms in the spaces provided. Some sentences may have more than one misspelled word. If the sentence is correct, write C. *Then check your answers with those at the end of the guide.*

_____	48.	I am writing to inform you of an ommission in my application.
_____	49.	Parking was unecessarily difficult because of construction.
_____	50.	Our order for 100 calenders didn't arrive until Febuary 2.
_____	51.	During the internship Jennifer worked with her superviser to update the company's mailing database.
_____	52.	Your checks will be automaticly canceled when they reach the bank.
_____	53.	Two local nonprofit organizations asked for assistance to develop their promotional pamflets.
_____	54.	The company's new president immediately set out to balance the buget.
_____	55.	The research division of Schering Plough must respond to the request by the goverment for more testing of its colon cancer drug.
_____	56.	The executive assistant filed the applications in seperate folders.
_____	57.	As interest rates drop to levels not seen in over 30 years, homeowners are choosing to refinance their morgages.

My Spelling Monsters

List each troublesome word. Be sure to spell it correctly. Then write it four or more times. Review this page often to help you vanquish these spelling demons.

_____

_____

_____

_____

_____

CAREER TRACK VOCABULARY

Use your dictionary to define the words in Column A. Then select the best definition in Column B to match each word in Column A.

	Column A		**Column B**
_____	58. discretionary	a.	inequality or unequal nature
_____	59. disperse	b.	humility, respect
_____	60. deign	c.	scatter, strew
_____	61. deference	d.	optional, voluntary
_____	62. disparity	e.	recognizable, perceptible
_____	63. discernable	f.	condescend, to see fit

Choose the best meaning for the following underlined words.

_____ 64.   Once the new policies were in place, a sense of dread <u>emanated</u> from the company.

a. emigrated   b. flowed from   c. erupted

_____ 65.   The basketball star told his fans not to <u>emulate</u> him; but then, paradoxically, he endorsed products on television.

a. imitate   b. quote   c. parody

_____ 66.   Problems with honesty in reporting were <u>endemic</u> to the department.

a. foreign   b. imported   c. native

_____ 67.   From executives, stockholders want performance that is <u>equivalent</u> to their lofty salaries.

a. transcendent   b. commensurate   c. inferior

_____ 68.   Reports are occasionally hard to read because writers like to use <u>esoteric</u> terms.

a. obscure   b. rapid   c. obvious

_____ 69.   This item is needed immediately; please <u>expedite</u> the order.

a. reserve   b. hand carry   c. rush

_____ 70.   Use care when putting paper in the fax; it is difficult to <u>extricate</u> when jammed.

a. smooth   b. remove   c. photocopy

_____ 71.   The organization's glamorous <u>facade</u> was shattered by recent scandals.

a. artificial appearance   b. prosperous clientele   c. entertainment schedule

Confusing Words

conscience	regard for fairness	*desert*	(n) arid land
conscious	aware		(v) abandon
		dessert	sweet food
credible	believable or reliable	*device*	invention or mechanism
creditable	bringing honor or praise	*devise*	to design or arrange

72. We rely on *The Wall Street Journal* for _____ financial news.

73. Jorge and Samuel were asked to _____ a wireless network for the office.

74. Sara's _____ performance resulted in her selection as the winner of the John F. Kennedy award.

75. After listening to the talk about ethics, Mr. Smith became more _____ of small ways in which he might possibly be violating company policy.

76. This new memory stick is a great _____ for carrying data.

77. The bakery's motto is "Eat _____ first; life's uncertain."

78. In the midst of the traffic jam, Melody wished she could _____ her car.

79. Before asking his employees to work overtime, the manager searched his _____.

Look back over the vocabulary words in this chapter. Select five or more new words to add to your vocabulary. Double-check the meanings of your selections in a dictionary. Then write a sentence for each of your words.

_____

_____

_____

_____

_____

COMPETENT LANGUAGE USAGE ESSENTIALS (C.L.U.E.)

Commas

Guide 21: Use commas to separate three or more items (words, phrases, or short clauses) in a series.

> The president was tanned, rested, and ready to return to work.
>
> Robert designed a questionnaire, collected data, and made recommendations.
>
> From the freezer section she selected corn, broccoli, peas, and carrots.

TIP. Some writers omit the comma before *and*. However, business writers prefer to retain the comma because it prevents misreading the last two items as one. Notice in the previous example how the final two vegetables (peas and carrots) could be misread if the comma had been omitted.

Guide 22: Use commas to separate introductory clauses and certain phrases from independent clauses. This guideline describes the comma most often omitted by business writers. Sentences that open with dependent clauses (often introduced by words such as *since, when, if, as, although,* and *because*) require commas to separate them from the main idea. The comma helps readers recognize where the introduction ends and the main idea begins. Introductory phrases of more than five words or phrases containing verbal elements also require commas.

> Since she does all her writing at her computer, she needed a laptop for traveling. (Introductory dependent clause requires a comma.)
>
> When you purchase a small truck, you have many models from which to choose. (Introductory dependent clause requires a comma.)
>
> If necessary, you may have a co-signer help you with the purchase. (You may assume the subject and verb of the introductory clause *If it is necessary.*)
>
> In the fall of next year, we plan to hire new representatives. (Introductory phrases of five or more words require a comma.)
>
> Having studied our competitor's techniques, we see many areas for improvement. (Introductory phrase containing a verbal element requires a comma.)
>
> To succeed, we must cut costs and improve quality. (Introductory phrase containing a verbal element requires a comma.)

Guide 23: Use a comma before the coordinating conjunction in a compound sentence.

> Interest rates were falling, and homeowners were eager to refinance.
>
> Some homeowners refinanced immediately, but others waited for even lower rates.

TIP. Before inserting a comma, test the two clauses. Can each of them stand alone as a complete sentence? If either is incomplete, skip the comma.

> Lenders require a letter from your employer *or* a copy of your W-2 forms from the past two years. (Note that the words following *or* do not form an independent clause; hence, no comma is needed.)

> Judy majored in communications *and* took a job in public relations. (No comma is required because the words following *and* do not form an independent clause.)

C.L.U.E. Checkpoint

Use proofreading marks to insert necessary commas.

80. When she enrolled at Midwestern University Tina was unsure of a major.

81. When proofreading for problems in grammar check to see whether the pronouns agree with their antecedents.

82. After writing a dynamite résumé he sent it to 11 companies on his list.

83. Government in this country is intended to be of the people by the people and for the people.

84. Mike researched 15 companies in the Midwest and he finally found one that needed someone with a background in robotics.

85. In the spring of this year Unitech received hundreds of résumés.

86. A cover letter is meant to introduce your résumé and to help you secure a personal interview.

87. She submitted a résumé to eight companies and began thinking about friends relatives and acquaintances to serve as a network in her job search.

88. A few companies send recruiters to college campuses in the fall but many more send representatives and conduct interviews in the spring.

89. When you expect the audience will be receptive to the message use the direct pattern.

Super C.L.U.E. Review

In this cumulative review, use proofreading marks to correct punctuation, number usage, capitalization, spelling, and confusing word use. Mark C if a sentence is correct.

90. Approximatly twenty to thirty percent of all companies must restructure to reduce errors delays and returns.

91. When coca-cola and pepsi compete in asia they spend hundreds of thousands of dollars in marketing efforts.

92. Employees are encouraged to ask questions and these questions become a valuable source of feedback to management.

93. 34% of the twelve hundred job applicants in one study falsified information on their résumés.

94. When GM began selling daewoo cars under the chevrolet brand it hoped to overcome negative perceptions in europe.

95. Our human resources manager schedules and attends all job interviews but the hiring managers make all final selections.

96. The house was apprised at 125,000 dollars, however we felt its actual worth was at least twenty percent more.

97. We reccommend that fifteen real estate agents visit the property at ten a.m. and that the remaining twenty-three inspect it between 3:30 and five p.m.

98. When the recruiter visited indiana state university she was conscience of increased campus interest in ethics.

99. If you caused the accident and have liability insurance with state farm expect the company to pay for the damages you caused and any medical expenses arising from your negligince.

Chapter 7

Writing Process Phase 3: Revise, Proofread, Evaluate

CHAPTER REVIEW

Indicate whether the following statements are true or false by using T *or* F.

_____ 1. Revising means correcting grammar, spelling, punctuation, and mechanics. (Obj. 1, p. 191)

_____ 2. Some experts recommend devoting about half of the total composition time to revising and proofreading. (Obj. 1, p. 192)

_____ 3. Clarity is enhanced by writing that sounds professional and formal; you should avoid a conversational tone. (Obj. 1, p. 193)

_____ 4. Messages without flabby phrases and redundancies are easier to comprehend. (Obj. 2, p. 193)

_____ 5. Familiar phrases and words such as *case, degree,* and *the fact that* help readers feel comfortable and enhance the quality of the writing. (Obj. 2, p. 196)

_____ 6. Business writers can improve message clarity by using noun phrases (*perform an analysis of*) instead of using action verbs (*analyze*). (Obj. 3, p. 196)

_____ 7. Numbered lists improve readability, comprehension, and retention. (Obj. 4, p. 198)

_____ 8. Graphic techniques such as underlining and using all capital letters focus attention and can be relied on to increase readability. (Obj. 4, p. 199)

_____   9.   When proofreading messages on a computer screen, the safest method is to read one screen at a time. (Obj. 5, p. 202)

_____   10.   Because evaluation is such an important part of the writing process, you should encourage the receiver to provide feedback. (Obj. 6, p. 204)

Fill in the Blank

Use the listed words to complete the following sentences. You may use each word only once.

Revising Messages

bulleted	first draft	parallelism	recognize
concise	heading	persuade	redundant
final draft	impress	readability	retention

11.   Many professional writers compose the _____ quickly without worrying about language, precision, or correctness. (Obj. 1, p. 192)

12.   One reason communicators fail to craft simple messages is a desire to _____ their boss. (Obj. 1, p. 192)

13.   Expressions that repeat meaning or include unnecessary words are _____. (Obj. 2, p. 194)

14.   Business messages should be _____, meaning that they make their point in the fewest possible words. (Obj. 2, p. 193)

15.   A writing technique that involves balanced construction is called _____. This technique matches nouns with nouns, verbs with verbs, and phrases with phrases. (Obj. 4, p. 197)

16.   Numbered and _____ lists can be used to organize information and aid comprehension. (Obj. 4, p. 198)

17.   A well-written _____ enables readers to separate major ideas from details. This writing device helps readers skim familiar or less important information. (Obj. 4, p. 199)

18.   The Fog Index is a formula that measures _____. Long sentences and long words (those over two syllables) make writing foggy. (Obj. 4, p. 199)

19.   Even short words can cause trouble if readers don't _____ them. (Obj. 4, p. 200)

Proofreading and Evaluating Messages

analysis	easy	rough draft	time
content	expertise	spelling	two
difficult	numbers	three	words

20. Two items that require special care in proofreading are names and _____ because inaccuracies are not immediately visible. (Obj. 5, p. 201)

21. Because a common excuse for sloppy proofreading is lack of _____, you should develop and follow a careful schedule for writing projects. (Obj. 5, p. 203)

22. When proofreading, read the message at least _____ times for meaning and grammar/mechanics. (Obj. 5, p. 203)

23. Proofreading complex documents requires that you concentrate on individual _____ instead of ideas. (Obj. 5, p. 195)

24. Computer programs can help analyze writing, calculate readability, and locate some errors in grammar and _____. (Obj. 5, p. 203)

Multiple Choice

Choose the best answer.

_____ 25. Communicators fail to craft simple, direct messages for *all but which* of the following reasons?
a. Unethical writers intentionally obscure a message to hide the truth.
b. Unskilled writers create foggy messages because they haven't learned to communicate clearly.
c. Untrained employees haven't learned to impress their boss.
d. Untrained executives worry that plain messages don't sound important. (Obj. 1, p. 192)

_____ 26. Which of the following examples is free of clichés, fillers, and compound prepositions?
a. This is to inform you that the meeting will be held next Thursday.
b. Due to the fact that many people were busy, the meeting was postponed.
c. The meeting has been rescheduled for Thursday.
d. Please do not hesitate to call if you have any questions about the meeting. (Objs. 1 & 2, pp. 192–193)

_____ 27. The sentence *There are five employees who serve on the committee* could be made more concise by eliminating a(n)
a. opening filler.
b. compound expression.
c. redundancy.
d. trite business expression. (Objs. 1 & 2, pp. 192–193)

_____ 28. The sentence *I am writing this letter to inform you that our meeting location has changed*
- a. contains a redundancy.
- b. contains a long lead-in.
- c. contains a trite business expression.
- d. is an example of good business writing. (Obj. 2, pp. 193–196)

_____ 29. Locating and excising wordiness involves eliminating *all but which* of the following?
- a. Fillers
- b. Adverbs
- c. Redundancies
- d. Long lead-ins (Obj. 2, p. 194)

_____ 30. Which of the following expressions is free from redundancy?
- a. *Proposed meeting*
- b. *Midway between*
- c. *Exactly identical*
- d. *Collect together* (Obj. 2, pp. 194–195)

_____ 31. Business expressions that have been used excessively over the years and are no longer original are called
- a. noun phrases.
- b. parallel construction.
- c. trite expressions.
- d. noun constructions. (Obj. 3, p. 197)

_____ 32. Which of the following statements is incorrect?
- a. Headings can be used effectively to highlight information.
- b. Headings enable readers to skim documents for familiar information.
- c. Graphic techniques help readers group ideas.
- d. Because graphic techniques add length, they should be avoided. (Obj. 4, p. 199)

_____ 33. Bullets, enumerated lists, headings, boldface, and italics help writers to
- a. improve comprehension.
- b. eliminate redundancies.
- c. reduce trite phrases.
- d. apply the KISS formula. (Obj. 4, p. 198)

_____ 34. *All but which* of the following is important when revising documents?
- a. Keep the message simple.
- b. Don't convert verbs to nouns.
- c. Shun parallelism.
- d. Consider readability. (Obj. 4, p. 200)

Short Answer

35. Name four strategies to help readers anticipate and comprehend ideas quickly. (Obj. 4, pp. 197–200)

36. List four items that proofreaders should check carefully. (Obj. 5, pp. 201–202)

Clarity

Revise the following sentences to make them direct, simple, and conversational. (Obj. 1)

37. As you recommended in your report, the managers of each department will initiate and conduct a thorough and complete examination of our company's personnel policy to determine if it is possible and probable that it needs to be changed.

38. If on our part there is any doubt entertained regarding an optimal solution to the problem of acquisition of new computers, it is my suggestion that we commence an investigation of our usage of our current computer equipment.

39. It would be advantageous for you to enlighten your employees regarding the company's new e-mail guidelines.

40. It is our considered opinion that you should not attempt to advance or proceed with this project until you seek and receive approval of said project from the department head prior to beginning the project.

41. This organization is honored to have the pleasure of extending a welcome to you as a new customer.

Conciseness

Revise and shorten the following sentences. (Obj. 2)

42. There are seventeen new vehicles that need to be priced prior to making them available for sale.

43. Due to the fact that the statement seemed wrong, I sent a check in the amount of $200.

44. In the case of Mattel and Fisher-Price, the two toy companies merged their lines.

45. It is my personal opinion that we cannot create a reduction in our inventory unless we lower prices.

46. Until such time as we can locate all addresses that are duplicates, this is to notify you that mass mailings must be avoided.

47. Despite the fact that there is only one van available, response to the program designated for employee van pooling is remarkable.

48. According to the staff's recent survey of applicants for the small number of private parking spaces, over 66 percent, or two-thirds, of the applicants do not believe that parking is a problem that should be investigated.

49. Those who are functioning as vendors may not have a complete and full understanding of our difficulty.

50. This is just to let you know that applications will be accepted at a later date for positions that are at the entry level.

51. There are many words that can be eliminated through revision that is carefully executed.

Vigor

Revise the following sentences to reduce noun conversions, trite expressions, and other wordiness. (Obj. 2)

52. There are three members of our staff who are making every effort to locate your order.

53. Enclosed please find the contract we have prepared for you.

54. Please give consideration to our latest proposal, despite the fact that it comes into conflict with our original goals.

55. If you are in need of any further assistance, please do not hesitate to make a call to me at (212) 499-3029.

Parallelism

Revise the following sentences to improve parallelism. (Obj. 3)

56. As a successful entrepreneur, I wrote a business plan and cash flow was analyzed, as well as designed promotional materials and was responsible for the marketing of the business.

57. Researchers examined data concerning our employees' income, health, and situations involving stress levels.

58. Ensuring equal opportunities and the elimination of age discrimination are our goals.

59. Employers can avoid complaints of discrimination if they ask each applicant the same questions, limit questions to job-related issues, and trained interviewers are used.

60. In my last job I set up a log of all incoming materials, the contents were inspected and findings documented, after which I reported results to shipping.

CAREER TRACK SPELLING

Underline misspelled words. Write correct forms in the spaces provided. Some items may have more than one misspelled word. If all words in an item are correct, write C. Then check your answers with those at the end of the guide.

_____	61.	analyze	destroy	embarrass	separate
_____	62.	supervisor	schedule	refered	yield
_____	63.	division	employee	development	practicle
_____	64.	correspondence	ocurred	advisable	paid
_____	65.	remittance	emphasis	consecutive	calandar
_____	66.	describe	ninty	fascinate	profited
_____	67.	courteous	insidentally	grateful	excellent
_____	68.	maintinance	fiscal	forty	qualify
_____	69.	extraordinary	incredible	exempt	foriegn
_____	70.	friend	useage	yield	surprise

My Spelling Monsters

List each troublesome word. Be sure to spell it correctly. Then write it four or more times. Review this page often to help you vanquish these spelling demons.

_____

_____

_____

_____

_____

CAREER TRACK VOCABULARY

Use your dictionary to define the words in Column A. Then select the best definition in Column B to match each word in Column A.

	Column A		**Column B**
_____	71. egress	a.	unpredictable, irregular
_____	72. erratic	b.	list, detail
_____	73. enumerate	c.	exact copy, duplication
_____	74. equitable	d.	eloquent, well-spoken
_____	75. facsimile	e.	equal or identical in value
_____	76. fluent	f.	emergence, exit

Choose the best meaning for the following underlined words.

____ 77.   Dr. Loy's neat desk illustrates his <u>fastidious</u> personality.

   a. indifferent   b. meticulous   c. creative

____ 78.   As a result of the opposing party's <u>filibuster</u>, the latest government budget failed to pass.

   a. delaying speeches   b. investment   c. support

____ 79.   Demonstrators worked hard to <u>foment</u> a riot, but their words were ignored.

   a. delay   b. incite   c. avoid

____ 80.   California leads the nation in <u>fraudulent</u> auto accident claims.

   a. honest   b. expensive   c. deceitful

____ 81.   Pictures can't impart the <u>grandeur</u> of Niagara Falls.

   a. majesty   b. tranquility   c. ferocity

____ 82.   Some companies offer stock options as a <u>gratuity</u> for years of service.

   a. compliment   b. gift   c. salary

_____ 83.   In the hotel business a <u>gregarious</u> personality is an asset.

a. defiant   b. placid   c. sociable

_____ 84.   Unfamiliar with the storeroom, the secretary <u>groped</u> for the light switch.

a. looked   b. fumbled   c. lunged

Confusing Words

disburse	to pay out		*elicit*	to draw out
disperse	to scatter wildly		*illicit*	unlawful

envelop	to wrap, surround, or conceal
envelope	a container for a letter

85.   Our treasurer promised to _____ all funds in accordance with the by-laws.

86.   David's humorous comments are sure to _____ laughter from his audience.

87.   The executive was charged with _____ behavior for attempting to bribe the government official.

88.   Because clouds often _____ Mount McKinley, photographers have difficulty getting a clear picture.

89.   The officers asked the crowd to _____ to open up a secure space for the motorcade.

Look back over the vocabulary words in this chapter. Select five or more new words to add to your vocabulary. Double-check the meanings of your selections in a dictionary. Then write a sentence for each of your words.

_____

_____

_____

_____

_____

COMPETENT LANGUAGE USAGE ESSENTIALS (C.L.U.E.)

Commas (cont.)

Guide 24: Use commas appropriately in dates, addresses, geographical names, degrees, and long numbers.

> November 3, 1976, is his birthday. (For dates use commas before and after the year.)
>
> Send the announcement to Rob Silver, 1901 NW 23 Avenue, Portland, OR 97210, as soon as possible. (For addresses use commas to separate all units except the two-letter state abbreviation and the zip code.)
>
> The Lees plan to move from Naperville, Illinois, to Waterloo, Iowa, in June. (For geographical areas use commas to enclose the second element.)
>
> Mark Hendricks, Ph.D., and Davonne Williams, C.P.A., were the speakers. (For professional designations and academic degrees following names, use commas to enclose each item.)
>
> We have budgeted $135,000 for new equipment. (In figures use commas to separate every three digits, counting from the right.)

Guide 25: Use commas to set off internal sentence interrupters. Sentence interrupters may be verbal phrases, dependent clauses, contrasting elements, or parenthetical expressions (also called transitional phrases). These interrupters often provide information that is not grammatically essential.

> Globex International, having registered its name in Washington, started business. (Use commas to set off an interrupting verbal phrase.)
>
> The new company, which planned to ship cargo only, was headquartered in Juneau. (Use commas to set off nonessential dependent clauses.)
>
> Jake Franklin, who helped organize the new company, invested energy and capital. (Use commas to set off nonessential dependent clauses.)
>
> It was Michael Williams, not Michael Thomas, who became the company attorney. (Use commas to set off a contrasting element.)
>
> Several investors, on the contrary, were eager to meet the organizers. (Use commas to set off a parenthetical expression.)

Parenthetical (transitional) expressions are helpful words that guide the reader from one thought to the next. Here are representative parenthetical expressions that require commas:

as a matter of fact	consequently	in addition	nevertheless	on the other hand
as a result	for example	in the meantime	of course	therefore

TIP. Always use *two* commas to set off an interrupter, unless it begins or ends a sentence.

C.L.U.E. Checkpoint

Insert necessary commas.

90. Send the material to Harlan D. Miller 20 Hawthorne Street Boston MA 02114 as soon as possible.

91. Our manager is from Raleigh North Carolina.

92. Joan Winkoff who is one of the executives attending the conference plans to leave Thursday June 5.

93. Business at our Allentown branch which was opened last February has boosted company profits considerably.

94. In the meantime please list David Smith as a contract not a permanent employee.

Super C.L.U.E. Review

In this cumulative review, use proofreading marks to correct punctuation, number usage, capitalization, spelling, and confusing word use. Mark C if a sentence is correct.

95. Among the topics discussed at the staff meeting held on April 5th 2004 were schedules deadlines and suppliers.

96. Eric Sims one of the four company foundars invested capitol of just under thirty thousand dollars.

97. Companys now include disclaimers saying that the employee policy manual is not a contract that policies may be changed or withdrawn and that the individual and the company may seperate at any time for any reason.

98. Our new policy manual which was adapted from an industry publication is twenty-six pages long.

99. We hired Dr. Nocaponte who is known for his expertise in tropical diseases as a consultant for the upcoming project in Mexico which begins on June 10th at a monthly rate of $2300 dollars.

100. In today's fast-paced global marketplace companies that can move products through the development process fastest enjoy a cost advantage through increased efficeincy.

CAREER APPLICATION

Using the proofreading marks shown in Chapter 7 or in Appendix D of Guffey's Business Communication: Process and Product, *revise the following letter. Rectify wordy and trite phrases, sexist language, spelling, capitalization, number expression, and other faults. When you finish, compare your revision with that shown in Appendix B.*

October 5, 200x

Ms. Michele Taylor
Abonte Guaranty Company
3401 Providence Avenue
New York, NY 10001

Dear Michele:

Pursuant to our telephone conversation of October 4, this is to advise you that two (2) agent's packages will be sent to you October 6th. Due to the fact that you need these immediatly; we are using federal express.

Although we cannot offer a 50/50 commission split, we are able to offer new agents a 60/40 commission split. There are two new agreement forms that show this commission ratio. When you get ready to sign up a new agent have her fill in both forms.

When you send me an executed agency agreement, please make every effort to tell me what agency package was assigned to the agent. On the last form that you sent, you overlooked this information. We need this information to distribute commissions in an expeditious manner.

If you have any questions, don't hesitate to call on me.

Very truly yours,

Chapter 8

Routine
E-Mail Messages
and Memos

CHAPTER REVIEW

Indicate whether the following statements are true or false by using T *or* F.

_____ 1.   E-mail is the communication channel of choice in the U.S. and abroad. (Obj. 1, p. 218)

_____ 2.   When you want to convey enthusiasm, warmth, or other emotion, e-mail is the most effective communication channel to use. (Obj. 1, p. 219)

_____ 3.   Memos and e-mail generally follow similar structure and formatting; in both an informative subject line is mandatory. (Obj. 2, p. 220)

_____ 4.   Most e-mails cover sensitive information that needs to be handled carefully. (Obj. 2, p. 220)

_____ 5.   When typing the body of an e-mail message, use all lowercase characters for efficient keystroking. (Obj. 2, p. 223)

_____ 6.   Those who use e-mail wisely are aware of its benefits and dangers. (Obj. 3, pp. 227–228)

_____ 7.   Information and procedure messages generally flow upward from employees to management. (Obj. 4, p. 231)

_____ 8. When seeking answers to questions, one of your best options is to use a polite command such as *Please answer the following questions.* (Obj. 5, p. 233)

_____ 9. When responding to requests, consider using a standard opener such as *In response to your message of the 15th.* (Obj. 5, p. 235)

_____ 10. Because individuals may forget, alter, or retract their words, it's wise to create a written record of oral decisions in a confirmation memo. (Obj. 6, p. 236)

Fill in the Blank

Use the listed words to complete the following sentences. You may use each word only once.

Routine Memos and E-Mail Messages

abilities	evaluation	lists	summary
closings	goals	openings	text
e-mail	length	subject	topic

11. Developing skill in writing e-mail messages and memos brings two benefits. The first is that well-written documents are likely to achieve their _____. (Obj. 1, p. 218)

12. Careful writing always takes time, especially for inexperienced writers. Following a systematic plan like the 3-x-3 writing process enables communicators to work at maximum speed while producing a good product. Remember that your speaking and writing _____ can determine how much influence you'll have in your organization. (Obj. 1, p. 218)

13. When writing e-mail, avoid amassing huge blocks of _____. (Obj. 1, p. 219)

14. A mandatory part of an e-mail message or a memo is the _____ line, which summarizes a memo's central idea and provides quick topic identification for the reader. (Obj. 2, p. 220)

15. When writing e-mail messages or memos, effective writers limit the _____ to help the receiver act on it and file it appropriately. (Obj. 2, p. 220)

16. The body of a memo often includes numbered or bulleted _____, headings, or other graphic techniques that facilitate comprehension. (Obj. 2, p. 221)

17. Memos may conclude with action information such as dates and order deadlines, a _____ of the message, or a closing thought. (Obj. 2, p. 221)

18. Writers of e-mail messages within organizations may omit _____ and even skip their names at the end of messages. (Obj. 2, p. 223)

Using E-Mail and Memos Effectively

channel	cultural	personal	requests
compose	delete	private	scan
correct	letter	procedure	thread

19. When an e-mail message travels outside a company, the writer may include a salutation to make the message seem less curt and unfriendly and more like a _____. (Obj. 3, p. 223)

20. Despite its dangers and limitations, e-mail has become a mainstream _____ of communication. (Obj. 3, p. 227)

21. Avoid sending sensitive, confidential, or inflammatory messages via e-mail because it is not _____. (Obj. 3, p. 228)

22. When using e-mail, you should organize your thoughts, _____ carefully, and pay close attention to grammar and punctuation. (Obj. 3, 227)

23. Messages with misleading subject lines may not be opened or read because receivers may think they are junk e-mail and _____ them. (Obj. 3, p. 227)

24. To save time and frustration when reading and answering e-mail, you should _____ all messages in your inbox before replying to each individually. (Obj. 3, p. 229)

25. When replying to incoming e-mail messages, don't return the entire _____ (sequence of messages) on a topic. Instead, cut and paste the relevant parts. (Obj. 3, p. 230)

26. Because e-mail may be used to expedite business with companies in other countries, be aware of _____ differences. (Obj. 3, p. 230)

27. In writing information and _____ messages, be careful of tone. (Obj. 4, p. 233)

28. When replying to _____, direct opening statements can also be cheerful and emphatic. (Obj. 5, p. 235)

Multiple Choice

_____   29. Generally, memos may be grouped by function into *all but which* of the following categories?
   a. Procedure and information memos
   b. Claim adjustment memos
   c. Confirmation memos
   d. Request and reply memos (Obj. 4, p. 231)

_____ 30. Which of the following would *not* be considered either a procedure or information memo?
   a. A memo about the upcoming company picnic
   b. A memo stating the specific holidays employees will have off
   c. A memo confirming responsibilities of members of the budget committee
   d. A memo stating guidelines for using company e-mail (Obj. 4, p. 231)

_____ 31. An effective opening for a request memo is
   a. *Please send me your answers to the following questions by December 1.*
   b. *Thank you in advance for answering the following questions.*
   c. *Here are the answers to the questions you had about our new software product called "Personal Assistant."*
   d. *Please answer the following questions about your new software product called "Personal Assistant."* (Obj. 5, p. 233)

_____ 32. In the body of a request or reply memo, you should
   a. explain and justify your request or reply.
   b. include action information and deadlines.
   c. begin with a polite command.
   d. ask the most important question first. (Obj. 5, pp. 233–235)

_____ 33. A direct e-mail message or memo that requests information should begin by
   a. requesting the information without providing elaborate explanations and justifications.
   b. giving the reasons for the request.
   c. giving the date a response is needed.
   d. introducing the writer by name and title. (Obj. 5, p. 233)

_____ 34. What is the best closing for an e-mail message or memo that requests information?
   a. *I am looking forward to receiving your reply.*
   b. *Please send me the answers to these questions by May 15.*
   c. *Please send me the answers to these questions at your earliest convenience.*
   d. *I need the answers to these questions as soon as possible.* (Obj. 5, p. 234)

Short Answer

35. List five questions you should ask yourself before writing an e-mail or memo. (Obj. 1, pp. 218–219)

36. List the three ways messages generally end. (Obj. 2, p. 221)

37. List four key issues to consider to help you get off to a good start in using e-mail smartly and safely. (Obj. 3, pp. 225–226)

38. List four of the six rules of polite online interaction involving e-mail. (Obj. 3, p. 229)

39. Name three items to be included in a confirmation memo or e-mail. (Obj. 6, p. 236)

CAREER TRACK SPELLING

Underline misspelled words. Write correct forms in the spaces provided. Some sentences may have more than one misspelled word. If the sentence is correct, write C. Then check your answers with those at the end of the guide.

_____	40.	On the forth call Lisa was able to reach the director.
_____	41.	She wondered, never the less, why he was never in.
_____	42.	Gary considered his spell checker indespensible.
_____	43.	Jeremy decided on two instruments to gather data: an online survey and a questionaire administered in person.
_____	44.	The friends refused to be drawn into an arguement.
_____	45.	Consistant business practices and a tight budget enabled the franchise to succeed.
_____	46.	Carlos asked his supervisor for a recommendation.
_____	47.	Janine saw an extrodinery opportunity in computer sales.
_____	48.	The new vacation and leave policy had a noticable effect on productivity.
_____	49.	The third colume of figures appears to have an error.
_____	50.	On this floor, we do not permit metal objects, not even metal buttons on jackets.

My Spelling Monsters

List each troublesome word. Be sure to spell it correctly. Then write it four or more times. Review this page often to help you vanquish these spelling demons.

_____

_____

_____

_____

_____

CAREER TRACK VOCABULARY

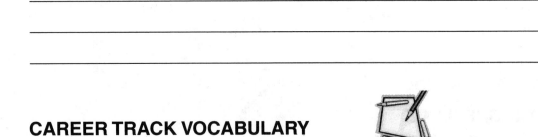

Use your dictionary to define the words in Column A. Then select the best definition in Column B to match each word in Column A.

	Column A		Column B
_____	51. franchise	a.	smooth-talking, fluent
_____	52. fraudulent	b.	break, disruption
_____	53. glib	c.	deceitful, fake
_____	54. gratis	d.	execute, put into action
_____	55. hiatus	e.	free, without charge
_____	56. implement	f.	right to vote, permission

Choose the best meaning for the following underlined words.

_____ 57.　Weak response in consumer trials is a sure <u>harbinger</u> of product failure.

　　　　a. interpretation　　　b. signal　　　　　　c. conduit

_____ 58.　Many companies realize that choosing employees who are <u>hospitable</u> to customers often results in repeat business.

　　　　a. attractive　　　　b. predictable　　　　c. gracious

_____ 59.　During the 1990s, many small companies were victims of <u>hostile</u> takeovers.

　　　　a. unfriendly　　　　b. happy　　　　　　c. inexpensive

_____ 60.　Price and quality determine consumer spending, not advertising <u>hyperbole</u>.

　　　　a. exaggeration　　　b. restraint　　　　　c. jingles

_____ 61.   Because <u>icons</u> simplify computer use, many software programs feature them.

a. documentation   b. guides   c. images

_____ 62.   The false reports created an <u>illusion</u> that the production line was meeting its quota.

a. reality   b. actuality   c. false impression

_____ 63.   With the hundreds of class action lawsuits waiting to be filed, the drug company faces an <u>imminent</u> decision about filing for Chapter 11 bankruptcy.

a. impending   b. completed   c. doubtful

Confusing Words

every day	each single day	_flair_	natural talent, aptitude
everyday	ordinary	_flare_	to blaze up or spread out

farther	a greater distance
further	additional

64. Paula's _____ for decorating shows in her well-appointed office.

65. The team starts _____ with a short meeting to set the agenda.

66. Ms. Dwinelle asked the benefits coordinator for _____ guidance during their meeting.

67. Because the synthetic material has the potential to _____ quickly when exposed to fire, the company saturates it with retardant.

68. Although it's _____ from Tucson than Phoenix, Sedona is worth the trip.

69. In this company, emergencies are a(n) _____ occurrence.

Look back over the vocabulary words in this chapter. Select five or more new words to add to your vocabulary. Double-check the meanings of your selections in a dictionary. Then write a sentence for each of your words.

_____

_____

_____

_____

_____

COMPETENT LANGUAGE USAGE ESSENTIALS (C.L.U.E.)

Semicolons and Colons

Guide 27: Use a semicolon to join closely related independent clauses. Mature writers use semicolons to show readers that two thoughts are closely associated. If the ideas are not related, they should be expressed as separate sentences. Often, but not always, the second independent clause contains a conjunctive adverb (such as *however, consequently, therefore,* or *furthermore*) to show the relation between the two clauses.

> Good visual aids need no explanation; they speak for themselves.

> He invested wisely; consequently, he became a wealthy man.

> Some stores were open on the holiday; however, most were closed.

TIP. Don't use a semicolon unless each clause is truly independent. Try the sentence test. Omit the semicolon if each clause is not independent.

> **Faulty:** Although some employees work on weekends; the main office is closed. (The initial clause here is dependent, not independent. It fails the sentence test. It can't stand alone; therefore, a comma instead of a semicolon should be used.)

Guide 28: Use a semicolon to separate items in a series when one or more of the items contain internal commas.

> Attending the conference were Roberta Carrera, president, Carrera Industries; William Franker, C.P.A., General Systems; and Gail Gomez, vice president, Sun Company.

> Production sites being considered include Canton, Ohio; Mesa, Arizona; and Waterford, Connecticut.

Guide 29: Use a colon after a complete thought that introduces a list of items. Words such as *these, the following,* and *as follows* may introduce the list or they may be implied.

> At the top of our list are the following cities: Portland, San Diego, and Virginia City.

> An alternate list includes cities in the South: New Orleans, Miami, and Atlanta.

TIP. Be sure that the statement before the colon is grammatically complete. An introductory statement that ends with a preposition (such as *by, for, at,* or *to*) or a verb (such as *is, are,* or *were*) is incomplete. The list following a preposition or a verb actually functions as an object or as a complement to finish the sentence.

> **Faulty:** Send invitations to: Jim, Pat, and Tim. (Omit the colon because the introductory statement is incomplete.)

> **Faulty:** Some of the best colors are: salmon, red, and green. (Do not use a colon after an incomplete statement.)

Guide 30: Use a colon after business letter salutations and to introduce long quotations.

Ladies and Gentlemen: Dear Ms. Lee: Dear Lisa:

The advertising executive said: "As opposed to nations in the West, Asia is a growing market. By the year 2020, two-thirds of the world's consumers will live around the edge of the Pacific Rim."

C.L.U.E. Checkpoint

Use proofreading marks to add or delete commas, semicolons, and colons.

70. Kristin prepared a chronological résumé, Michael preferred a functional résumé.

71. Travis was determined to become a CPA consequently he majored in accounting.

72. Although hotel managers say that customers' needs are met nearly all the time; only 40 percent of travelers agree.

73. General Electric interviewed marketing candidates from: Central Michigan University, Ohio University, and Texas Tech.

74. Nominees for president included: Jacki Ames, Miami, Thomas Hart, Atlanta, and Tamala Wilson, Tampa.

Super C.L.U.E. Review

In this cumulative review, use proofreading marks to correct punctuation, number usage, capitalization, spelling, and confusing word use. Mark C if a sentence is correct.

75. After we investigate the matter farther; we hope to develop a set of every day procedures that all employes can follow.

76. Underinflation reduces the life of a tire overinflation may cause a blowout.

77. Some people thought that technology would mean they would be doing less writing on the job however just the opposite has occured.

78. Recruiters were looking for three principle qualitys; Initiative, Reliability, and Enthusiasm.

79. The american bar association elected dennis r. radiman, president, harriet lee-thomas, vice president, and e. m. miles, secretary.

80. All the mexican restaurants were further away than we realized therefore we decided to have our staff lunch at a nearby thai restaurant.

81. We are greatful that twenty-four companies submitted bids, unfortunately only 3 will be selected.

82. Reports from: ms sampson, mr tomas, and mrs jay are overdo.

83. All employees will persenally recieve copies of their Performance Evaluations; which the President said would be the primary basis for promotion.

84. Our manager gives many oral complements to deserving workers, however the praise would be more lasting if written in notes or reports.

CAREER APPLICATION

Your boss, Pauline M. Wu, director, Human Resources, asks you to draft a memo for her signature. It announces the open enrollment period for employees to change their benefit coverage. This is an important announcement because employees may make changes to their benefits only during this period. The cutoff date is November 29; all applications must be in by that time.

Pauline is very concerned about the attitude of employees in the past. They don't seem to realize that changes to health, dental, and life insurance programs can be made only once a year, during the month of November. She wants you to get this announcement out by November 3. Emphasize that the decisions employees make are important—to themselves and to their families as well. You will want to caution employees that voluntary changes can be made only in November, although qualified changes in family status, of course, may be made during the year.

She wants you to tell employees that most of the benefit program is unchanged. However, dental coverage is a little different; two carriers now offer dental coverage. Family members are also eligible for increased coverage in life insurance, and medical coverage now offers a basic plan plus a prudent buyer plan. You don't have to describe these improvements; just encourage employees to read about them in the enrollment package you will enclose.

She asks you to select times on three days when representatives from Human Resources will be available to answer employee questions. When you push her for more details, she says that you will be one of the representatives. Therefore, consult with another representative to work out a schedule. But do choose two-hour blocks of time. She suggests that these question-and-answer sessions be held in the East Lounge.

You know that Pauline appreciates concise, straightforward expression. Before drafting your memo, answer the following questions.

Critical Thinking Questions

85. In the first phase of the writing process, you'll want to analyze the audience for your message. Who is the audience for this memo?

86. In analyzing your employee audience, what assumptions can you make about these readers?

87. What assumptions can you make about your boss's reaction to your memo?

88. What is the purpose of this memo? What do you want employees to do?

89. What research will you have to do to collect information for this memo?

90. Should the memo be developed directly or indirectly? Why?

91. The opening sentence should tell the main idea for writing. Prepare a rough draft of your opening here.

92. What three benefit programs have changes?

93. What two sets of information could be itemized for improved readability?

94. What action information should be contained in the closing?

Check your responses with the solutions for this chapter. Then write your memo on a separate sheet of paper or at your computer. Use proper formatting techniques. When you finish, compare your version with that in Appendix B. How does yours measure up? Did you include enough information? Too much?

Chapter 9

Routine Letters
and
Goodwill Messages

CHAPTER REVIEW

Indicate whether the following statements are true or false by using T *or* F.

_____ 1. Letters are used primarily to deliver internal messages within an organization. (Obj. 1, p. 253)

_____ 2. Business letters are important only when a writer wants to add a personal touch to a message. (Obj. 1, p. 253)

_____ 3. Everyday transactions of a business consist mainly of routine requests and responses, which generally do not require special techniques to be convincing or tactful. (Obj. 2, p. 255)

_____ 4. The indirect strategy is most effective for routine, everyday messages. (Obj. 2, p. 255)

_____ 5. For routine requests the best way to elicit the most information is to pose open-ended questions such as *What features do your calling plans offer?* (Obj. 3, p. 259)

_____ 6. Written claims are often taken more seriously, and they also establish a record of what happened. (Obj. 4, p. 261)

_____ 7. Using a subject line in a response to a direct request is redundant and serves only to confuse the reader. (Obj. 5, p. 265)

_____ 8.   One goal in writing adjustment letters is to promote further business. (Obj. 6, p. 268)

_____ 9.   Many companies prohibit their managers from writing personnel recommendations because they fear lawsuits. (Obj. 7, p. 273)

_____ 10.   Sending a ready-made card is the most effective method to express thanks and recognition because it enables you to be prompt. (Obj. 8, p. 277)

Fill in the Blank

Use the listed words to complete the following sentences. You may use each word only once.

action	clear purpose	goodwill	questions
block	correct form	main idea	sentences
business partners	customers	paragraph	visualizing

11.   Letters to _____ receive a high priority because they encourage product feedback. (Obj. 1, p. 253)

12.   The three key goals in the first step of the 3-x-3 writing process for routine letters are (a) analyzing your purpose, (b) _____ the reaction of your audience, and (c) anticipating the response. (Obj. 1, p. 253)

13.   In routine letters you should avoid starting with introductory material, history, justifications, or old-fashioned "business" language. Instead, you should start directly with the action desired or the _____. (Obj. 2, p. 255)

14.   In the last paragraph of a routine letter, the reader looks for _____ information: schedules, deadlines, and activities to be completed. (Obj. 2, p. 257)

15.   Three characteristics of good letters include clear content, a tone of goodwill, and _____. (Obj. 2, p. 257)

16.   For letters with considerable information, you should develop each idea in a separate _____. (Obj. 2, p. 257)

17.   Clearly written letters answer all the reader's _____ or concerns so that no further correspondence is necessary. (Obj. 2, p. 257)

18.   Presenting messages from the reader's perspective is an effective method to achieve _____. (Obj. 2, p. 257)

19.   When using the _____ style, all the parts of your letter are set flush left on the page. This means that all parts begin at the left margin. (Obj. 2, pp. 257–258)

Writing Routine Letters

adjustment	claim	foreign	order
applicants	costs	information	payment
appreciation	customs	justification	
chronologically	employers	logically	

20. Before writing any letter, think about its _____ in terms of your time and workload. Whenever possible, don't write! Consider using a telephone call or an e-mail message to accomplish your goal. (Obj. 2, pp. 258–259)

21. The majority of business letters are written to request _____ or action. For these direct messages put the main idea first. (Obj. 3, p. 259)

22. The body of a direct request letter should explain your purpose for writing and provide _____ to explain the request. (Obj. 2, p. 259)

23. In direct request letters, it's always appropriate to show _____. Try to do it, though, in a fresh way. Avoid *Thank you for your cooperation.* (Obj. 3, p. 259)

24. The closing paragraph of an order letter should clearly state the method of _____. (Obj. 3, p. 260)

25. When a customer must write to identify or correct a wrong, the letter is called a _____. (Obj. 4, p. 261)

26. When answering a group of questions or providing considerable data, arrange the information _____ and make it readable by using graphic devices such as lists. (Obj. 5, p. 267)

27. In the body of a(n) _____ letter, your goal is to win back the confidence of the consumer. (Obj. 6, p. 269)

28. When writing a recommendation letter, you have an ethical duty to the candidate and to other _____. (Obj. 7, p. 271)

29. American businesspeople appreciate efficiency, straightforwardness, and conciseness, but _____ correspondents may look upon such directness and informality as inappropriate or even abrasive. (Obj. 9, p. 281)

30. When sending letters abroad, it is wise to have someone familiar with local _____ read and revise the letter. (Obj. 9, p. 282)

Multiple Choice

Choose the best answer.

_____ 31. For short messages responding to routine inquiries, you might
a. use a cluster diagram to generate ideas for the letter's content.
b. outline the letter's content on a separate page.
c. organize the letter by presenting the desired action in the first paragraph.
d. jot down notes on the document being answered. (Obj. 1, pp. 253–255)

_____ 32. The body of a routine request letter should
a. have at least two paragraphs.
b. announce the purpose immediately.
c. present details that explain the purpose of the letter.
d. state an end date for action from the reader. (Obj. 2, p. 256)

_____ 33. If you must ask a series of questions in a routine request letter, what is the best way to present these questions?
a. In a paragraph in the body of your letter
b. In a separate attached document
c. In a bulleted or numbered list in the body of your letter
d. In the closing paragraph of your letter so that they're not overlooked (Obj. 2, p. 256)

_____ 34. A written claim
a. establishes a record of the problem.
b. gives the writer a chance to vent frustrations.
c. guarantees the problem will be solved.
d. needs to establish the blame for the problem. (Obj. 4, p. 261)

_____ 35. Which of the following is the best closing for a routine claim letter?
a. *Thank you for your cooperation.*
b. *We would appreciate receiving the additional items by July 23 because our current supply is low and your cassettes are popular with our customers.*
c. *We will expect to receive the rest of our order by July 23.*
d. *We look forward to receiving the corrected order soon.* (Obj. 4, p. 263)

_____ 36. The final paragraph of a letter of recommendation should
a. present traits of the candidate, supported by evidence.
b. offer global, nonspecific statements.
c. offer an overall evaluation of the candidate.
d. encourage the receiver to hire the candidate. (Obj. 7, p. 275)

_____ 37. When granting a claim,
a. always apologize if an error has been made.
b. include only a brief apology in the closing paragraph of the letter.
c. focus on how you are complying with the customer's claim.
d. be sure to indicate who or what is to blame for the error. (Obj. 7, p. 275)

_____ 38. Goodwill letters
    a. should demonstrate the sender's creative writing ability.
    b. should not use pretentious or overly formal language.
    c. should focus on the sender as much as possible.
    d. are longer than most other business messages. (Obj. 8, p. 276)

_____ 39. When you receive a congratulatory note or a written pat on the back, you should
    a. respond but show proper humility by minimizing your achievements.
    b. respond by saying that you appreciate the kindness you were shown.
    c. be appreciative but not overly so.
    d. say that you don't really deserve the praise. (Obj. 8, p. 279)

_____ 40. Which of the following should you avoid in a message of sympathy?
    a. Mention the loss tactfully.
    b. Recognize good qualities of the deceased (in the case of a death).
    c. Assure the receiver that you know exactly how he or she feels and describe similar situations you have experienced.
    d. Offer assistance. (Obj. 8, p. 280)

_____ 41. What is the best advice for writing goodwill messages?
    a. Place as much focus on the writer as possible.
    b. You'll make a better impression by giving a ready-made card than by writing your own message.
    c. Goodwill messages should be sent promptly.
    d. All of the above are good tips for writing goodwill messages. (Obj. 8, pp. 279–280)

_____ 42. Most international business letters should be written
    a. in an informal, conversational manner.
    b. following generally accepted principles for American business letters.
    c. using only active-voice verbs.
    d. to conform to the conventions of the receiver's country. (Obj. 9, p. 281)

Short Answer

43. List three strategies for writing a direct claim letter. (Obj. 4, p. 265)

44. List three goals of an adjustment letter. (Obj. 6, p. 268)

45. List four *don'ts* to consider when writing adjustment letters. (Obj. 6, p. 270)

46. List six cautions that writers of recommendations should heed. (Obj. 7, p. 273)

47. List six tips for writing effective letters of recommendation. (Obj. 7, p. 274)

48. List the five S's in writing goodwill messages. (Obj. 8, p. 277)

CAREER TRACK SPELLING

Underline misspelled words. Write correct forms in the spaces provided. Some sentences may have more than one misspelled word. If the sentence is correct, write C. Then check your answers with those at the end of the guide.

_____	49.	We do not ordinarilly make cash refunds.
_____	50.	The claim submitted for $200 is legitamate.
_____	51.	Although the manager's mistake was costly, it proved valuble because it highlighted a problem in the supply procedure.
_____	52.	We are making a conscience effort to improve service.
_____	53.	Management thought the divesion of duties was fair.
_____	54.	One office tennant refused to pay the rent increase.
_____	55.	Not one of the three proposals is feasable at this time.
_____	56.	Investors profitted when international sales soared.
_____	57.	The new generator we purchased has a limited guarantee.
_____	58.	When he learned of the death of his secretary's mother, Mr. Potter offered his condolences.

My Spelling Monsters

List each troublesome word. Be sure to spell it correctly. Then write it four or more times. Review this page often to help you vanquish these spelling demons.

_____

_____

_____

_____

_____

CAREER TRACK VOCABULARY

Use your dictionary to define the words in Column A. Then select the best definition in Column B to match each word in Column A.

	Column A		Column B
_____	59. impede	a.	unwise, hasty
_____	60. imprudent	b.	start, get going
_____	61. inaugurate	c.	hamper, prevent
_____	62. indiscernible	d.	encroach
_____	63. indolent	e.	unclear, vague
_____	64. infringe	f.	lazy, shiftless

Choose the best meaning for the following underlined words.

_____ 65.   Large energy trading companies, in danger of becoming <u>insolvent</u>, are considering the option of going public.

     a. dangerous   b. bankrupt   c. prosperous

_____ 66.   When offered the opportunity to make money on insider trading, the broker declined, knowing that his <u>integrity</u> was worth more.

     a. interests   b. intellect   c. ethical values

_____ 67.   The dispute between the FCC chairman and the cable companies seems <u>irreconcilable</u>.

     a. unsolvable   b. compatible   c. compulsive

____ 68. Through the <u>largess</u> of a successful graduate, the local community college received a new computer lab.

      a. wrath   b. displeasure   c. generosity

____ 69. Chuck will act as <u>liaison</u> between the employees' union and management.

      a. arbitrator   b. link   c. informer

____ 70. Tenants submitted a <u>litany</u> of complaints about the aging apartment building.

      a. list   b. letter   c. tirade

____ 71. The union members were pleased to have a representative who was capable of providing <u>lucid</u> explanations of the contractual details.

      a. clear   b. cryptic   c. demented

____ 72. Many analysts believe that marketing to the leading-edge baby boomers is the nation's most <u>lucrative</u> business opportunity.

      a. wasteful   b. troublesome   c. profitable

Confusing Words

formally	in a formal manner	*hole*	an opening
formerly	in the past	*whole*	entire

grate	(n) lattice
	(v) to rub on a rough surface, irk, or irritate
great	(adj) large, numerous, distinguished

73. To make the right decision, you must read the _____ report.

74. The engineer repaired the loose valve, knowing that the constant squeaking would _____ on the pilot's nerves.

75. The promotion of Margaret Rose to president has yet to be announced _____.

76. "Managing at IBM is like sandbagging a levee," said a _____ employed executive.

77. The undersea tunnel linking England and France is a _____ engineering feat.

78. Please bore a _____ large enough for this cable to fit through.

Look back over the vocabulary words in this chapter. Select five or more new words to add to your vocabulary. Double-check the meanings of your selections in a dictionary. Then write a sentence for each of your words.

_____

_____

_____

_____

_____

COMPETENT LANGUAGE USAGE ESSENTIALS (C.L.U.E.)

Apostrophes

Guide 31: Add an apostrophe plus *s* to an ownership word that does not end in an *s* sound.

> Today's economy is brighter than in the past. (Add *'s* because the ownership word *today* does not end in an *s*.)
>
> Put the folder on Bryan's desk. (Add *'s* because the ownership word *Bryan* does not end in an *s*.)
>
> All the women's organizations sent representatives. (Add *'s* because the ownership word *women* does not end in *s*.)

TIP. To determine whether an ownership word ends in an *s*, use it in an *of* phrase. For example, *today's economy* becomes *economy of today*. By isolating the ownership word without its apostrophe, you can decide whether it ends in an *s* and where to place the apostrophe.

Guide 32: Add only an apostrophe to an ownership word that ends in an *s* sound—unless an extra syllable can be pronounced easily.

> All employees' health benefits will be examined. (Add only an apostrophe because the ownership word *employees* ends in an *s*.)
>
> Several years' profits were reinvested. (Add only an apostrophe because the ownership word *years* ends in an *s*.)
>
> We need the boss's signature. (Add *'s* because an extra syllable can be pronounced easily.)

TIP. Only a few words ending in an *s* sound require an extra syllable formed with *'s*. Some of these words are *actress, boss, class, fox,* and names like *Ross, Betz,* and *Davis.* Examples: *the actress's voice, the fox's den, Ross's car, Mr. Betz's house, Mrs. Davis's office.* For all these words we would pronounce an extra syllable in forming the possessive; therefore, we add *'s*.

Guide 33: Use *'s* to make a word possessive when it precedes a gerund, a verb form used as a noun.

Fellow workers protested *Beth's* (not *Beth*) smoking in the office.

We appreciate *your* (not *you*) writing the final report.

His (not *Him*) talking interfered with the video.

TIP. When words provide description or identification only, the possessive form is *not* used. Writers have most problems with descriptive nouns ending in *s*, such as *Claims* Department. No apostrophe is needed; *Department* is not possessed by *Claims*. Note the lack of apostrophe in these examples: *sales staff, electronics division, Los Angeles Dodgers.*

C.L.U.E. Checkpoint

Correct all possessive constructions in the following sentences. Tip: Don't be tempted to add apostrophes to all nouns ending in *s*. Some are merely plurals, not possessives.

79. Ms. Wilsons staff is responsible for all accounts receivable contracted by customers purchasing electronics parts.

80. In less than a years time, both attorneys offices were moved.

81. Luke would appreciate you answering his telephone while he is gone.

82. Three months interest on the two notes will be due February 1.

83. After a months delay, Lucy Johnson car registration finally arrived.

Super C.L.U.E. Review

In this cumulative review, use proofreading marks to correct punctuation, number usage, capitalization, spelling, and confusing word use. Mark C *if a sentence is correct.*

84. Although I refered to figure 12 on page 4 I was dissappointed when I could not find Paul Stanleys sales figures.

85. The unions officers sincerly hope that employees will exceed to managements latest wage proposals.

86. A key factor to be observed in our hiring program, is that all candidates references must be checked thoroughly.

87. Everyone has noticed Mistys flare for words, therefore she is being promoted to our editorial department.

88. Because of her recent accident Mrs. Wilson insurance premium will be increased one hundred twelve dollars for every six-month billing period.

89. Todays weather is much better than yesterdays consequently, we'll work outside.

90. Ted Bowman the new marketing manager offerred 9 suggestions for targeting potential customers.

91. We are hoping that Teds suggestions are feasable, and that they will succede in turning around our sales decline.

92. Both companys offices will open at eight a.m. however only the atlantic branch will offer full counter service until five PM.

93. Zacharys spring schedule includes the following courses english, history, and business law.

CAREER APPLICATION

As a student intern in the office of a magazine publisher, you are given a group of sample letters to evaluate. Read the letter below and then answer the following critical thinking questions.

April 14, 200x

Mrs. Thomas Dobbin
2950 King Street
Alexandria, VA 22313

Dear Mrs. Dobbin:

We appreciate your letter of April 4 in which you complain that you are receiving two issues of *Home Computing* every month.

My staff has looked into the matter and ascertained that the misunderstanding resulted when you placed an order under the name of Patricia R. Dobbin. You claim that this new subscription was made as part of your son's magazine fund-raising program at his school. You must be aware that the entire circulation operation of a large magazine is computerized. Obviously, a computer cannot distinguish between your current subscription for Mrs. Thomas Dobbin and a new one for another name.

But we think we've straightened the problem out. We're extending your subscription for 14 months. That's a bonus of two issues to make up for the double ones you've received. However, we can't prevent you from receiving one or two more double issues.

Sincerely,

Roger W. Hobart
Circulation Manager

Critical Thinking Questions

94.   Is the format of this letter satisfactory?

95.   What expressions create a negative tone for this letter?

96.   Should this letter be organized directly or indirectly? Why? How is it now organized?

97.   In an adjustment letter, what three goals should the writer seek to achieve? Is the writer successful in this letter?

98.   What good news does the writer have to offer?

99.   In this instance, should the writer explain why the double mailing took place? When must a writer be careful in offering explanations to customers?

100.   How should this claim adjustment letter end?

Revise the letter on a separate sheet of paper or at your computer. Then compare your revision with that shown in Appendix B.

Chapter 10

Persuasive and Sales Messages

CHAPTER REVIEW

Indicate whether the following statements are true or false by using T *or* F.

_____ 1. Successful persuasion results from a reasonable request, a credible source, and a well-presented argument. (Obj. 1, p. 299)

_____ 2. The first step in planning a persuasive message is adapting the message to the audience. (Obj. 1, p. 299)

_____ 3. To gain attention, the opening statement in a persuasive request should be brief, relevant, and engaging. (Obj. 2, p. 302)

_____ 4. Attempting to deceive others when using persuasive techniques is considered ethical behavior. (Obj. 2, p. 305)

_____ 5. Focusing primarily on indirect reader benefits is usually necessary when requesting favors such as time, money, special privileges, or cooperation. (Obj. 3, pp. 306–307)

_____ 6. Instructions or directives moving downward from superiors to subordinates usually require persuasion. (Obj. 3, p. 309)

_____ 7. Although you may never write sales letters, understanding their organization and appeals will make you a more perceptive consumer of ideas, products, and services. (Obj. 4, p. 314)

____   8.   Your primary goal in writing a sales message is to establish a relationship with the reader. (Obj. 4, p. 316)

____   9.   The body of a sales message carries the punch line and tells readers what you want them to do. (Obj. 4, p. 318)

____   10.   The most important ingredient of a press release is news. (Obj. 6, p. 321)

Fill in the Blank

Use the listed words to complete the following sentences. You may use each word only once.

Persuasive Messages

action	direct	indirect	persuasion
agreement	documentation	logical	purpose
attention	given	needs	resistance

11.   Using argument or discussion to change an individual's beliefs or actions is known as _____. Few businesspeople can succeed without developing this valuable skill. (Obj. 1, p. 299)

12.   _____ credibility results from position or reputation, such as that of the head of an organization or a highly regarded scientist, whereas acquired credibility is earned. (Obj. 1, p. 300)

13.   The opening paragraph of a persuasive request should gain the _____ of the reader. (Obj. 1, p. 302)

14.   When writing persuasive messages, consider both your purpose and the receivers' _____. How well you convince receivers that your message helps them achieve some of life's major goals (such as money, power, comfort, confidence, importance, and peace of mind) will determine the success of your message. (Obj. 1, p. 301)

15.   One of the biggest mistakes writers make when composing persuasive messages is failure to anticipate and offset audience _____. (Obj. 2, p. 304)

16.   Knowing exactly what _____ you favor before you start to write enables you to create effective arguments with strong conclusions. (Obj. 2, p. 304)

17.   A college student organization offers a local C.P.A. a $200 honorarium to speak to a group of students about the accounting profession. The student group is offering the C.P.A. a(n) _____ benefit. (Obj. 3, p. 307)

18.   When employees are asked to perform outside their work roles or to accept changes that are not in their best interests, persuasive memos using the _____ pattern may be most effective. (Obj. 3, pp. 309-310)

19.   Effective claim letters make a reasonable request, present a _____ case with clear facts, and adopt a moderate tone. (Obj. 3, p. 310)

20. In the opening of a claim or complaint letter, consider opening with sincere praise, an objective statement of the problem, a point of _____, or a review of the steps you have taken to resolve the problem. (Obj. 3, p. 312)

Sales Messages

act	competitor	illustration	stimulating
appeals	desire	letter	target
benefits	electronic	postscript	telephone

21. Companies now employing direct marketing may soon turn to _____ marketing, which involves sales messages delivered by e-mail, Web sites, and even wireless devices. (Obj. 4, p. 314)

22. Direct-mail sales packages typically contain a brochure, a price list, illustrations of the product, testimonials, and a carefully written sales _____. (Obj. 4, p. 314)

23. One way to improve the response rates when sending blanket direct mailings is to _____ the audience through selected mailing lists. (Obj. 4, p. 316)

24. One of the most critical elements of a sales message is its opening paragraph. To make readers want to continue, the opening should be short (one to five lines), honest, relevant, and _____. (Obj. 4, p. 316)

25. Emotional _____ are generally used when products are inexpensive, short-lived, or nonessential. (Obj. 4, p. 317)

26. When price is an obstacle, you can (a) delay mentioning it until after you have created a desire for the product, (b) show the price in small units, (c) demonstrate how the receiver can save money, or (d) compare your prices with those of a(n) _____. (Obj. 4, p. 318)

27. An important technique for building interest in a product involves translating cold facts into warm feelings and reader _____. (Obj. 4, p. 317)

28. Marketing pros use a number of techniques to overcome resistance and build _____. (Obj. 4, p. 318)

29. Providing a reply card, a stamped envelope, a toll-free number, an easy-to-use Web site, or a promise of a follow-up call are all ways to make sure the reader will _____ on the sales message. (Obj. 4, p. 318)

30. When you are trying to motivate action, put the strongest motivator in a(n) _____. (Obj. 4, p. 319)

Multiple Choice

Choose the best answer.

_____ 31. Successful persuasion results from all but which of the following?
a. A reasonable request
b. A receptive audience
c. A credible source
d. A well-presented argument (Obj. 1, p. 299)

_____ 32. You are writing a sales letter for a new compact car and have decided to focus the letter on how much drivers will save on gas costs. This can best be accomplished by
a. using a direct organizational strategy.
b. gaining your reader's attention.
c. gathering statistics about fuel economy.
d. adapting the message to the audience. (Obj. 1, pp. 301–302)

_____ 33. The statement *How would you like to save 20 percent on your home heating costs this winter?*
a. builds interest with a product description.
b. motivates action by telling readers how to save money.
c. gains attention by asking a question that focuses on reader benefits.
d. presents an indirect benefit. (Obj. 2, pp. 302–303)

_____ 34. Which of the following situations requires an indirect strategy?
a. An invitation to a local firm's CEO to speak at your professional organization's awards banquet
b. An e-mail message asking for information about student loan programs
c. A letter requesting a copy of your credit report
d. All of the above should use an indirect strategy (Obj. 3, p. 307)

_____ 35. Persuasive claim letters typically involve *all but which* of the following?
a. Damaged products
b. Mistaken billing
c. Recommendation requests
d. Warranty problems (Obj. 3, p. 310)

_____ 36. When you are writing to complain about something and you're worried that your reader might be reluctant to grant your claim, you should use
a. the indirect strategy.
b. the direct strategy.
c. both direct and indirect appeals.
d. circular reasoning. (Obj. 3, p. 310)

_____ 37. Professionals who specialize in traditional direct-mail services have done all but which of the following?
   a. Analyzed a market
   b. Built a Web site
   c. Developed an effective mailing list
   d. Studied the product (Obj. 4, p. 314)

_____ 38. Which of the following is a technique likely to result in an effective online sales message?
   a. Place the most important information near the top of the message.
   b. Keep the message short and conversational.
   c. Convey urgency to encourage fast action.
   d. All of the above. (Obj. 4, p. 315)

_____ 39. The most effective news releases
   a. concentrate on advertising a company's products.
   b. emphasize the most important information by placing it near the end.
   c. attempt to answer the five _W's_ and one _H_ in the first sentence.
   d. look and sound credible by avoiding typos, punctuation errors, and factual errors. (Obj. 5, p. 321)

_____ 40. The most important information in a news release should be
   a. saved for the last paragraph for dramatic effect.
   b. focused totally on selling the writer's company and its products.
   c. concentrated at the beginning of the release.
   d. highlighted briefly in the middle paragraphs. (Obj. 5, p. 321)

Short Answer

41. List four questions that help you adapt a persuasive request to a receiver. (Obj. 1, p. 301)

42. Describe the four parts of the indirect pattern for a persuasive or sales message. (Obj. 1, p. 302)

43. Identify six techniques that gain attention in opening a persuasive request. (Obj. 1, p. 303)

44. Name six devices that build interest in a persuasive request. (Obj. 1, p. 289)

45. Name eight techniques for gaining attention in the opening of a sales message. (Obj. 6, p. 302)

46. List five techniques for overcoming resistance and proving the credibility of a product. (Obj. 6, p. 304)

CAREER TRACK SPELLING

Underline misspelled words. Write correct forms in the spaces provided. Some items may have more than one misspelled word. If all words in an item are correct, write C. *Then check your answers with those in Appendix B.*

_____	47.	challenge	grateful	critisize	financially
_____	48.	operate	knowledgible	almost	suppose
_____	49.	almost	decision	bankrupsy	physical
_____	50.	freind	muscle	separation	deceive
_____	51.	advertising	restaurant	forty	fiskal
_____	52.	studying	neccessery	significance	medicine
_____	53.	irresponsible	fulfill	safety	qualafy
_____	54.	buziness	naturally	enough	noticible
_____	55.	misspell	opportunaty	summary	recognize
_____	56.	familiar	interest	adaquate	studying

My Spelling Monsters

List each troublesome word. Be sure to spell it correctly. Then write it four or more times. Review this page often to help you vanquish these spelling demons.

_____

_____

_____

_____

_____

CAREER TRACK VOCABULARY

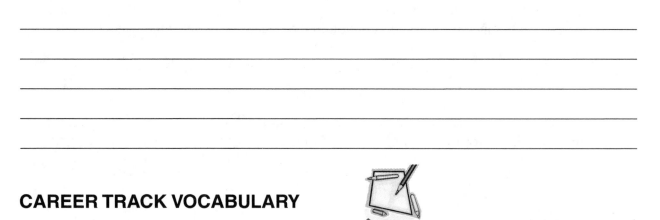

Use your dictionary to define the words in Column A. Then select the best definition in Column B to match each word in Column A.

	Column A		**Column B**
_____	57. lenient	a.	slander, defame
_____	58. litigious	b.	kind, merciful
_____	59. liability	c.	exact, factual
_____	60. literal	d.	command, requirement
_____	61. malign	e.	financial obligation, handicap
_____	62. mandate	f.	actionable, disputable

Choose the best meaning for the following underlined words.

_____ 63. To avoid the <u>maelstrom</u> on the trading floor caused by the falling market, the young reporter climbed on one of the platforms.

      a. photographers   b. fans   c. frenzy

_____ 64. The new plastic is <u>malleable</u>, which makes it more attractive to the auto industry.

      a. immature   b. pliant   c. vigorous

_____ 65. The reasons for approving the new zoning for the chemical plant are many; only one—its <u>malodorous</u> by-products—caused the town council to delay the vote.

      a. pleasant   b. foul-smelling   c. manly

_____ 66. Two Silicon Valley software companies asked a judge to <u>mediate</u> their trade secret controversy.

      a. ignore   b. inflame   c. reconcile

_____ 67.   Intelligence and a <u>mellifluous</u> voice contribute to his success as a talk-show host.

      a. shrewish, harsh   b. loud   c. honeyed, mellow

_____ 68.   Once he stepped down as CEO of General Electric, Jack Welch wrote a <u>memoir</u> describing his experiences.

      a. chronicle   b. lecture   c. fantasy

_____ 69.   The sales representative's <u>mercenary</u> attitude hurt the company's reputation.

      a. ambitious   b. fast-talking   c. greedy

_____ 70.   College students proved their <u>mettle</u> by sandbagging levees and rescuing stranded motorists during the flood.

      a. strength   b. courage   c. brilliance

Confusing Words

imply	to suggest indirectly	*liable*	legally responsible
infer	to reach a conclusion	*libel*	a damaging written statement

lean   (v) to rest against; to incline toward
             (adj) not fat
lien   a legal right or claim to property

71.   Newspapers must guard against _____ suits by printing facts, not rumors.

72.   Because he wasn't paid, the electrician placed a _____ on the property.

73.   The company was held _____ for the injury Ms. Sothward sustained when on a plant tour.

74.   If you _____ against the ladder, it will give way.

75.   Can we _____ from these test results that our product will sell?

76.   Vitamin makers don't promise health benefits, but they often _____ them.

Look back over the vocabulary words in this chapter. Select five or more new words to add to your vocabulary. Double-check the meanings of your selections in a dictionary. Then write a sentence for each of your words.

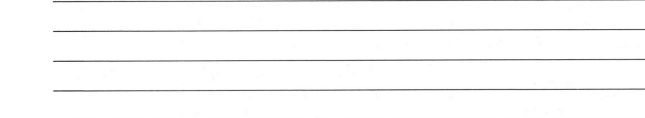

COMPETENT LANGUAGE USAGE ESSENTIALS (C.L.U.E.)

Other Punctuation

Guide 34: Use a period to end a statement, command, indirect question, or polite request.

> Our meeting starts at 2 p.m. (Statement. Note that only one period ends a sentence.)
>
> Bring the report to our next meeting. (Command)
>
> Steven asked if he could attend the meeting. (Indirect question)
>
> Will you please send a catalog to Lamps, Inc. (Polite request)

TIP. Polite requests often sound like questions. To determine the punctuation, apply the action test. If the request prompts an action, use a period. If it prompts a verbal response, use a question mark. *Example: Would you please send me a corrected statement.* Use a period instead of a question mark because this polite request suggests an action rather than an answer.

Guide 35: Use a question mark after a direct question and after statements with questions appended.

> Did you send a meeting agenda to each person?
>
> Most departmental members are planning to attend, aren't they?

Guide 36: Use a dash to (a) set off parenthetical elements containing internal commas, (b) emphasize a sentence interruption, or (c) separate an introductory list from a summarizing statement. The dash has legitimate uses. However, some writers use it whenever they know that punctuation is necessary, but they're not sure exactly what. The dash can be very effective, if not misused.

> Three outstanding employees—Reba, Thomas, and Erik—were promoted. (Use dashes to set off elements with internal commas.)
>
> Officials at General Motors—despite rampant rumors in the stock market—remained silent about dividend earnings. (Use dashes to emphasize a sentence interruption.)
>
> McDonald's, Coca-Cola, and Ford—these are among the most famous U.S. brands. (Use a dash to separate an introductory list from a summarizing statement.)

Guide 37: Use parentheses to set off nonessential sentence elements, such as explanations, directions, questions, or references.

> Prices on framing lumber (see last week's detailed report) have fallen 38 percent.
>
> Only two dates (November 2 and November 17) are acceptable for the meeting.

TIP. Careful writers use parentheses to de-emphasize and the dash to emphasize parenthetical information. One expert said, "Dashes shout the news; parentheses whisper it."

Guide 38: Use quotation marks to (a) enclose the exact words of a speaker or writer, (b) distinguish words used in a special sense, such as slang, or (c) enclose titles of articles, chapters, or other short works.

"To most of us," said Damion Moore, "the leading economic indicator is our bank account." (Use quotation marks to enclose the exact words of a speaker.)

The recruiter said that she was looking for candidates with good communication skills. (Omit quotation marks because the exact words of the speaker are not quoted.)

Sheila feared that her presentation before management would "bomb." (Use quotation marks for slang.)

In *U.S. News & World Report,* I saw an article titled "Trade Show Turn-Offs." (Use quotation marks around article titles; use all caps, underlines, or italics for names of magazines and books.)

TIP. Never use quotation marks merely for emphasis, as in *Our "summer" sale starts July 15.*

C.L.U.E. Checkpoint

Use proofreading marks to add all necessary capitalization, italics, and punctuation.

77. (Direct quotation) Someone who never asks anything said Malcolm Forbes either knows everything or knows nothing

78. Could you please send a corrected statement of my credit account

79. (De-emphasize) Directions for assembly see page 15 are quite simple.

80. (Emphasize) Only two possible dates May 5 and June 6 are available for a team videoconference.

81. Learning, earning, and yearning these are natural pursuits for most of us.

82. Our next conference is scheduled for Monday at 3 p.m. isn't it

83. In Business Week I saw an article titled Outsourcing: a look at the facts.

84. A business office filled with cubicles is often called a cube farm.

85. (Emphasize) Two of our researchers Emily Smith and José Real resigned yesterday.

86. (De-emphasize) Three employees in our Marketing Department David, Debbie, and Joy were responsible for all product promotional materials.

Super C.L.U.E. Review

In this cumulative review, use proofreading marks to correct punctuation, number usage, capitalization, spelling, and confusing word use. Mark C if a sentence is correct.

87. The treasurer will disperse all excess dues collected won't she

88. You may cancel **your** calling plan see page 3 of your customer agreement within fifteen days of excepting.

89. The two recruiters remarks seemed to infer that they were most interested in candidates' with computer and accounting skills.

90. (De-emphasize) The major functions of a manager planning directing and controling will be covered in management 301.

91. Any letter sent to the banks customers must have a professional appearance, otherwise it's message may be disregarded.

92. 40 people enrolled in the class however only 32 actually appeared at 7 p.m..

93. (Direct quotation) When you are right said Martin Luther King, Jr. you cannot be too radical when you are wrong you cannot be too conservative.

94. (Emphasize) States with the best export assistance programs California, Illinois, Minnesota, and Maryland offer seminars and conferences.

95. When we promote our "inventory reduction sale" in June you'll find the years best prices.

96. (Emphasize) Each of these citys Rochester Albany and Purchase has substantial taxes all ready in affect.

CAREER APPLICATION

The following request for an adjustment needs revision. Read it over and answer the critical thinking questions about it.

Current Date

Mr. James Ferraro
Vice President, Sales
Copy World
2510 East Pine Street
Tulsa, OK 74160-2510

Dear Mr. Ferraro:

Three months ago we purchased four of your CopyMaster Model S-5 photocopiers, and we've had nothing but trouble ever since.

Our salesperson, Kevin Woo, assured us that the S-5 could easily handle our volume of about 3,000 copies a day. This seemed strange since the sales brochure said that the S-5 was meant for 500 copies a day. But we believed Mr. Woo. Big mistake! Our four S-5 copiers are down constantly; we can't go on like this. Because they're still under warranty, they eventually get repaired. But we're losing considerable business in downtime.

Your Mr. Woo has been less than helpful, so I telephoned the district manager, Keith Sumner. I suggested that we trade in our S-5 copiers (which we got for $2,500 each) on two S-55 models ($13,500 each). However, Mr. Sumner said he would have to charge 50 percent depreciation on our S-5 copiers. What a ripoff! I think that 20 percent depreciation is more reasonable since we've had the machines only three months. Mr. Sumner said he would get back to me, and I haven't heard from him since.

I'm writing your headquarters because I have no faith in either Mr. Woo or Mr. Sumner, and I need action on these machines. If you understood anything about business, you would see what a sweet deal I'm offering you. I'm willing to stick with your company and purchase your most expensive model—but I can't take a 30 percent loss on the S-5 copiers. The S-5 copiers are relatively new; you should be able to sell them with no trouble. And think of all the money you'll save by not having your repair technicians making constant trips to service our S-5 copiers! Please let me hear from you immediately.

Sincerely,

Tracy W. Quincy
Manager

Critical Thinking Questions

97. Who is the primary audience for this adjustment request? Do you think this person is responsible for the problem described? Is it necessary to fix the blame for the problem here?

98. What is the specific purpose of this letter? To vent anger? To point fingers? What action does Tracy want taken?

99. Is Copy World likely to resist her request? Why?

100. What three arguments can be used to reduce resistance and encourage Copy World to approve the trade-in of four S-3 copiers with only 20 percent depreciation?

101. Should Tracy also appeal to Copy World's sense of responsibility and pride in its good name? Why?

102. Would Tracy's letter be stronger if she gave a day-by-day account of what happened with the copiers and how angry it made her and the staff? Explain.

103. Should this letter be developed directly (with the request made immediately) or indirectly (with an explanation coming first)? Why?

104. Name four possible openers for a claim letter. Which would be best for this letter?

105. What's wrong with Tracy's closing? What would be better?

106. How can Tracy make it easy for Copy World to approve her request?

Chapter 11

Negative Messages

CHAPTER REVIEW

Indicate whether the following statements are true or false by using T *or* F.

_____ 1. Organizing bad-news messages indirectly guarantees that the reader will understand and accept the bad news. (Obj. 1, p. 337)

_____ 2. Bad news is generally easier to accept when it is received gradually. (Obj. 1, p. 337)

_____ 3. Writing bad-news messages requires less attention to the 3-x-3 writing process than other types of business messages. (Obj. 1, p. 338)

_____ 4. The most important part of a bad-news letter is the buffer. (Obj. 2, p. 342)

_____ 5. To keep the reader in a receptive mood, avoid negative expressions such as *claim, error, failure, fault, mistaken,* and *violate.* (Obj. 2, p. 343)

_____ 6. Unlike the active voice, the passive voice highlights the action and is, therefore, a good choice when stating bad news. (Obj. 2, p. 344)

_____ 7. When situations involve sending information to many unhappy customers, companies should use a standard form letter. (Obj. 3, p. 351)

_____ 8. You should never apologize in a bad-news letter to a customer because doing so admits legal liability. (Obj. 4, p. 351)

_____ 9.   Although organizations are experimenting with a variety of delivery channels for bad news, the most effective means seems to be hard copy memos because they provide a permanent record. (Obj. 5, p. 359)

_____ 10. To minimize disappointment, Americans generally prefer to present negative messages directly. (Obj. 6, p. 362)

Fill in the Blank

Use the listed words to complete the following sentences. You may use each word only once.

accepts	indirect	problem	refusal
blame	libel	reader	slander
compromise	praise	reasons-first	subordinate

11. One primary goal in communicating bad news is to make sure your reader understands and _____ the bad news. (Obj. 1, p. 337)

12. When abusive language is spoken, it's called _____. (Obj. 1, p. 339)

13. One useful technique for reducing the pain associated with a bad-news message is to place the refusal in a(n) _____ clause. (Obj. 2, p. 343)

14. A refusal is not so depressing—for the sender or the receiver—if a suitable _____, substitute, or alternative is available. (Obj. 2, p. 344)

15. In the body of a refusal letter, show how your decision benefits the _____ or others, if possible. (Obj. 3, p. 349)

16. When closing a bad-news letter, supply more information about an alternative, look forward to future relations, or offer good wishes and _____. (Obj. 3, p. 349)

17. When dealing with unhappy customers, identify the _____ and accept responsibility if your organization is to blame. (Obj. 4, p. 353)

18. When denying claims, do not _____ customers, even if they are at fault. (Obj. 4, p. 354)

19. If you are delivering bad news to an employee and you know that the news will upset the receiver, the _____ strategy is most effective. (Obj. 5, p. 358)

20. In many high-context cultures, because saving face is important, a(n) _____ is a potential loss of face for both parties. (Obj. 6, p. 362)

Multiple Choice

Choose the best answer.

_____   21.   The bad feelings associated with negative news can sometimes be reduced if
a.   the receiver knows the reasons for the rejection.
b.   an apology is immediately offered.
c.   the writer tells a joke and tries to make the receiver laugh.
d.   the bad news is immediately announced. (Obj. 1, p. 337)

_____   22.   In delivering bad news, your goals should include
a.   making sure the reader understands and accepts the bad news.
b.   promoting and maintaining a good image of yourself and your organization.
c.   making sure the message is clear but also avoids creating legal responsibility.
d.   all of the above. (Obj. 1, p. 337)

_____   23.   Many bad-news letters are best organized indirectly with the reasons preceding the bad news. However, the direct pattern may be more appropriate when
a.   the receiver may overlook the bad news.
b.   organization policy or the receiver prefers directness.
c.   firmness is necessary or when the bad news is not damaging.
d.   all of the above (Obj. 1, p. 338)

_____   24.   In delivering bad news, writers sometimes get into legal difficulties by using abusive language, by using careless language, or by
a.   failing to apologize.
b.   falling into the "bad-guy" syndrome.
c.   falling into the "good-guy" syndrome.
d.   using the direct method to announce the bad news. (Obj. 1, pp. 339–341)

_____   25.   Which of the following statements is *not* true of buffers?
a.   A buffer should be relevant and concise.
b.   A buffer should provide a natural transition to the explanation that follows.
c.   An effective buffer might be *Thank you for your letter.*
d.   A buffer should include a neutral but meaningful statement that makes the reader continue reading. (Obj. 2, p. 341)

_____   26.   The most effective statement in a letter refusing a request from an outsider would be
a.   *Even though our budget won't allow a contribution this year, we hope to be able to contribute next year.*
b.   *Please accept our sincerest apologies for being unable to donate to your cause.*
c.   *We are unable to contribute this year because of budget constraints.*
d.   *Unfortunately, company policy prevents us from donating to your cause.*
(Obj. 3, p. 345)

_____ 27. When refusing routine requests, it is best to open with a buffer that does all but which of the following?
   a. Pays a compliment to the reader
   b. Supplies information about future relations
   c. Shows appreciation for something done
   d. Mentions some mutual understanding (Obj. 3, pp. 348–349)

_____ 28. What is the first thing most companies do when a problem arises?
   a. Consult the company's legal counsel
   b. Call the individual involved, if possible
   c. Write a letter to the individual involved
   d. Ignore the problem if it is unlikely to happen again (Obj. 4, p. 351)

_____ 29. Select the best subject line for a memo delivering bad news to employees.
   a. Discontinuation of Free Parking
   b. Change in Parking Benefit
   c. Parking
   d. Major Reduction in Parking Privileges (Obj. 5, p. 359)

_____ 30. In announcing bad news, British writers tend to
   a. consider it disrespectful and impolite to report bad news to superiors.
   b. use a similar approach to that of Americans.
   c. be straightforward because they see no reason to soften the blow.
   d. soften the message by including a buffer. (Obj. 6, p. 362)

Short Answer

31. List and describe the four parts of the indirect pattern for revealing bad news.

32. What are three specific causes of legal problems that can expose you and your employer to legal liability when you write negative messages? Give an example of each.

33. Name six possibilities for buffers in a bad-news message.

34. List five techniques for cushioning bad news.

35. Discuss four ways to close a bad-news message.

36. List four reasons why written messages are important.

37. In Asian cultures what are some signals that a request is being denied?

CAREER TRACK SPELLING

In the spaces provided write the correct version of the word in parentheses. If the word is spelled correctly, write C. Then check your answers with those in Appendix B.

_____ 38. Fashions in car colors and clothes are equally (changible).

_____ 39. Many stockholders read the annual report looking for answers to the (legitimite) questions they had asked during the year.

_____ 40. (Usualy) 5 percent of stockholders attend the annual meeting, but this year the number increased to 15 percent because of the controversy over the proposed takeover.

_____ 41. The state's attorney general was (disatisfyed) with the company's explanations concerning its reporting procedures.

_____ 42. Because of the stock's poor performance, several major shareholders of the company's stock in attendance chose to (harass) Mr. Florsehn, the chief financial officer, when he spoke.

_____ 43. Mr. Paterson, a (promminant) financial analyst with 20 years of experience in the textile industry, spoke as part of a panel organized by the CEO.

_____ 44. Unfortunately, the panel's presentation was (unneccessarily) technical.

_____ 45. After the meeting, the general feeling (prevalent) among stockholders was one of concern.

_____   46.   Only those in attendance were (permited) to vote.

_____   47.   One result of the annual meeting was the decision that no one in management would be (exemp) from salary cutbacks.

My Spelling Monsters

List each troublesome word. Be sure to spell it correctly. Then write it four or more times. Review this page often to help you vanquish these spelling demons.

_____

_____

_____

_____

_____

CAREER TRACK VOCABULARY

Use your dictionary to define the words in Column A. Then select the best definition in Column B to match each word in Column A.

	Column A		**Column B**
_____ 48.	miscreant	a.	hard, inflexible
_____ 49.	mitigate	b.	impertinent, pushy
_____ 50.	notoriety	c.	smooth, soften
_____ 51.	obdurate	d.	delinquent, criminal
_____ 52.	obtrusive	e.	concealed, unintelligible
_____ 53.	obscure	f.	shame, disfavor

Choose the best meaning for the following underlined words.

_____   54.   Managers who keep track of <u>mundane</u> details often find themselves overwhelmed.

a. accounting   b. extraordinary   c. commonplace

_____   55.   The <u>onus</u> of proving a product's safety rests with the manufacturer.

a. burden   b. method   c. cost

____ 56.   In an <u>ominous</u> proposal, government officials discussed taxing the assets of pension plans.

   a. threatening   b. lengthy   c. liberal

____ 57.   Every day a different personality <u>officiates</u> over the opening of the New York Stock Exchange (NYSE).

   a. rules   b. presides over   c. watches

____ 58.   To ensure privacy when talking to employees, Fred installed <u>opaque</u> plastic panels instead of glass in the conference room.

   a. transparent   b. darkened   c. not transparent

____ 59.   A financial columnist <u>opines</u> that Microsoft should diversify its software business.

   a. demands   b. maintains   c. writes

____ 60.   Upset by the decline in the company's stock price, several key shareholders threatened to <u>oust</u> Mr. Soledad, the company's founder and current CEO.

   a. control   b. eject   c. chastise

____ 61.   Investors, dissatisfied with <u>paltry</u> bond returns, have turned to stocks.

   a. insignificant   b. grandiose   c. average

Confusing Words

loose	not fastened	*patience*	calm perseverance
lose	to misplace	*patients*	people getting medical care

miner	person working in a mine
minor	a lesser item; underage person

62. Dr. Evans tries to give all his _____ at least 30 minutes each.

63. With parental permission a _____ may marry.

64. Mrs. Stevenson has the _____ to handle the irate customers during the holidays.

65. If you don't want to _____ your computer work, save it often.

66. Every _____ dreams of striking a rich gold vein someday.

67. The _____ bolt in the landing gear was tightened by the observant mechanic.

Look back over the vocabulary words in this chapter. Select five or more new words to add to your vocabulary. Double-check the meanings of your selections in a dictionary. Then write a sentence for each of your words.

_____

_____

_____

_____

COMPETENT LANGUAGE USAGE ESSENTIALS (C.L.U.E.)

Verb Tenses

Guide 4: Use correct verb forms for present tense, past tense, and past participle. The list below shows selected irregular verbs. To use these verbs correctly, practice them in the patterns shown. For example, *Today I begin, yesterday I began,* and *I have begun.*

Present Tense	Past Tense	Past Participle
Today I _____	*Yesterday I* _____	*I have* _____
am	was	been
begin	began	begun
break	broke	broken
bring	brought	brought
choose	chose	chosen
come	came	come
do	did	done
give	gave	given
go	went	gone
know	knew	known
pay	paid	paid
see	saw	seen
steal	stole	stolen
write	wrote	written

TIP. Probably the most frequent mistake in tenses results from substituting the past participle for the past tense. Remember that the past-participle tense requires auxiliary verbs such as *has, had, have, would have,* and *could have.*

> **Faulty:** When he *come* over last night, he *brung* pizza.
> **Correct:** When he *came* over last night, he *brought* pizza.
> **Faulty:** If he *had came* earlier, we *could have saw* the video.
> **Correct:** If he *had come* earlier, we *could have seen* the video.

Guide 5: Use the subjunctive mood to express hypothetical (untrue) ideas. The most frequent use of the subjunctive mood involves the use of *was* instead of *were* in clauses introduced by *if* and *as though* or containing *wish.*

> If I *were* (not *was)* you, I would take a business writing course.
>
> Sometimes I wish I *were* (not *was)* the manager of this department.
>
> He acts *as though* he *were* (not *was)* in charge of this department.

TIP. If the statement could possibly be true, use *was*. For example, If I *was* to blame, I accept the consequences.

C.L.U.E. Checkpoint

Use proofreading marks to correct any errors. Mark C if correct.

68. If I was you, I would have brung a backup for our presentation slides.

69. Craig must have knew the salary, or he would never have took the job.

70. When I seen Jan's letter, I immediately gave her a call.

71. I wish I was finished with my degree so that I could have went to work at LaserTech.

72. Many computer users wished they had choose a different printer.

Super C.L.U.E. Review

In this cumulative review, use proofreading marks to correct punctuation, number usage, capitalization, spelling, and confusing word use. Mark C if a sentence is correct.

73. If Courtney was manager I'm convinced she would have more patients with employees.

74. We payed every credit card bill when it arrived, however we still recieved late charges.

75. If the package had came earlier we could have finished by five o'clock PM

76. The Herald Post Dispatch our local newspaper suprised me with an article titled How To Keep Employees Safe.

77. Unless he's more careful than he's been in the past, we are in danger of being sued for libel.

78. John should have knew that our competitors products would be featured at the Denver home and garden show.

79. If I was you I would schedule the conference for one of these cities Atlanta Memphis or Nashville.

80. We choose the Madison hotel because it can acommodate two hundred convention guests, and has parking facilities for one hundred cars.

81. The CEOs management book was wrote long before a publisher excepted it.

82. When she come to our office yesterday she brung a hole box of printer cartridges.

CAREER APPLICATION

Assume that you are Nelson R. Raymond, partner in the firm of Powell, Raymond, and Robbins Professional Accountancy Organization. Sherry A. Lopez, the daughter of one of your best clients, has asked you for a favor that you must refuse.

Sherry is president of Alpha Gamma Sigma, a student business honorary on the campus of Miami-Dade College. She wrote to you asking that you speak at a meeting February 17 on the topic of careers in public accounting. You are very pleased to learn that Sherry is studying business administration and that she is taking a leadership role in this organization. You're also flattered that she thought of you.

But you must refuse because you will be attending a seminar in Lake Worth, at which you will represent your accountancy organization. This seminar will focus on recent changes in tax laws as they relate to corporations. Your organization handles many corporate clients; therefore, it's something you don't feel that you can miss.

You start to write Sherry a letter saying that you can't make it, when you remember that your local C.P.A. organization has a list of speakers. These accountants are prepared to make presentations on various topics, and you have a list of those topics somewhere. When you find the list, you discover that Paul Rosenberg, a Miami C.P.A. with 14 years of experience, is the expert on careers in accountancy and preparation for the C.P.A. examination. You can't decide whether to call him and ask him to speak to Alpha Gamma Sigma on February 17 or leave that decision up to Sherry. Perhaps Sherry would prefer to find another speaker herself.

Make a decision about what to do and write a refusal to Sherry A. Lopez, President, Alpha Gamma Sigma, 1150 Del Ray Avenue, Miami, FL 33178. But before you begin composing, answer the following questions.

Critical Thinking Questions

83. Should you use a direct or indirect approach in delivering this bad news? Why?

84. Of all the possible techniques for developing a buffer, what would be most appropriate for this letter?

85.   What should follow the buffer in this letter to Sherry?

86.   In delivering the bad news, is it necessary to state it directly? How could it be implied?

87.   What compromise is available to you? When should you present the compromise?

88.   What should you strive to accomplish in the closing?

Check your responses with the solutions in Appendix B before writing your version. Then compare your version with that shown in Appendix B.

Chapter 12

Preparing to Write Business Reports

CHAPTER REVIEW

Indicate whether the following statements are true or false by using T *or* F.

_____ 1. Although reports vary in length, content, form, and formality level, they have one common purpose: to answer questions and solve problems. (Obj. 1, p. 380)

_____ 2. Reports organized in the direct pattern usually begin with an introduction or description of the problem, followed by facts and interpretations from the writer. (Obj. 1, p. 381)

_____ 3. It's best for business report writers to concentrate solely on preparing their reports for a primary reader. (Obj. 2, p. 388)

_____ 4. Preparing a work plan keeps you on schedule and provides management with a means of measuring your progress. (Obj. 2, p. 389)

_____ 5. You are reading an article in *The Wall Street Journal* that discusses the research findings of a Centers for Disease Control study on workplace hazards. This newspaper article is an example of primary data. (Obj. 3, pp. 392–394)

_____ 6. Primary data can be generated from surveys, interviews, observation, and experimentation. (Obj. 4, p. 399)

_____ 7. The most effective questions for surveys are open-ended questions because they provide quantifiable data that are easily tabulated. (Obj. 4, p. 400)

_____   8.   Although documentation is viewed differently in the business world than in the academic world, business writers must be able to produce their source materials. (Obj. 5, p. 404)

_____   9.   Graphics can be used in a business report to clarify data, make numeric data meaningful, and create visual interest. (Obj. 6, p. 407)

_____   10.   Bar charts enable you to show changes over time, thus indicating trends. (Obj. 6, p. 408)

Fill in the Blank

Use the listed words to complete the following sentences. You may use each word only once.

Report Basics

analytical	informational	memo	purpose
factoring	letter	persuasive	schedule
indirect	limitations	problem	strategy

11. Reports that involve routine operations, compliance with regulations, and company policies and procedures are classified as _____ reports. (Obj. 1, p. 380)

12. Reports that provide data, analyses, and conclusions are _____. These reports generally intend to persuade readers to act or to change their beliefs. (Obj. 1, p. 380)

13. Many readers prefer the _____ pattern because it seems logical and mirrors the way they solve problems. (Obj. 1, p. 381)

14. The format of a report depends on its length, audience, topic, and purpose. Most reports are prepared in one of four formats: memo, manuscript, printed form, or _____. (Obj. 1, p. 385)

15. The _____ format works best for most short informal reports within an organization. (Obj. 2, p. 384)

16. The first step in the 3-x-3 writing process for reports involves analyzing the _____ and purpose. (Obj. 2, p. 386)

17. Preparing a written _____ statement is always wise for a report writer; doing so defines the focus of a report and provides a standard that keeps the project on target. (Obj. 2, p. 387)

18. Many report projects require an expanded statement of purpose in order to set boundaries on a project. This expanded statement of purpose should consider the project's scope, significance, and _____. (Obj. 2, p. 388)

19. Breaking the main problem to be investigated into smaller subproblems, issues, or possible solutions is called _____. (Obj. 2, p. 389)

20. A good work plan consists of a research _____ that includes a description of potential sources and methods of collecting data. (Obj. 2, p. 389)

Gathering Report Information

accuracy	database	periodicals	search
Boolean	designs	pilot study	secondary
commercial	observation	primary	survey

21. Most research projects should begin with _____ data collection to locate information that someone else has gathered. (Obj. 3, p. 392)

22. Print sources are generally books and _____. The latter includes magazines, pamphlets, and journals. (Obj. 3, pp. 392–393)

23. A _____ is a collection of information stored electronically so that it is accessible by computer and is digitally searchable. (Obj. 3, p. 394)

24. InfoTrac, LexisNexis, and ABI/Inform are _____ electronic databases. (Obj. 3, p. 394)

25. Yahoo!, Google, and AskJeeves are popular _____ engines or tools used to locate information on the Web. (Obj. 3, p. 395)

26. Using _____ operators such as "and," "or," and "not" will help you save time when searching the Internet for information. (Obj. 3, p. 397)

27. In evaluating a Web source, you should ask questions about its currency, authority, content, and _____. (Obj. 3, p. 399)

28. One way to collect primary data is through a mailed _____. This source provides efficient and economical data, but response rates may be low. (Obj. 4, pp. 399–400)

29. Valid experiments require sophisticated research _____ and careful attention to matching the experimental and control groups. (Obj. 4, p. 403)

30. Some of the best report data come from firsthand _____ and investigation. Seeing for yourself produces rich data, but that information is especially prone to charges of subjectivity. (Obj. 4, p. 403)

Illustrating and Documenting Data

bar charts	documentation	line charts	percentages
bibliographies	emphasize	organization charts	plagiarism
budget	flow charts	paraphrase	trends

31. Giving credit to your information sources is called _____. (Obj. 5, p. 403)

32. Using the words or ideas of another person without properly acknowledging the source is called _____. (Obj. 5, p. 404)

33. Effective report writers _____ an original passage by restating it in their own words and in their own style. (Obj. 5, p. 405)

34. You can direct readers to your sources with parenthetical notes inserted into the text and with _____. (Obj. 5, p. 406)

35. Tables, charts, graphs, pictures, and other visuals perform important functions for report writers and readers. Visual aids clarify, condense, simplify, and _____ data. (Obj. 5, p. 407)

36. Although tables are the most frequently used graphic, they do not display _____ readily. (Obj. 6, p. 408)

37. Although they lack the precision of tables, _____ enable readers to compare related items, see changes over time, and understand how parts relate to a whole. (Obj. 6, p. 408)

38. Pie graphs enable readers to see a whole and the proportion of its components; thus, they are useful in showing _____. (Obj. 6, p. 410)

39. Procedures may be simplified and clarified by diagramming them in _____, which generally use conventional symbols to illustrate the beginning and end of a process, decision points, or major activities. (Obj. 6, p. 411)

40. Before you incorporate graphics into a report, consider the reader, the content, your schedule, and your _____. (Obj. 6, p. 412)

Short Answer

41. What are the differences between formal and informal writing styles? (Obj. 1, p. 385)

42. How does primary information differ from secondary information? What are the principal sources of each? (Objs. 3 and 4, pp. 392–403)

43. List four Internet search tips and techniques. (Obj. 3, pp. 395–396)

44. List four strategies for preparing surveys. (Obj. 4, pp. 399–402)

45. List four kinds of data you should document. (Obj. 5, p. 404)

CAREER TRACK SPELLING

Underline misspelled words. Write correct forms in the spaces provided. Some sentences may have more than one misspelled word. If a word is correct, write C. Then check your answers with those in Appendix B.

_____ 46. Our budget did not factor in the impact of the declining value of the dollar in foriegn markets this year.

_____ 47. In the exit briefing following his visit, Mr. Smelzer told the manager that it was a privilige to meet such pleasant employees.

_____ 48. The consensus of the comittee is to investigate the candidate's credentials thorougly.

_____ 49. Will packaging the software separately result in a significant increase in shipping costs?

_____ 50. Our skedule calls for three restaurant openings in six months.

_____ 51. Experts will analize sales and returns for February.

_____ 52. In my judgment his services are totally indespensible.

_____ 53. Some copying expenditures are deductable as business expenses.

_____ 54. Incidentally, did you check the length of the guaranty?

_____ 55. The manufacturer evidentally issues its own catalog.

My Spelling Monsters

List each troublesome word. Be sure to spell it correctly. Then write it four or more times. Review this page often to help you vanquish these spelling demons.

_____

_____

_____

_____

_____

CAREER TRACK VOCABULARY

Use your dictionary to define the words in Column A. Then select the best definition in Column B to match each word in Column A.

	Column A		**Column B**
_____	56. passé	a.	investments, documents
_____	57. paucity	b.	drinkable, pure
_____	58. portfolio	c.	scarcity, lack
_____	59. potable	d.	quarrelsome, peevish
_____	60. procure	e.	purchase, secure
_____	61. querulous	f.	dated, old-fashioned

Choose the best meaning for the following underlined words.

_____ 62. Recently the word *basic* has become a <u>pejorative</u> term in the fashion industry.

      a. negative   b. commonplace   c. trendy

_____ 63. Several manufacturers relocated to the <u>periphery</u> of the city.

      a. suburbs   b. center   c. outskirts

_____ 64. To gain an edge in the <u>perpetual</u> videogame race, Nintendo and Silicon Graphics have merged.

      a. exciting   b. aggressive   c. constant

_____ 65.   Small World Toys' <u>perspicacious</u> policy of selling to specialty stores helps it survive.

     a. shrewd   b. foolish   c. standard

_____ 66.   His excuse for being late was too outrageous to be <u>plausible</u>.

     a. imaginary   b. unlikely   c. possible

_____ 67.   The start-up company's fate is <u>precarious</u> in the face of stiff competition and a lack of venture capital.

     a. distinct   b. uncertain   c. prosperous

_____ 68.   After the lab personnel developed the procedure for hazardous waste disposal, they received <u>profuse</u> praise.

     a. polite   b. lavish   c. restrained

_____ 69.   Caught in the banking <u>quagmire</u> were top executives who acted unethically.

     a. swamp   b. fantasy   c. disaster

Confusing Words

personal	private, individual		_precede_	to go before
personnel	employees		_proceed_	to continue

populous	(adj) having a large population
populace	(n) people, masses

70.   One difficult question facing employees is whether they may use their company Internet account for _____ e-mail.

71.   For tomorrow's panel discussion, Victor will _____ you, and Joanne will follow you.

72.   All _____ receive employment packets describing company benefits.

73.   Tokyo is Japan's most _____ city.

74.   After donning the proper gear, visitors to the biotechnology lab _____ with caution.

75.   The _____ of Brazil face tough questions concerning the coming election and the development of the Amazon River Basin.

Look back over the vocabulary words in this chapter. Select five or more new words to add to your vocabulary. Double-check the meanings of your selections in a dictionary. Then write a sentence for each of your words.

_____

_____

_____

_____

_____

COMPETENT LANGUAGE USAGE ESSENTIALS (C.L.U.E.)

Verb Agreement

Guide 6: Make subjects agree with verbs despite intervening phrases and clauses. Become a real detective in locating *true* subjects. Don't be deceived by prepositional phrases and parenthetic words that often disguise the real subject of a sentence.

> The range of colors, models, and sizes *is* (not *are)* amazing. (The true subject is *range.)*
>
> One candidate from the hundreds of applicants *is* (not *are)* sure to meet our qualifications. (The true subject is *candidate.)*
>
> Lee's original plan, together with ideas from other employees, *is* best. (The true subject is *plan.)*

TIP. Subjects are nouns or pronouns that control verbs. To find subjects, cross out prepositional phrases beginning with words such as *about, at, by, for, from, of,* and *to.* Subjects of verbs are not found in prepositional phrases. Moreover, don't be tricked by expressions introduced by *together with, in addition to,* and *along with.*

Guide 7: Subjects joined by *and* require plural verbs. Watch for true subjects joined by the conjunction *and.* They require plural verbs.

> Our CEO and one vice president *have* (not *has)* accepted speaking invitations.
>
> Exercising in the gym and running every day *are* (not *is)* how he keeps fit.
>
> The letter that we sent and a memo that we received in return *are* (not *is)* missing.
>
> Considerable time and energy *were* (not *was)* spent in developing an acceptable alternative plan.

Guide 8: Subjects joined by *or* or *nor* may require singular or plural verbs. The verb should agree with the closer subject.

Either the attorney or the judge *is* (not *are*) responsible for the delay.

Neither the computer nor the printer *has* (not *have*) been working properly.

TIP. In joining singular and plural subjects with *or* or *nor*, place the plural subject closer to the verb. Then the plural verb sounds natural. For example, *Neither the president nor the faculty members favor the tuition increase.* Notice that the plural verb *favor* agrees with the plural subject *members*.

Guide 9: Use singular verbs for most indefinite pronouns. For example, *anyone, anybody, anything, each, either, every, everyone, everybody, everything, neither, nobody, nothing, someone, somebody*, and *something* all take singular verbs.

Everybody in both classes *has* (not *have*) received the materials.

Each of the printers *is* (not *are*) ready for replacement.

Guide 10: Use singular or plural verbs for collective nouns, depending on whether the members of the group are operating as a unit or individually. Words such as *faculty, administration, class, crowd*, and *committee* are considered collective nouns. If the members of the collective are acting as a unit, treat them as singular subjects. If they are acting individually, it's usually better to add the word members and use a plural verb.

The Admissions Committee *is* working harmoniously. (*Committee* is singular because its action is unified.)

The Finance Committee are having difficulty agreeing. (*Committee* is plural because its members are acting individually. If the action is individual, the sentence will sound better if it's recast: *The Finance Committee members are having difficulty agreeing.*)

TIP. Collective nouns in America are generally considered singular. In Britain these collective nouns are generally considered plural.

C.L.U.E. Checkpoint

Use proofreading marks to correct any errors in verb use. Mark C if a sentence is correct.

76. The Council on Consumer Prices have taken a firm position.

77. Neither Sofia nor Alysia were able to install her new computer firewall.

78. A revised list of customers' names and e-mail addresses are being sent today.

79. Our president, along with the manager and three sales representatives, are flying to the meeting.

80. The tone and wording of each personnel message is important in creating goodwill.

81. A group of players, coaches, and fans are booking a personal charter flight.

82. Each of the recently hired staff members are scheduled for a private performance review.

83. One of your duties, in addition to the tasks already outlined, involve budgeting department expenses.

84. The renovation and the landscaping, which cost over $200,000, was finished in June.

85. Legal experts say that the extent of the company's contract rights are murky.

Super C.L.U.E. Review

In this cumulative review, use proofreading marks to correct grammar, punctuation, number usage, capitalization, spelling, and confusing word use. Mark C if a sentence is correct.

86. An increase in our companies sales in the united states have prompted us to insure our stockholders that we plan to expand overseas.

87. Research and development of course is essential. If we plan to have new products available for global expansion.

88. Although we called several bookstores neither of the dictionarys are available.

89. Either of the two applicants are satisfactory, however our personell department must check their references.

90. A set of guidelines to standardize input and output have allready been submitted to our document production department.

91. If stock prices has sank to their lowest point our broker will begin buying.

92. Something about these insurance claims appear questionable therefore I want the hole investigation reopened.

93. Anyone in the class action suit are eligible to make a personnal claim.

94. Mr. Wilson asked a clerk to help him select a tie and shirt that has complimentary colors.

95. Any one of the auditors are authorized to procede with an independant investigation.

CAREER APPLICATION

Your boss, Stew Beltz, vice president, Operations, asks you to help him research information leading to a decision about lighting in all offices where computers are used heavily. Your company, 21st Century Insurance, employs hundreds of administrative workers using computers. Within eight months the company will be remodeling many offices, and Stew is considering switching from standard lighting to indirect lighting.

As an administrative assistant, you are to find out all you can about both kinds of lighting. You will not be expected to conduct any primary research yet; Stew first wants you to search secondary sources. What has already been learned about lighting for computer working environments?

Immediately, you start to work. You learn that indirect lighting (uplighting) distributes the light across the ceiling and upper walls, lighting a room evenly and comfortably. Standard direct lighting (parabolic), on the other hand, shines directly onto the working environment, creating glare and harsh shadows.

Your research also shows that the use of indirect lighting is growing. The American Institute of Lighting collects data on the number of people working in computer environments where indirect lighting is installed. Here's what you found for 1991 through 2005.

Year	Workers
1991	487,000 workers
1993	751,000
1995	1,012,000
1997	3,045,000
1999	3,441,000
2001	5,150,000
2003	6,033,000
2005	6,552,000

Even more interesting is a study done by Cornell University's Department of Design and Environmental Analysis. Researchers set out to learn the most effective lighting for computer working environments. They studied the performance, satisfaction, and visual health of 200 workers. Here are some specific results from the Cornell Study:

- Eleven percent of participants working under standard lighting reported losing time due to itching, watering eyes. Only four percent working under indirect light reported the same problem.

- Twenty-one percent had trouble focusing their eyes under standard lighting. Just one percent reported the problem with indirect lighting.

- Six percent complained of tired, lethargic eyes resulting from indirect lighting. Twenty-six percent had the same problem under standard lighting.

- Overall, more than 72 percent of the participants preferred indirect lighting over standard lighting, finding it more pleasant, more comfortable, and more likable.

- Indirect lighting produced production time losses estimated at 15 to 20 minutes per day.

Critical Thinking Questions

96. Who is the audience for your findings?

97. How could the data on use of indirect lighting from 1991 to 2005 be best presented? Table? Bar chart? Line chart? Pie graph? What influenced your choice?

98. You know that Stew will want you to interpret your findings. You think that he leans toward keeping the old direct, parabolic lighting because it is cheaper than installing indirect lighting. You, on the other hand, would like to see indirect lighting installed because it seems more attractive. When you draw conclusions from this set of data, should you emphasize the data that support indirect lighting? Why?

99. What did you learn that could be used against the installation of indirect lighting? How should you treat it? Forget it? Bury it? Emphasize it?

100. Based on the information you collected, would you recommend indirect lighting? Why?

101. To make the most readable line chart, what information should be plotted vertically, up the left side of the chart? What information should be plotted horizontally, across the bottom? In charting the number of workers, should you work with the numbers exactly as shown or round them off to even millions?

Check your responses with those shown in Appendix B. Then prepare a chart reflecting the worker figures from 1991 through 2005. Add appropriate legends and a title. Use a computer program to make your chart, or fill in the chart started below. You may wish to add vertical lines to divide the chart into squares. (Review the suggestions for making line charts on pages 409–410 of Guffey's Business Communication: Process and Product, 5th ed.*) On a separate sheet, write the Conclusions and Recommendations section of the report you will submit to your boss. When you finish, compare your chart and Conclusions/Recommendations with those shown in Appendix B.*

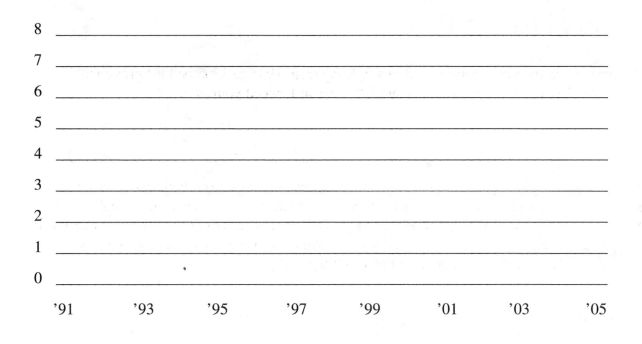

Chapter 13

Organizing and Writing Typical Business Reports

CHAPTER REVIEW

Indicate whether the following statements are true or false by using T *or* F.

_____ 1. Unprocessed data become meaningful information through sorting, analysis, combination, and recombination. (Obj. 1, p. 423)

_____ 2. Data become more meaningful when cross-tabulated, a process that allows analysis of at least four variables together. (Obj. 1, p. 423)

_____ 3. The median represents the value in a group of figures that occurs most frequently. (Obj. 1, p. 425)

_____ 4. Using consistent evaluation criteria is one method report writers use to remain as objective as possible when drawing conclusions from collected data. (Obj. 2, p. 428)

_____ 5. Recommendations explain a problem; conclusions offer specific suggestions for solving the problem. (Obj. 2, p. 429)

_____ 6. Regardless of which of the five methods you use for organizing information, reader comprehension should govern the overall structure of a report. (Obj. 3, p. 432)

_____ 7. Transitional expressions (*on the contrary, however, first*) help reveal the logical flow of report ideas. (Obj. 3, p. 434)

____ 8. Investigative or informational reports should generally offer a writer's interpretation or recommendations about a specific situation. (Obj. 4, p. 443)

____ 9. The three typical analytical reports that answer business questions are justification/recommendation reports, feasibility reports, and progress reports. (Obj. 5, p. 445)

____ 10. A typical feasibility report presents the decision, background information, benefits, problems, costs, and a schedule. (Obj. 5, p. 450)

Fill in the Blank

Use the listed words to complete the following sentences. You may use each word only once.

Interpreting and Organizing Data

answers	grid	mean	tables
commands	ideas	median	time
conclusions	importance	schedule	transitions

11. Data you've collected for a report often seem like a jumble of isolated facts. You must sort and analyze this information so that you can find meanings, relationships, and _____ to your research questions. (Obj. 1, p. 423)

12. Numerical data from questionnaires or interviews are usually summarized and simplified in _____, which use columns and rows to organize the data. (Obj. 1, p. 423)

13. Three statistical devices used to help researchers organize data are the three *M*'s. When people say "average," they most frequently intend to indicate the _____, which is an arithmetic average. (Obj. 1, p. 424)

14. Knowledgeable readers normally read the section devoted to _____ first to see what the report writer thinks the data mean. (Obj. 2, p. 427)

15. Whenever possible, phrase your recommendations as _____. (Obj. 2, p. 431)

16. Of the five methods for organizing data, organizing by _____ should not be overused because it tends to be boring, repetitious, and lacking in emphasis. (Obj. 3, p. 432)

17. When organizing information by _____, the writer imposes a value judgment. (Obj. 3, p. 432)

18. Writers can guide readers through a report by providing the equivalent of a map and road signs. Cues that provide such direction include introductions, _____, and headings. (Obj. 2, p. 433)

19. Good headings provide organizational cues and spotlight key _____. (Obj. 3, p. 435)

Writing Reports

analytical	direct	internal	persuaded
conclusions	external	management	topic
customers	informational	measures	yardstick

20. In informational reports readers do not have to be _____; they are usually neutral or receptive. (Obj. 4, p. 436)

21. Trip, convention, and conference reports generally inform _____ about new procedures, equipment, and laws and supply information affecting products, operations, and service. (Obj. 4, p. 438)

22. Progress or interim reports may go to _____, perhaps advising them of the headway of their projects, or to management, informing them of the status of some activity. (Obj. 4, p. 440)

23. Investigative or information reports are usually arranged in a(n) _____ pattern with three segments: introduction, body, and conclusions. (Obj. 4, p. 443)

24. Analytical reports seek to collect and present data clearly, but they also try to persuade the reader to accept the _____ and act on the recommendations presented. (Obj. 5, p. 445)

25. Organizing _____ reports with the conclusions and recommendations first is appropriate when the reader has confidence in the writer. (Obj. 5, p. 445)

26. When writers are free to organize justification/recommendation reports, they should let the audience and _____ determine the choice of direct or indirect structure. (Obj. 5, p. 445)

27. Feasibility reports typically are _____ reports written to advise on matters such as consolidating departments, offering a wellness program, or hiring an outside firm to handle some aspect of company operations. (Obj. 5, pp. 448–449)

28. Yardstick reports earn their name because they tend to examine problems with two or more solutions, using criteria by which the author compares and _____ alternatives. (Obj. 5, p. 450)

Short Answer

29. For this group of figures, calculate the mean, median, mode, and range: 2, 2, 3, 3, 3, 4, 5, 10. (Obj. 1, pp. 424–425)

30. List six tips for writing conclusions. (Obj. 2, p. 429)

31. Describe the organizational patterns for informational and analytical reports. (Obj. 3, pp. 431–432)

32. List the basic guidelines for creating effective headings. (Obj. 3, p. 435)

33. Assume that you must write a report on the status of a company ride-sharing promotional drive (or some other activity that you name). Discuss the information that your progress report should contain. (Obj. 4, pp. 440–442)

34. Give an original example of a business problem that could be solved by a yardstick report. Explain how the report would be organized using examples from your selected problem. (Obj. 5, pp. 450–452)

CAREER TRACK SPELLING

For each group below identify misspelled words and write corrected versions in the spaces provided. Write C if all words are correct. Then check your answers with those in Appendix B.

_____	35. dominant	controversial	itinerery	conceive
_____	36. affible	accidentally	beginning	dropped
_____	37. transfered	until	fluctuate	vegetable
_____	38. cylinder	apparent	shining	criterian
_____	39. defendant	mechanics	referring	peculiar
_____	40. shoulder	poison	huge	imprudent
_____	41. disparity	courage	emphazise	knowledge
_____	42. existance	safety	rhythm	regard
_____	43. suspense	genuine	interupt	importance
_____	44. efficient	miscelanous	parallel	miniature

My Spelling Monsters

List each troublesome word. Be sure to spell it correctly. Then write it four or more times. Review this page often to help you vanquish these spelling demons.

_____

_____

_____

_____

_____

CAREER TRACK VOCABULARY

Use your dictionary to define the words in Column A. Then select the best definition in Column B to match each word in Column A.

	Column A		Column B
_____	45. quell	a.	repetitious, superfluous
_____	46. quiescent	b.	deny, revoke
_____	47. quixotic	c.	imaginary, impractical
_____	48. realm	d.	still, latent
_____	49. recant	e.	subdue, suppress
_____	50. redundant	f.	region, field

Choose the best meaning for the following underlined words.

____ 51. Five members constitute a <u>quorum</u>; therefore, we can't pass this motion.

      a. ratio   b. legal assembly   c. representation

____ 52. We hired the computer consultant to <u>rectify</u> the security problem.

      a. analyze   b. acknowledge   c. fix

____ 53. Evening air along the coast was <u>redolent</u> with seaweed and sea spray.

      a. fragrant   b. heavy   c. offensive

____ 54. The company's board of directors <u>reiterated</u> its recommendation concerning employee 401K plans.

      a. abandoned   b. drafted   c. restated

____ 55. Vision is <u>requisite</u> for any chief executive officer.

      a. mandatory   b. optional   c. dispensable

____ 56. Despite pressure from manufacturers, the Air Quality Board refused to <u>rescind</u> its paint emission standards.

      a. increase   b. repeal   c. decrease

____ 57. Enjoined against using his own name, Wally Amos <u>retaliated</u> with the Noname Cookie Co.

      a. reciprocated   b. protested   c. joined

_____ 58.   Although he was <u>reticent</u> initially, the CEO outlined the restructuring plan he had developed to address the serious concerns of the labor unions.

a. smiling   b. silent   c. talkative

Confusing Words

precedence	priority	_persecuted_	oppressed
precedents	events used as an example	_prosecuted_	sued

plaintiff	a party to a lawsuit
plaintive	mournful

59.   After Mr. Jasper was diagnosed with cancer, he joined a class action suit and became a _____ against the asbestos manufacturer.

60.   The state's attorney general _____ the tobacco companies.

61.   Although few _____ exist, our company decided to establish its own clean environment rules.

62.   In the early part of the twentieth century, workers who identified union members were dismissed from work, and union leaders were threatened and _____.

63.   The young man's plight was becoming desperate, and his letters home were increasingly _____.

64.   Your health should take _____ over your job.

Look back over the vocabulary words in this chapter. Select five or more new words to add to your vocabulary. Double-check the meanings of your selections in a dictionary. Then write a sentence for each of your words.

_____

_____

_____

_____

_____

COMPETENT LANGUAGE USAGE ESSENTIALS (C.L.U.E.)

Pronouns

Guide 11: Learn the three cases of pronouns and how each is used. Pronouns are substitutes for nouns. Every business writer must know the following pronoun cases or categories:

Nominative or Subjective Case	Objective Case	Possessive Case
(Used for subjects of verbs and subject complements)	(Used for objects of prepositions and objects of verbs)	(Used to show possession)
I	me	my, mine
we	us	our, ours
you	you	you, yours
he	him	his
she	her	her, hers
it	it	its
they	them	their, theirs
who, whoever	whom, whomever	whose

Guide 12: Use nominative case pronouns as subjects of verbs and as complements.
Complements are words that follow linking verbs (such as *am, is, are, was, were, be, being,* and *been*) and rename the words to which they refer.

> *He* and *I* (not *him* and *me*) are studying management. (Use nominative case pronouns as the subjects of the verb *are studying*.)

> We're convinced that *she* and *he* will win the election. (Use nominative case pronouns as the subjects of the verb *will win*.)

> It must have been *he* (not *him*) who left the package. (Use a nominative case pronoun as a subject complement following the linking verb *been*.)

TIP. If you feel awkward using nominative case pronouns after linking verbs, rephrase the sentence to avoid the dilemma. Instead of *It is he who is the manager,* say *He is the manager.*

Guide 13: Use objective case pronouns as objects of prepositions and verbs.

> Please send catalogs to *her* and *me* (not *she* and *I*). (The pronouns *her* and *me* are objects of the preposition *to*.)

> Professor James asked *me* (not *I*) to write a report. (The pronoun *me* is the object of the verb *asked*.)

TIP. When a pronoun appears in combination with a noun or another pronoun, ignore the extra noun or pronoun and its conjunction. Then the case of the pronoun becomes more obvious. For example, *The CEO gave Derrick and* me (not *I*) *the assignment*. Ignoring *Derrick and* helps you see that the objective case, not the nominative case, is needed.

TIP. Be especially alert to the following prepositions: *except, between, but,* and *like*. Be sure to use objective case pronouns as their objects. For example, *Just between you and me* (not *I*), *those shoes are made from recycled rubber. Everyone except Jake and him* (not *he*) *received raises*.

Guide 14: Use possessive case pronouns to show ownership. Possessive pronouns (such as *hers, yours, whose, ours, theirs,* and *its*) require no apostrophes.

> My car is here. Where is *yours* (not *your's*)?
>
> We rented the office and *its* (not *it's*) furnishings.

TIP. Don't confuse possessive pronouns and contractions. Contractions are shortened forms of subject-verb phrases (such as *it's* for *it is, there's* for *there is, who's* for *who is,* and *they're* for *they are*).

C.L.U.E. Checkpoint

Use proofreading marks to correct any errors in pronoun use. Mark C if a sentence is correct.

65. Although the manager and me are interested in this laptop, it's price seems high.

66. The list of customers' names and addresses intended for her and I was delivered to Jeffrey and he by mistake.

67. Just between you and I, our C.P.A. said that the company and it's profits might be investigated.

68. All my luggage was found, but your's and her's are still missing.

69. Do you think it was him who sent the gift?

Super C.L.U.E. Review

In this cumulative review, use proofreading marks to correct grammar, punctuation, number usage, capitalization, spelling, and confusing pronoun use. Mark C if a sentence is correct.

70. At the last Department meeting, the Manager and him reminded all newly-hired employes about the importence of submitting regular progress reports.

71. Her knowledge of computing and her genuine interest in people is what appealed to the recruiter and I.

72. If anyone is dissapointed it will be me, however I do not anticipate bad news.

73. The body of the feasibility report and it's footnotes are on seperate pages.

74. Because we have no precedents for problems like these Ms. Sheridan and me will seek advise from a management consultant.

75. All class members except Karen and he knew the assignment, and were prepared with there reports when they were do.

76. Just between you and I, do you think it was him who complained?

77. If you will send the shipment to Tran or I; we will inspect it's contents throughly.

78. The itinerary for Jason and he included these countrys holland france and germany.

79. The use of concrete nouns and active verbs are important. If you want to improve your writing.

CAREER APPLICATION

Your friend and fellow worker Rick Seid, assistant to the vice president for Human Resources, was asked by his boss to explore ways to begin training young managers for global assignments. Your company is already developing markets in Europe and Asia, but it has done little to prepare American managers to operate in these markets. The CEO and management council hope to begin training company employees to manage overseas production and marketing efforts, rather than relying on foreign nationals. Rick is to investigate ways to train our managers and to examine what other companies are doing. His boss expects a full report in two months and a progress report after one month.

Rick writes the following draft of his progress report, and he asks you to critique it.

In evaluating this report, answer the questions that follow it. Then prepare a progress report outline that might help Rick revise his report.

Draft of Progress Report—To Be Revised

DATE: Current
TO: John R. Zurawski, Vice President, Human Resources
FROM: Rick Seid, Administrative Assistant
SUBJECT: Progress Report for International Training Programs

I am writing this progress report, as you requested, to inform you of the status of my research into developing training programs for young international managers. My research includes both secondary and primary sources. I have read lots of magazine, newspaper, and government articles on cross-cultural training and skills required of global managers. I have also talked with consultants and training schools. Because the topic is so broad, I have divided it into internal programs that could be conducted within our environment and external programs outside the company.

Let me describe what I have done thus far, John. Under internal training programs, I've learned that many companies are preparing employees for international assignments by using videotapes, in-house seminars, and intensive language and culture courses during work hours. Consultants and trainers conduct these short-term training sessions. Some companies are also improving their pool of young international managers by recruiting more globally oriented new employees who already possess many of the skills required.

In investigating external programs, I have found (primarily through reading tons of articles!) that at least six U.S. companies have developed extensive global management trainee programs. These companies are American Express, Colgate-Palmolive Company, General Electric aircraft-engine unit, PepsiCo international beverage division, and Raychem Corporation. Most of these companies use both short- and long-term assignments abroad as training for prospective international managers. They also send trainees to intensive training programs offered by specialized (and very expensive!) schools in this country.

Thus far, to investigate internal training programs, I have ordered some training videos, which I hope to evaluate in the next two weeks. I'm also talking with a training consultant who offers in-house seminars that can be individualized to our needs. For external training, I have ordered literature from some specialized schools, such as International Orientation Resources (Denver) and Business Services for Global Understanding (Chicago) to learn about their programs and costs. These intensive programs generally prepare prospective managers and their families for immediate transfer abroad, but I was assured that they will develop any program we want. I also plan to conduct telephone interviews with the six companies listed above to learn about their international training programs.

The biggest problem in gathering this information is the telephone interviewing of busy executives. I may not be able to reach representatives from all six companies. In that case, I hope you will forgive me for including in my report only as much information as I could gather by my deadline of November 15.

Critical Thinking Questions

80. Who is the audience for Rick's report?

81. Is the tone of the report, including its word choice and degree of formality, appropriate for its audiences? Cite specific examples. How could the tone be improved?

82. Although his report may not show it, Rick has already done considerable thinking to organize his research and findings. Why, then, is this report so hard to read? What three reader cues could Rick use to help readers comprehend his organization?

83. Readers of progress reports expect to find what general categories? How could Rick make sure the organization is easier to comprehend?

84. What critical data has Rick omitted from the closing of his report?

After comparing your responses to these questions with those in the solutions in Appendix B, prepare an outline here or on a separate page to guide Rick in improving this progress report. When you finish, compare your outline to the one in Appendix B.

Chapter 14

Proposals and Formal Reports

CHAPTER REVIEW

Indicate whether the following statements are true or false by using T *or* F.

_____ 1. Proposals may be divided into three categories: solicited, unsolicited, and business plans. (Obj. 1, p. 465)

_____ 2. Unsolicited proposals are written when an individual or company sees a problem that needs to be solved and offers to solve it. (Obj. 1, p. 465)

_____ 3. Because the goal when writing an unsolicited proposal is to convince the reader that a problem exists, most writers include a background section in which they present the problem in detail. (Obj. 1, p. 466)

_____ 4. Formal proposals often include an abstract, which describes how the writer learned about a problem or how the proposal will respond to it. (Obj. 2, p. 469)

_____ 5. When individuals are thinking about starting a business, the Small Business Association (SBA) says that the importance of a carefully written business plan cannot be overemphasized. (Obj. 3, p. 472)

_____ 6. Formal reports differ from formal proposals in length, organization, and tone. (Obj. 4, p. 473)

_____ 7. When putting formal reports together, writers should avoid redundancy, particularly in the letter of transmittal, executive summary, and introduction. (Obj. 4, p. 476)

_____   8.   The principal section in a formal report is the body. (Obj. 5, p. 477)

_____   9.   The second phase of writing a formal report consists of an analysis of the problem. (Obj. 6, p. 478)

_____   10.   When writing formal reports, use *I* and *we* whenever possible to establish a friendly tone. (Obj. 6, p. 479)

Fill in the Blank

Use the listed words to complete the following sentences. You may use each word only once.

Formal and Informal Proposals

appendixes	credentials	mission	request for proposal
business plan	feedback	online	staffing
contract	market	proposal	timetable

11.   A written offer to solve a problem, provide services, or sell equipment is referred to as a(n) _____. (Obj. 1, p. 465)

12.   Government agencies and large companies often prepare a(n) _____ to announce their specifications for a project and to solicit competitive bids. (Obj. 1, p. 465)

13.   The _____ section of an informal proposal should include résumés of key people. (Obj. 1, p. 468)

14.   Most proposal writers establish credibility by describing the project leaders' _____ and expertise. (Obj. 1, p. 468)

15.   A central item in most proposals is the budget, which must be prepared carefully because it represents a _____. (Obj. 1, p. 469)

16.   Formal proposals often contain _____, which is where writers place ancillary material that may interest readers. (Obj. 2, p. 470)

17.   Proposals in the past were always paper-based and delivered by mail or special messenger. Companies today, however, increasingly prefer _____ proposals. (Obj. 2, p. 470)

18.   An important part of a business plan is a letter of transmittal and/or executive summary that includes a(n) _____ statement. (Obj. 3, p. 472)

19.   A(n) _____ analysis discusses market characteristics, trends, projected growth, customer behavior, complementary products and services, and barriers to entry. (Obj. 3, p. 473)

Formal Reports

bibliography	indirect	recommendations	timetable
direct	investigation	research findings	tone
formatting	outline	scope	topic

20. Instead of making an offer, formal reports represent the end product of thorough _____ and analysis. (Objs. 3 and 4, p. 473)

21. Although front and end items such as a title page, table of contents, and executive summary lengthen formal reports, they serve to enhance a professional _____ and help the multiple audiences find and use the information included. (Obj. 3, pp. 474–476)

22. A letter or memorandum of transmittal typically functions to announce the _____, describe the project, highlight the findings, and close appropriately (e.g., express appreciation for the assignment or offer instructions for follow-up actions). (Obj. 3, p. 475)

23. The introduction sets the scene and announces the subject, typically covering the following elements: background, problem or purpose, significance, _____, and organization. (Obj. 4, p. 476)

24. The principal section in any formal report is the body, which discusses, analyzes, interprets, and evaluates the _____ in relation to the initial problem. (Obj. 5, p. 476)

25. When requested, writers should submit _____ that make precise suggestions for actions that are practical and reasonable in solving the report problem. (Obj. 5, p. 477)

26. An alphabetic list of references on a topic is called a _____. Arranged by author, it may include all the works consulted as well as those actually cited in the report. (Obj. 5, p. 478)

27. To avoid the problem of being disappointed by running out of time, report writers develop a realistic _____ and stick to it. (Obj. 6, p. 478)

28. A big project like a formal report needs the order and direction provided by a clear _____, even if its parts have to be revised as the project unfolds. (Obj. 6, p. 478)

29. The best way to proofread a formal report is to read a printed copy slowly for word meanings and content. Then read it again for spelling, punctuation, grammar, and other mechanical errors. Finally, scan the entire report for _____ and consistency. (Obj. 6, p. 478)

Short Answer

30. What are some techniques for capturing the interest of the reader in the introduction to a proposal? (Obj. 1, p. 465)

31. In a solicited proposal responding to an RFP, what is your aim? (Obj. 1, p. 466)

32. Why is the budget section of a proposal so important? (Obj. 1, p. 469)

33. List four special components of formal proposals and explain their function. (Obj. 2, pp. 469–470)

34. List eight elements most commonly found in business plans. (Obj. 3, pp. 472–473)

35. How does the executive summary of a formal report differ from its introduction? (Obj. 4, pp. 475–476)

36. How many times should a formal report be proofread? Why? (Obj. 6, p. 479)

CAREER TRACK SPELLING

In the space provided write the correct version of the word in parentheses. If the word is correct, write C.

_____ 37. Every language has a (grammer) or system of rules for use.

_____ 38. Our company's new salary plan is (contingint) on the vote of the labor union.

_____ 39. The office building is located in a (dezireable) section of town.

_____ 40. Is it (fezable) to convert these three rooms into four offices?

_____ 41. The board of directors and the CEO had (opposete) views.

_____ 42. What (milage) do you expect from your new truck?

_____ 43. The (consensus) of the board is to recommend a merger.

_____ 44. We are solidly (commited) to service and quality.

_____ 45. The company made an (encredable) recovery last year.

_____ 46. When offering (advice) to Mr. Symantos, focus on the benefits of the suggestion.

My Spelling Monsters

List each troublesome word. Be sure to spell it correctly. Then write it four or more times. Review this page often to help you vanquish these spelling demons.

_____

_____

_____

_____

_____

CAREER TRACK VOCABULARY

Use your dictionary to define the words in Column A. Then select the best definition in Column B to match each word in Column A.

	Column A		**Column B**
_____	47. schism	a.	examination, review
_____	48. scrutiny	b.	discord, split
_____	49. sequester	c.	terse, concise
_____	50. succinct	d.	chain, restrain
_____	51. teem	e.	abound, overflow
_____	52. tether	f.	separate, seclude

Choose the best meaning for the following underlined words.

____ 53.   The board of directors <u>sanctioned</u> the stock split.

a. prevented   b. authorized   c. forbade

____ 54.   When interest rates are down, <u>savvy</u> homeowners refinance.

a. wealthy   b. complacent   c. shrewd

____ 55.   Our accountant is <u>scrupulous</u> when he conducts an audit.

a. casual   b. careful   c. fleeting

____ 56.   The company was indicted for marketing <u>sham</u> name-brand watches.

a. fake   b. reliable   c. colorful

____ 57.   A series of scandals left the company's finances in <u>shambles</u>.

a. debt   b. prosperity   c. disorder

____ 58.   The <u>tally</u> at the end of the day indicated that the store had a successful opening.

a. count   b. performance   c. showing

____ 59.   To obtain U.S. <u>tariff</u> rates for specific imported products, contact the local customs office.

a. stipend   b. penalty   c. tax

____ 60.   Chinese student demonstrators threw <u>taunts</u> at the police.

a. ridicule   b. stones   c. projectiles

Confusing Words

principal	(n) capital sum; school official	*reality*	that which is real
	(adj) chief, primary	*realty*	real estate
principle	rule of action		

stationary	immovable
stationery	writing material

61. After changing our company's logo, we had to order new office _____.

62. Critics complain that the _____ goal of taxes is the redistribution of wealth.

63. After earning a broker's license, Ruth opened her own _____ office specializing in commercial buildings.

64. The CEO had one fixed _____: Tell the truth when asked about the company's performance.

65. Although the bookshelves on the back wall are _____, those along the side walls can be moved.

66. Few people have experienced the _____ of an earthquake at its epicenter.

Look back over the vocabulary words in this chapter. Select five or more new words to add to your vocabulary. Double-check the meanings of your selections in a dictionary. Then write a sentence for each of your words.

_____

_____

_____

_____

_____

COMPETENT LANGUAGE USAGE ESSENTIALS (C.L.U.E.)

Pronouns (cont.)

Guide 15: Use *self*-**ending pronouns only when they refer to previously mentioned nouns or pronouns.**

> The manager *herself* signed all purchase orders.
>
> Send the check to Michael or *me* (not *myself*).

TIP. Trying to sound less egocentric, some radio and TV announcers incorrectly substitute *myself* when they should use *I*. For example, "Robin and *myself* (should be *I*) will be jetting to Acapulco." Remember that a *self*-ending pronoun can be used only when it refers to a previously mentioned antecedent.

Guide 16: Use *who* **or** *whoever* **for nominative case constructions and** *whom* **or** *whomever* **for objective case constructions.** In determining the correct choice, it's helpful to substitute *he* for *who* or *whoever* and *him* for *whom* or *whomever*.

> To *whom* did he address the letter? (The letter was addressed to *him*?)
>
> *Who* did you say left the message? (You did say *he* left the message?)
>
> Give the award to *whoever* deserves it. (In this sentence the clause *whoever deserves it* functions as the object of the preposition *to*. Within the clause *whoever* is the subject of the verb *deserves*. Again, try substituting *he: he deserves it*.)

C.L.U.E. Checkpoint 1

Use proofreading marks to correct all errors in *self*-ending pronouns and *who/whoever, whom/whomever*.

67. Please distribute the supplies to whomever ordered them.

68. Send all contributions to Mr. Rather or myself.

69. Who would you prefer to see elected president?

70. Our manager herself will give the award to whoever we recommend.

71. The CEO and myself plan to attend the morning session of the seminar.

Guide 17: Make pronouns agree in number and gender with the words to which they refer (their antecedents). When the gender of the antecedent is obvious, pronoun references are simple.

> One of the men left *his* (not *their*) car lights on. (The singular pronoun *his* refers to the singular antecedent *One*.)
>
> Each of the women received *her* (not *their*) license. (The singular pronoun *her* agrees with the singular antecedent *Each*.)

When the gender of the antecedent could be male or female, sensitive writers today have a number of options—some acceptable and others not.

Faulty: Any subscriber may cancel *their* subscription. (The plural pronoun *their* does not agree with its singular antecedent *subscriber*.)

Improved: All subscribers may cancel their subscriptions. (Make the subject plural so that the plural pronoun *their* is acceptable. This option is preferred by many writers today.)

All subscribers may cancel subscriptions. (Omit the possessive pronoun entirely.)

Any subscriber may cancel a subscription. (Substitute *a* for a pronoun.)

Every subscriber may cancel *his* or *her* subscription. (Use the combination *his* or *her*. However, this option is wordy and should be avoided.)

Guide 18: Be sure that pronouns such as *it, which, this,* and *that* refer to clear antecedents. Vague pronouns are confusing when they have no clear single antecedents. Replace vague pronouns with concrete words, or provide these pronouns with clear antecedents.

Faulty: Homeowners responded enthusiastically to separating their trash and recycling newspaper, but *it* caused more problems than solutions. [To what does *it* refer?]

Improved: Homeowners responded enthusiastically to separating their trash and recycling newspaper, but *these efforts* caused more problems than solutions. [Replace the vague pronoun *it* with more concrete words.]

Faulty: Stocks fell, the bond market slipped, and interest rates rose, *which* caused distress on Wall Street. [To what does *which* refer?]

Improved: Stocks fell, the bond market slipped, and interest rates rose. This combination of circumstances caused distress on Wall Street. [Remove the vague pronoun *which* and use a concrete reference.]

Faulty: We collected newsletters, brochures, announcements, and other printed samples. *This* helped us design our first newsletter. [To what does *This* refer?]

Improved: We collected newsletters, brochures, announcements, and other printed samples. *This sample collection* helped us design our first newsletter. [Add specific words to the pronoun to clarify its reference.]

TIP. Whenever you use the words *this, that, these,* and *those* by themselves, a red flag should pop up. These words are dangerous when they stand alone. Inexperienced writers often use them to refer to an entire previous idea, rather than to a specific antecedent, as shown in the preceding example. You can often solve the problem by adding another idea to the pronoun (*this sample collection*).

C.L.U.E. Checkpoint 2

Use proofreading marks to correct poor pronoun references.

72. Every employee must be prepared to show their picture identification.

73. In creating a successful business plan, you must define your overall company goals, identify customer characteristics, and project potential sales. This is what most beginning entrepreneurs fail to do.

74. Connecticut provides tax credits, customized job training, and fast-track permitting, which is why many companies are moving there.

75. Our new business had cash-flow problems, partnership squabbles, and a leaky roof; however, we didn't let it get us down.

76. Anybody who opens a new business is sure to have their own start-up problems.

Super C.L.U.E. Review

In this cumulative review, use proofreading marks to correct grammar, punctuation, number usage, capitalization, spelling, and confusing word use. Mark C if a sentence is correct.

77. You must send all newly-ordered supplies to myself or whomever submitted the purchase requisition.

78. Research and development of course is essential. If we plan to expand into the following key markets; pacific rim countys, the european community, and south america.

79. Exports from small companys has increased; but it is still insufficient to effect the balance of trade positively.

80. Our's is the only country with a sizable middle class and they are hungry for consumer goods.

81. Cell Phone Depot promised complementary cell phones to all new customers but it attracted only fifty-seven new accounts.

82. Every new employee must apply to recieve his permit to park in lot 5-A.

83. Jeffrey and myself was preparing a 4-page newsletter; each page consisting of 3 verticle columes.

84. Poor ventilation, inadequate lighting and hazardous working conditions were sighted in the complaint. This must be improved before negotiations may continue.

85. We reccommend therefore that a committee study our working conditions for a 3-week period, and submit a report of it's findings.

86. The rules of business etiquette is based primarily on the principals of good manners, every-one should exercise them in the workplace.

CAREER APPLICATION

Ramon Prentice is founder and president of Prentice Consultants, a national research group. Together with his staff, he is putting together a proposal that would test consumer satisfaction for a growing airline based in the Southeast. The airline solicited this proposal, as it plans to expand along the eastern seaboard and into Midwest markets. Before doing so, it wants to test its image and current levels of customer satisfaction. What is the airline doing right and what is it doing wrong?

Ramon assigns you the task of coordinating the final proposal. Here's what has been done thus far:

- "Sally has worked out a plan of focus groups and survey research (questionnaires) that should provide excellent data about customer feelings. She has also worked out a schedule showing when the focus groups would meet and when and how the questionnaires would be administered.

- "Tom looked over Sally's plan and prepared a budget showing how much time would be required and how much the total project would cost. The budget includes the costs of collecting and interpreting the data, plus preparing a final report with recommendations.

- "Ramon wants you to look in the files and find samples of satisfaction surveys that the company has done for other customers. He would also like you to include a partial list of "satisfied" customers. Incidentally, Ramon usually writes the introduction and background sections for proposals.

- "Amanda is the personnel expert. She has current résumés of the principal investigators who would work on this project. Amanda insists on submitting each person's complete résumé with the proposal because "these investigators have impressive qualifications and experience."

Ramon asks you to prepare a list showing all parts of the proposal package, in the proper order, along with the name of the person who is responsible for preparing that part. He'd also like you to include a brief description or reminder of what goes in each part.

Before preparing your list, answer the critical thinking questions that follow.

Critical Thinking Questions

87. Who is the audience for your list?

88. Would you classify this proposal as formal or informal? Does it make any difference for your project?

89. What proposal parts have been accounted for?

90. What parts have been omitted that you think would improve this proposal? How should you treat these omissions?

91. Ramon didn't mention the company's new computer software that facilitates factor and cluster analysis. All your data processing is now done in-house, unlike many other research firms. You know he would want this information included. Where does it go?

92. Who should establish a deadline for the budget submitted with the proposal? Where should it be listed?

After comparing your responses to the questions with the solutions in Appendix B, prepare your list. Then compare it with the sample solution in Appendix B.

Chapter 15

Speaking With Confidence

CHAPTER REVIEW

Indicate whether the following statements are true or false by using T *or* F.

_____ 1. Preparing for an oral presentation is much like preparing to write a report; both activities begin with analysis of purpose and audience. (Obj. 1, p. 504)

_____ 2. When you anticipate having an uninterested audience, it is best to use a delivery style that is controlled. (Obj. 1, p. 504)

_____ 3. Writing the introduction should always be the first step when preparing for an oral presentation. (Obj. 2, p. 506)

_____ 4. Ending a presentation with statements such as *As I end this presentation* is an effective strategy. (Obj. 2, p. 509)

_____ 5. The fastest way to connect with an audience is to offer a list of facts. (Obj. 3, pp. 510)

_____ 6. As a rule of thumb, a speaker should try to dress as well as the best-dressed person in the audience. (Obj. 3, p. 512)

_____ 7. Research shows that the use of visual aids, while helpful, extends the length of meetings. (Obj. 4, p. 512)

_____ 8. When making presentations to a small audience, smart speakers choose not to put their key points on-screen. (Obj. 4, p. 514)

_____ 9. Memorizing the entire presentation allows an inexperienced speaker to establish rapport with the audience through eye contact. (Obj. 5, p. 520)

_____ 10. When creating visuals for an international or cross-cultural audience, experienced speakers use the language of the audience as well as their own language. (Obj. 6, p. 524)

Fill in the Blank

Use the listed words to complete the following sentences. You may use each word only once.

Preparing Oral Presentations and Building Rapport

adaptations	audience	exceptions	remember
appearance	credibility	problem	signposts
attention	customize	rear of the room	stories

11. When preparing for a presentation, a key step is audience analysis, which may enable the speaker to anticipate the audience's reactions and make appropriate _____. (Obj. 1, p. 504)

12. The opening of an oral presentation should capture the audience's _____ and get them involved. (Obj. 2, p. 506)

13. Speakers establish their _____ by describing their qualifications, knowledge of a subject, or experience. (Obj. 2, p. 506)

14. Using an emotionally moving story or describing a serious _____ is an effective way to gain an audience's attention. (Obj. 2, p. 507)

15. A straightforward summary should review the major points and focus on what the speaker wants the listeners to do, think, or _____. (Obj. 2, p. 510)

16. To prevent listeners from getting "lost" during a presentation, speakers should use verbal _____. (Obj. 3, p. 511)

17. A speaker's _____, movement, and speech affect the success of a presentation. (Obj. 3, p. 511)

18. When using PowerPoint slides or transparencies during an oral presentation, talk to the _____, not to the slide. (Obj. 4, p. 519)

19. Adding a corporate logo, adjusting the color scheme, and selecting a different font are effective ways to _____ existing PowerPoint templates. (Obj. 4, p. 514)

Delivery Techniques, Cross-Cultural Presentations, and Other Media

beginning	end	stage fright	teleconferences
confidence	four-point	static	three-point
discussion	notes	storage	videoconferences

20. The most effective method for delivering an effective presentation is to use _____. (Obj. 5, p. 520)

21. Probably the most effective strategy for reducing _____ is to know the subject thoroughly. (Obj. 5, p. 521)

22. Eliminating verbal _____, such as *ah, er, you know,* and *um,* helps speakers gain credibility. (Obj. 5, p. 522)

23. In adapting to international and cross-cultural audiences, speakers should develop topics separately, encouraging _____ periods after each topic. (Obj. 6, p. 524)

24. Handouts should be translated and handed out at the _____ of a presentation. (Obj. 6, p. 524)

25. When placing a call, using a _____ introduction helps to develop a professional image. (Obj. 7, p. 527)

26. Voice mail saves companies money, eliminates telephone tag, and is an efficient method for message _____. (Obj. 7, p. 528)

27. Participants in _____, also known as conference calls, communicate by telephone. (Obj. 7, p. 529)

Short Answer

28. List the four audience categories. (Obj. 1, p. 505)

29. List five questions that help speakers determine the organizational pattern, delivery style, and supporting material necessary to meet the needs of the audience being addressed. (Obj. 1, p. 505)

30. How can ideas in an oral presentation be organized? (Obj. 2, p. 509)

31. What are verbal signposts in a speech, and why are they important? (Obj. 3, p. 511)

32. Name six kinds of visual aids that can enhance a presentation. Give an original example of how each could be used in a talk you might give in your profession. (Obj. 3, pp. 512–513)

33. Describe two ways to use multimedia elements to add interest to your presentation. (Obj. 4, pp. 517–518)

34. Name six tips for preparing and using electronic presentation slides. (Obj. 5, p. 519)

CAREER TRACK SPELLING

Underline misspelled words. Write correct forms in the spaces provided. Some sentences may have more than one misspelled word. If the sentence is correct, write C. Then check your answers with those in Appendix B.

_____ 35. Some critics argue that analyzing an audience is an exercise involving little more than conjectur.

_____ 36. All headings throughout the report must be consistant.

_____ 37. The new personnel manager was hired to change the staff's complasent attitude.

_____ 38. The stockholders were suprised and graiteful when the CEO announced that new products were being developed.

_____ 39. One way to gather valueable marketing information is to promise prizes.

_____ 40. We're genuinely hoping that every supervisor will succede.

_____ 41. As part of his introduction, Mr. Takomota presented the results from the questionaire that he and his colleagues developed as a way to gauge the reception of the newly designed cars.

_____ 42. Most often, audiences are courteous to speakers; sometimes, however, a few individuals with an axe to grind can create an unpleasant environment.

_____ 43. One of the attractions of the new restaurant is its excelent service.

_____ 44. You have undoubtlessly checked your maintenance agreement.

My Spelling Monsters

List each troublesome word. Be sure to spell it correctly. Then write it four or more times. Review this page often to help you vanquish these spelling demons.

_____

_____

_____

_____

_____

CAREER TRACK VOCABULARY

Use your dictionary to define the words in Column A. Then select the best definition in Column B to match each word in Column A.

	Column A		Column B
_____	45. tenable	a.	overused, banal
_____	46. tepid	b.	belligerent, cruel
_____	47. transgression	c.	transparent
_____	48. translucent	d.	lukewarm
_____	49. trite	e.	sin, indiscretion
_____	50. truculent	f.	reasonable, defensible

Choose the best meaning for the following underlined words.

_____ 51.   United Nations leaders issued an <u>ultimatum</u> to the warring countries.

      a. retaliation   b. demand   c. reward

_____ 52.   Administrative assistants may take <u>umbrage</u> at the president's remarks.

      a. offense   b. heart   c. fancy

_____ 53.   Fans at the international soccer match were <u>uncouth</u>.

      a. unshaved   b. vehement   c. vulgar

_____ 54.   Some oil companies seemed <u>unfettered</u> by regulations.

      a. unaffected   b. unrestrained   c. unchanged

_____ 55.   The staff was surprised when the vice president made a <u>unilateral</u> decision.

      a. dictatorial   b. forceful   c. one-sided

_____ 56.   One reason for the company's trouble was the inability of labor and management to act in <u>unison</u>.

      a. agreement   b. retaliation   c. compliance

_____ 57.   The new product was perceived as <u>unwieldy</u> when tested.

      a. heavy   b. ominous   c. cumbersome

_____ 58.   One reason Jon received an unsatisfactory rating was his tendency to <u>vacillate</u> when making a decision.

      a. argue   b. waver   c. dissent

Confusing Words

than	conjunction showing comparison		*to*	a preposition; the sign of the infinitive
then	at that time		*too*	also, to an extensive extent
			two	a number
their	possessive form of they			
there	at that place or point			
they're	contraction of *they are*			

59. Ms. Selzer argued that the current fleet of vehicles was _____ expensive to operate.

60. The audit led _____ some significant changes in accounting procedures.

61. Have you been _____ in the winter?

62. Most major organizations schedule _____ meetings in the winter rather _____ face the summer heat.

63. If he could have predicted the outcome, _____ he wouldn't have filed the lawsuit.

64. As possible convention sites, we're considering Tampa and St. Petersburg, _____ cities with excellent convention centers and reasonable hotel prices.

65. Jon Arnold and Patel Nebold asked Ms. Jessup whether she would like them to visit St. Petersburg in November when _____ in Tampa for the quality control visit.

Look back over the vocabulary words in this chapter. Select five or more new words to add to your vocabulary. Double-check the meanings of your selections in a dictionary. Then write a sentence for each of your words.

_____

_____

_____

_____

_____

COMPETENT LANGUAGE USAGE ESSENTIALS (C.L.U.E.)

Adjectives and Adverbs

Guide 19: Use adverbs, not adjectives, to describe or limit the action of verbs.

> Robin felt that she had done *well* (not *good*) on the employment test.
>
> How *quickly* (not *quick*) can you finish that spreadsheet?
>
> The engine runs *smoothly* (not *smooth*) after its tune-up.

Guide 20: Hyphenate two or more adjectives that are joined to create a compound modifier before a noun.

> A *once-in-a-lifetime* opportunity presented itself.
>
> We made *last-minute* preparations before leaving on a *two-week* vacation.

TIP. Don't confuse adverbs ending in *-ly* with compound adjectives. For example, *recently elected* official and *highly regarded* president would not be hyphenated. Words ending in *-ly* are almost never hyphenated.

C.L.U.E. Checkpoint

Use proofreading marks to make all necessary corrections.

66. Our recently-hired Web technician prepared a point by point analysis of our site.

67. Only the four year old printer was retained, and it will be inspected year by year.

68. Please don't take this comment personal.

69. We moved into the newly remodeled offices over the three day weekend.

70. Ron felt that he had completed the two hour aptitude test satisfactory.

Super C.L.U.E. Review

In this cumulative review, use proofreading marks to correct grammar, punctuation, number usage, capitalization, spelling, and confusing word use. Mark C if a sentence is correct.

71. Was any of the supervisers absent on the monday following the 4 day weekend.

72. Their going to visit there relatives in Toledo Ohio following they're coast to coast trip.

73. The three *C's* of credit is the following; character, capacity and capitol.

74. All branchs except the Peachtree Plaza Office is now using state of the art equipment.

75. After you have checked the matter farther please report to the CEO and myself.

76. Laura thought she had done good during the employment interview but she heard nothing.

77. Some trucks acceded the 5,000 pound weight limit, others were under it.

78. To attract people to our convention exhibit we rented a popcorn machine and hired a magician. This was very successful.

79. Each of the beautifully-printed art books have been priced at one hundred fifty dollars.

80. James Roosevelt said that his Father gave him this advise on making speeches "Be sincere, be brief; and be seated.

CAREER APPLICATION

Your friend and fellow employee Kevin must give his first oral presentation next week, and he asks you to look over his outline. He knows that you have recently studied business communication, and he hopes you can make constructive suggestions. You both work on the staff of a large construction company. Kevin is assistant safety officer.

As part of STOP (Safety Training Observation Program), Kevin must address new construction workers. His primary goal is to convince employees that safety begins with the way they act. The cause of over 96 percent of all workplace injuries is unsafe acts by workers.

Kevin has worked out the first two sections of his talk, and he wants you to critique and revise them. *Read over his draft, and then answer the questions following it.*

First Draft of Kevin's Safety Talk

First section: Tools
1. Hand tools
   a. You should use tools only for their designed purposes.
   b. Keep hand tools in peak condition. You want them to be sharp, clean, oiled, and dressed.
   c. Don't use "cheaters" to force tools beyond their capacity.
   d. Don't abuse tools, such as using a wrench as a pry bar.
2. Portable power tools
   a. You must not operate power tools unless you are trained and authorized to do so.
   b. Proper eye protection is important.
   c. Moving parts must be kept directed away from your body.
   d. Never touch a part unless its power source is disconnected.

Second section: Equipment
1. Some general suggestions
    a. You must inspect all equipment before using.
    b. Know the limitations of the equipment you use; do not exceed them.
    c. Equipment from other contractors must not be interchanged without permission.
2. Safety belts/harnesses
    a. Wear belts when working on sloping roofs, flat roofs without handrails, any suspended platform or stage, any scaffold, ladders near roof edges, and all elevated work.
    b. Demonstrate how to wear belts.
3. Welding and burning equipment. Contact your supervisor before performing these tasks.
4. Compressed air
    a. Hoses and couplings must be checked daily before use.
    b. Never crimp, couple, or uncouple a pressurized hose. Shut off valve and bleed down hose.
    c. Do not allow pressure to exceed 30 psi when cleaning workbenches and machinery.
    d. Hoses must be kept off the ground or floor whenever they interfere with walkways, roads, and so forth.

Critical Thinking Questions

81. You know the importance of good planning before a talk. You are especially concerned about audience analysis. What should Kevin know about his audience? Why? How can he learn more?

82. Did Kevin follow a standard outlining format? Should he?

83. Are Kevin's first two sections well organized? What suggestions would you make about the wording of his outline?

84. Should Kevin have an introduction? If so, what should it include?

85. Does this talk need visual aids? What would you suggest?

86. Kevin also wants to talk about flammable and corrosive liquids, but much of the information is available in a good brochure. How would you advise him to treat these two topics?

87. Should Kevin include transitions? If so, where? Give him one specific example of an effective transition.

88. What would you advise Kevin about using concrete examples in his talk?

89. What advice can you give about the conclusion?

After comparing your responses to these questions with those in Appendix B, revise Kevin's outline using the format shown in Activity 15.5 on page 539 of the textbook. Include a title and purpose. Also include, in outline form only, an introduction and conclusion. Revise the two sections he has written. When you finish, compare your outline with the one in Appendix B.

Chapter 16

Employment Communication

CHAPTER REVIEW

Indicate whether the following statements are true or false by using T *or* F.

_____ 1. The employment process begins with a job search. (Obj. 1, p. 538)

_____ 2. Employers are less willing to hire people into jobs with narrow descriptions. (Obj. 1, p. 539)

_____ 3. The goal of a persuasive résumé is obtaining a job. (Obj. 2, p. 543)

_____ 4. The most effective résumé is a chronological one. (Obj. 2, p. 545)

_____ 5. All résumés contain standard parts arranged in an established order. (Obj. 3, p. 549)

_____ 6. In preparing a résumé that will be scanned, you should focus on specific keywords that describe skills, traits, tasks, and job titles. (Obj. 4, p. 554)

_____ 7. When preparing an inline résumé for e-mailing, make it as attractive as possible and include it as an attachment. (Obj. 4, pp. 555–556)

_____ 8. The cover letter isn't nearly as important as a résumé; most people consider it outdated. (Obj. 5, p. 565)

_____ 9. Before listing anyone as a reference, remember to ask permission. (Obj. 6, p. 571)

_____ 10. To show your good manners, always wait for the interviewer to initiate a handshake at the beginning of an interview. (Obj. 7, p. 575)

Fill in the Blank

Use the listed words to complete the following sentences. You may use each word only once.

Writing a Résumé

chronological	functional	networking	proficiencies
computer	functions	objective	10–12
employment	graphic	qualifications	12–15

11. You can't expect to find the position of your dreams without first (a) knowing yourself, (b) knowing the job market, and (c) knowing the _____ process. (Obj. 1, p. 538)

12. Preparing for employment often means identifying your interests and evaluating your _____. Employers want to know what assets you have to offer them. (Obj. 1, p. 539)

13. The average employee will have worked at _____ jobs over the course of a career, staying an average of 3.6 years at each job. (Obj. 1, p. 540)

14. Many job openings are found in the "hidden" job market, through a process called _____, which involves developing a group of contacts and referrals who all know that you are looking for a job. (Obj. 1, p. 544)

15. Résumés that emphasize skill categories and deemphasize work history are classified as _____ résumés. This résumé can be used to focus on accomplishments and to hide a negative employment history. (Obj. 2, p. 545)

16. Opinion is divided on whether to include a career _____ on a résumé. Although this statement makes the recruiter's life easier, it can limit a candidate's opportunities. (Obj. 3, p. 549)

17. When listing capabilities and skills, describe _____ you have acquired through training and experience. (Obj. 3, p. 550)

18. The first reader of your résumé may well be a _____. (Obj. 4, p. 553)

19. A scannable résumé must sacrifice many of the _____ enhancements that you might use for a traditional print résumé. (Obj. 4, p. 554)

Writing Letters of Application and Other Employment Messages

contact	hire	needs	source
direct	indirect	outcomes	success
follow-up	introduce	qualifications	traditional

20. Cover letters _____ résumés and relate writer strengths to reader benefits. (Obj. 5, p. 565)

21. If an employment position has been announced and applicants are being solicited, use a(n) _____ approach in writing your letter. (Obj. 5, p. 566)

22. The opening of a letter applying for an advertised opening may begin with a reference to the _____ of information, such as the advertisement or job description. (Obj. 5, p. 566)

23. Once you have captured the attention of the reader, use the body of a cover letter to build interest and promote your _____. (Obj. 5, p. 567)

24. A good letter of application emphasizes a candidate's strong points in relation to the _____ of the employer. Recruiters want to know what candidates can do for them. (Obj. 5, p. 567)

25. In the closing, after asking for an interview, make it easy for the reader to _____ you. (Obj. 5, p. 569)

26. Like your résumé, your cover letter should look professional, which means using a _____ letter style such as block or modified block. (Obj. 5, p. 570)

27. If you've been rejected for a job, writing a _____ letter that emphasizes your continuing interest is a good idea. (Obj. 6, p. 573)

28. Before an interview, research the organization and prepare _____ stories. (Obj. 7, p. 575)

Short Answer

29. In identifying the position of your dreams, you first must understand your likes, dislikes, strengths, and weaknesses. List some key questions that will help you find a satisfying job. (Obj. 1, p. 539)

30. Examine the advice describing career path data. Name five activities to get you started in your job search. (Obj. 1, pp. 540–541)

31. How do traditional job search techniques differ from electronic job search techniques? (Obj. 1, pp. 542–543)

32. From a candidate's view, what are the advantages of chronological résumés? (Obj. 2, p. 545)

33. List the standard parts of a résumé and discuss the issue of arrangement. (Obj. 3, pp. 549–552)

34. List six tips for maximizing the scannability of your résumé. (Obj. 4, p. 554)

35. Discuss the value of an e-portfolio for a job candidate. (Obj. 4, p. 556)

36. Discuss three strategies for presenting information in the body of a cover letter. (Obj. 5, p. 571)

CAREER TRACK SPELLING

For each group below identify misspelled words and write corrected versions in the spaces provided. Write C if all words are correct. Then check your answers with those in Appendix B.

_____	37.	intelligence	luxary	rejuvenate	jealous
_____	38.	efficent	involve	explanation	sacrifice
_____	39.	ensue	automaticly	simply	hungry
_____	40.	generally	exaggerate	suspense	yield
_____	41.	noticeable	original	independant	secretaries
_____	42.	circumspict	exercise	dominant	beautiful
_____	43.	admitted	imediate	colume	define
_____	44.	discipline	vacuum	technique	facsemile
_____	45.	certain	represenative	dissatisfied	repetition
_____	46.	seperate	requirement	opinion	derogatory

My Spelling Monsters

List each troublesome word. Be sure to spell it correctly. Then write it four or more times. Review this page often to help you vanquish these spelling demons.

_____

_____

_____

_____

_____

CAREER TRACK VOCABULARY

Use your dictionary to define the words in Column A. Then select the best definition in Column B to match each word in Column A.

<u>**Column A**</u>   <u>**Column B**</u>

_____ 47.   vacuous   a.   word for word

_____ 48.   vagary   b.   empty, lacking content

_____ 49.   vapid   c.   truthfulness, accuracy

_____ 50.   vendor   d.   impulse, whim

_____ 51.   veracity   e.   seller

_____ 52.   verbatim   f.   insipid, uninteresting

Choose the best meaning for the following underlined words.

_____ 53.   When you write a cover letter, being concise is more effective than being <u>verbose</u>.

         a. portly   b. exuberant   c. wordy

_____ 54.   Even in New York City, Central Park is <u>verdant</u> in the summer.

         a. dangerous   b. green   c. cheerful

_____ 55.   Although <u>vernacular</u> expressions may be useful in the workplace, career advisors recommend against using them in a résumé or cover letter.

         a. informal   b. offensive   c. pushy

_____ 56.   Despite declaring bankruptcy, Globex maintained <u>viable</u> relationships with many long-time customers.

         a. sincere   b. working   c. adversarial

_____ 57.   Ms. Jessup was <u>voracious</u> when she returned home from a long day of interviewing.

         a. very hungry   b. exhausted   c. talkative

_____ 58.   Corporate profits began to <u>wane</u> when many of the experienced employees took early retirement.

         a. multiply   b. waver   c. diminish

_____ 59.   Police had difficulty finding the person who perpetrated the <u>wanton</u> act.

        a. bloody   b. cruel   c. beneficial

_____ 60.   In the annual report, the company's graphic designer created a <u>whimsical</u> picture of the chief financial officer wrestling with the budget.

        a. diminutive   b. lively   c. fanciful

Confusing Words

vary	to change	_weather_	(n) the state of the atmosphere
very	extremely		(v) to bear up against
		whether	an introduction to alternatives
waiver	abandonment of a claim		
waver	to shake or fluctuate		

61.   We're unsure _____ to fly or to drive to the conference.

62.   If the _____ is good, attendance at the conference workshops may suffer.

63.   Colors may _____ slightly from one dye lot to the next.

64.   Management was _____ anxious to proceed with the restructuring plan.

65.   Developers requested a _____ on local restrictions before proceeding with the office complex.

66.   Mitchell did not _____ in his decision to prosecute.

Look back over the vocabulary words in this chapter. Select five or more new words to add to your vocabulary. Double-check the meanings of your selections in a dictionary. Then write a sentence for each of your words.

_____

_____

_____

_____

_____

COMPETENT LANGUAGE USAGE ESSENTIALS (C.L.U.E.)

Review

This chapter introduces no new language guidelines. Instead, it gives you a chance to reinforce the 50 guidelines from previous chapters.

In the following two cumulative reviews, use proofreading marks to correct grammar, punctuation, number usage, capitalization, spelling, and confusing word use. Mark C if a sentence is correct.

Super C.L.U.E. Review 1

67. Nokia provides over night or 2 day delivery on it's Cell Phones for only twelve dollars and fifty cents; but it won't ship online orders to P.O. boxes.

68. City officials begged the two companies board of directors not to dessert they're locations, and not to abandon local employees.

69. China the worlds fastest growing economy, will be snapping up personal computers at a 30% rate by 2,010.

70. The registration of employees cars for parking permits had went smooth; until we run out of stickers.

71. If we are to remain freinds this personall information must be kept strictly between you and I.

72. The quality of e-mail messages, memos, and reports, in this organization need to be improved.

73. Although its usually difficult to illicit contributions I think you will find this charity drive incredibely fruitful.

74. Jeff Orenstein who was recently appointed Marketing Manager submitted 6 different suggestions for boosting sales, which everyone hopes will turn around this companys sales decline.

75. Stored on open shelves in room 15, is a group of office supplies and at least 7 reams of old stationary.

76. The additional premium you were charged which amounted to fifty-five dollars and 40 cents, was issued because of you're recent accident.

Super C.L.U.E. Review 2

77. Several copys of the sales' report was sent to the Manager and I immediatley after we requested it.

78. Any letter sent to a customer, must have a professional appearance, otherwise it's message may be disregarded.

79. Here are a group of participating manufactures, who you may wish to contact regarding there products.

80. As soon as the merger is completed we will inform the entire staff, until then its business as usual.

81. The entire team of thirty-five managers were willing to procede with the proposal for asian expansion.

82. The miami river is such a narrow and congested waterway, that tugboat captains joke about needing vaseline to slip freighters through.

83. Companys such as Amway and Avon, discovered that there unique door to door selling method was successful in japan and other asian countrys.

84. Locating foriegn markets and developing it requires aggressive efforts, however many companies dont know where to begin.

85. Some companies sell better at home then abroad; because they lack experience.

86. Smart organizations can boost profits almost one hundred percent by retaining just 5% more of there current customers.

CAREER APPLICATION

You are a recruiting specialist in the Human Resources Development Department of International Life Insurance Company. The business club from a nearby campus asks your boss to send a representative to tell club members about writing résumés, and you were selected to go. As you consider what you can say to these soon-to-be-graduated business majors, you decide to take two résumés as examples—a good one and a poor one.

Look over the two résumés shown on pages 185 and 186. You should see some real differences.

Now answer the following questions in preparation for drawing conclusions about these two résumés.

Critical Thinking Questions

87. You know something about your audience, but should you know more? What specific information should you have? How can you learn more?

88. Rather than speak in generalities, you want to show real résumés that have been submitted to your company. Should you feel any ethical conflict about showing these examples? What are some actions you can take to resolve this conflict in your mind? Should you speak to your boss?

89. In preparing your discussion of these two résumés, you try to decide how to use the samples. Should you make copies of the résumés and distribute them as handouts? Or should you project them as transparencies? Why?

90. Should you talk about the poor one first and then talk about the better one next? Or should you discuss major points—such as appearance, use of headings, description of experience—and flip back and forth from one résumé to the other as you discuss each point? Why?

91. What are some specific weaknesses of résumé No. 1?

92. What are specific strengths of résumé No. 2?

After comparing your responses to these questions with the solutions in Appendix B, prepare a list of conclusions that could be drawn from your analysis of these two résumés. You should have six to ten conclusions. They may include advice to student writers. Then compare your list with that shown in Appendix B.

Résumé No. 1
(Poor Example)

JOSEPH J. RADER
5402 Ferndale Avenue
Brockton, MA 02402
(215) 419-4421

CAREER OBJECTIVE

I'm looking for a challenging entry-level position in accounting with a progressive firm. Desire opportunity for advancement into management.

EDUCATION

Degree in Business Administration, Accounting and Management Information Systems, Mid-State University, 2006. Relevant courses completed:

> Accounting I and II
> Computer Applications in Business
> Income Tax I
> Cost Accounting
> Auditing Principles
> Senior Seminar in Accounting Theory and Practice

EXPERIENCE

V.I.T.A. campus program. Was responsible for helping local individuals fill out their tax returns; two years as a volunteer. 2005–2006.

Part-time bookkeeper, 2004–2006. Commonwealth International. Completed various functions demanding accounting and computer expertise. Assisted owner; helped prepare financial statements.

Counter person, assistant manager, Pizza Bob's, Westmoreland, 2002–2004. Responsibility for all managerial duties when manager was gone.

ACTIVITIES AND OTHER

Computer Lab assistant, work study program 2001–2002. Responsible for overseeing students in campus lab.

Familiar with personal computer, Macintosh, and Internet environments.

Counselor/manager, Mid-State University. Summer, 2002.

Enjoy outdoor sports. Active in Big Brothers, Westland County.

REFERENCES

Available on request.

Résumé No. 2
(Better Example)

DAVID M. GROSS
330 Water Street
Augusta, ME 04330
(405) 344-2109

OBJECTIVE

Position as underwriter with International Life Insurance Company.

EXPERIENCE

Atlantic Federal Bank, Boston, MA
Courier—Corporate Distribution Services—2003 to present
- Contribute to Atlantic Federal's efficiency and productivity by expediting information throughout its ten-building complex, providing courier service for internal distribution
- Maintain consistent and timely delivery schedule

J. C. Penney, Greenfield, MA
Management Trainee Intern—Summer, 2005
- Successfully met department quotas by targeting customer's needs, setting goals for sales associates, and providing incentives through recognition and reward
- Developed marketing management skills in purchase of seasonable merchandise through direct broadcast satellite systems
- Systemized department inventory and visual displays
- Prepared detailed computerized reports to senior management
- Developed customer service and communication skills through training and experience with retail customers

Mid-Atlantic University, Boston, MA
Language Lab Assistant—Work Study—2002–2004
- Reproduced over 500 master and student tapes; maintained tape inventory
- Instructed and monitored over 200 students a semester in use of lab equipment

Mid-Atlantic University, Boston, MA
Summer Resident Manager—2004
- Managed logistics of summer conferences and seminars; prepared function rooms, processed registrations, administered front desk management
- Supervised 140 student residents; coordinated student orientation, peer counseling, and academic and social activities

EDUCATION

Mid-Atlantic University, Boston, MA
B.S., Business Administration, 2006. GPA in major: 3.2
Concentration: Business Finance, Investment Management, and Commercial Banking

COMPUTER SKILLS

Languages: C, C++, Java Perl, HTML
Software Packages: Excel, Word, PowerPoint, FrontPage

Chapter 16
Employment Interview Kit

Should you be nervous about an upcoming job interview? Of course! Everyone is uneasy about being scrutinized, judged, and possibly rejected. But think of how much more nervous you would be if you had no idea what to expect in the interview and if you were unprepared.

This interview kit supplements the suggestions provided in Chapter 16. It helps you get ready for an interview by introducing the kinds of interviews and showing you how to learn about the employer. It will help you reduce your nervousness by teaching you to practice for the interview, check your body language, and fight fear. You'll pick up tips for responding to recruiters' favorite questions, as well as coping with illegal questions and salary matters. Moreover, you'll receive pointers on questions you can ask. Finally, you'll learn what you should do to successfully follow up an interview.

Yes, you can expect to be nervous. But you can also expect to ace an interview when you know what's coming and when you prepare thoroughly.

Succeeding in Two Kinds of Employment Interviews

Job applicants generally face two kinds of interviews: (a) screening interviews and (b) hiring/ placement interviews. You must succeed in the first to proceed to the second.

Screening Interviews

Screening interviews do just that—they screen candidates to eliminate those who fail to meet minimum requirements. Telephone conversations, sometimes as short as five minutes, are often used for screening interviews. The important thing to remember about screening interviews is being prepared!

- Keep a list near the telephone of positions for which you have applied.

- Have your résumé, references, a calendar, and a note pad handy.

- If caught off guard, defer your response: *I was just going out the door,* or *We just sat down to dinner. May I call you back in ten minutes from the telephone in my office?*

- Sell your qualifications and sound enthusiastic.

Hiring/Placement Interviews

These interviews are the real thing. Conducted in depth, hiring/placement interviews may take many forms.

- *One-to-one interviews* are most common. You can expect to sit down with a company representative and talk about the job and your qualifications. If the representative is the hiring manager, questions will be specific and job-related. If the representative is from human resources, the questions will probably be more general.

- *Sequential and group interviews* are common with companies that rule by consensus. You may face many interviewers in sequence, all of whom you must listen to carefully and respond to positively. In group interviews, the employer may be looking for signs of leadership. Strive to stay focused, summarize important points, and ask good questions.

- *Stress interviews* are meant to test your reactions. If asked rapid-fire questions from many directions, take the time to slow things down. For example, "I would be happy to answer your question Ms. X, but first I must finish responding to Mr. Z." If greeted with silence, another stress technique, you might say, "Would you like me to begin the interview?" "Let me tell you about myself." Or ask a question such as "Can you give me more information about the position?"

Investigating the Target

The more you know about a prospective employer, the better you'll be able to tailor your responses to the organization's needs. Moreover, companies are impressed by candidates who have done their homework. For companies that are publicly held, you can generally learn a great deal from annual reports and financial disclosure reports. Company information is available at many Web sites, including Hoovers Online (www.hoovers.com), Annual Reports Library (www.zpub.com/sf/arl), and Corporate Financials Online (www.cfonews.com). If these URLs don't work, use your favorite search tool to locate the sites. Another way to get information is to call the receptionist or the interviewer directly. Ask what you can read to prepare you for the interview. Here are some specifics:

- Find out all you can about company leaders. Their goals, ambitions, and values often are adopted by the entire organization—including your interviewer.

- Investigate the business philosophy of the leaders, involving their priorities, strategies, and managerial approach. Are you a good match with your target employer? If so, be sure to let the employer know that there is a correlation between their needs and your qualifications.

- Learn about the company's accomplishments and setbacks. This information should help you determine where you might make your best contribution.

- Study the company's finances. Are they so shaky that a takeover is imminent?

- Examine its products and customers. What excites you about this company?

For smaller companies and those that are not publicly owned, you'll probably have to do a little more footwork.

- Start by searching for a company site on the Web.

- Try your local library. Ask the reference librarian to help you locate information. Newspapers might contain stories or press releases with news of an organization.

- Visit the Better Business Bureau to discover if the company has had any difficulties with other companies or consumers.

- Check out the competition. What are its products, strengths, and weaknesses?

- Investigate the chamber of commerce to see what you can learn about the target company.

- Analyze the company's advertising. How does it promote its products or service?

- Talk with company employees. They are probably the best source of inside information. Try to get introduced to someone who is currently employed—but not working in the immediate area where you wish to be hired. Seek someone who is discreet.

Preparing and Practicing

After you have learned about the target organization,

- Study the job description. It not only helps you write a focused résumé but also helps you prepare to match your education, experience, and interests with the employer's position. Finding out the duties and responsibilities of the position will enable you to practice your best response strategies.

- Itemize your (a) most strategic skills, (b) greatest areas of knowledge, (c) strongest personality traits, and (d) key accomplishments. Be ready to relate these items to the kinds of questions frequently asked in interviews.

- Practice giving responses in a mock interview with a friend. Remember to be concise. You might wish to videotape or tape record a practice session to see and hear how you really come across.

- Be ready to answer questions about alcohol and drug use.

- Expect to explain problem areas on your résumé. For example, if you have little or no experience, you might emphasize your recent training and up-to-date skills. If you have gaps in your résumé, be prepared to answer questions about them positively and truthfully.

- Try to build interviewing experience with less important jobs first. You will become more confident and better able to sell your strengths with repeated interviewing exposure.

Sending Positive Nonverbal Messages

What comes out of your mouth and what's written on your résumé are not the only messages an interviewer receives about you. Nonverbal messages also create powerful impressions on people. Here are suggestions that will help you send the right nonverbal messages during interviews.

- Arrive on time or a little early. If necessary, find the location on a trial run a few days before the interview so that you know where to park and how much time the drive takes.

- Be courteous and congenial to everyone. Remember that you are being judged not only by the interviewer but by the receptionist and anyone else who sees you before and after the interview. They will notice how you sit, what you read, and how you look. Introduce yourself to the receptionist and wait to be invited to sit.

- Dress professionally. Even if some employees in the organization dress casually, you should look qualified, competent, and successful. Dress the part!

- Greet the interviewer confidently. Extend your hand, look him or her directly in the eye, and say, "I'm pleased to meet you Mr. X. I am Z." In this culture a firm, not crushing, handshake sends a nonverbal message of poise and assurance.

- Wait for the interviewer to offer you a chair. Make small talk with upbeat comments, such as "This is a beautiful headquarters. How many employees work here?" Don't immediately begin rummaging in your briefcase for your résumé. Being at ease and unrushed suggest that you are self-confident.

- Control your body. Keep your hands, arms, and elbows to yourself. Don't lean on a desk. Sit erect, leaning forward slightly. Keep your feet on the floor.

- Make eye contact frequently but don't get into a staring contest. In this culture a direct eye gaze suggests interest and trustworthiness.

- Smile enough to convey a positive attitude. Have a friend give you honest feedback on whether you generally smile too much or not enough.

- Sound enthusiastic and interested—but sincere.

Fighting Fear

Expect to be nervous. It's natural! Other than public speaking, employment interviews are the most dreaded events in people's lives. You can, however, reduce your fears by focusing on a few suggestions.

- Practice interviewing as much as you can—especially with real companies. The more times you experience the interview situation, the less nervous you will be.

- Prepare 110 percent! Know how you will answer the most frequently asked questions. Be ready with success stories. Rehearse your closing statement. One of the best ways to reduce butterflies is to know that you have done all you can to be ready for the interview.

- Take deep breaths, particularly if you feel anxious while waiting for the interviewer. Deep breathing makes you concentrate on something other than the interview and also provides much-needed oxygen.

- Remember that the interviewer isn't the only one who is gleaning information. You have come to learn about the job and the company. In fact, during some parts of the interview, you will be in charge. This should give you courage.

Answering Questions

The way you answer questions can be almost as important as what you say. The following tips will help you make the best impression.

- Use the interviewer's name and title from time to time when you answer. "Ms. Lyon, I would be pleased to tell you about . . . ." People like to hear their own names. But be sure you are pronouncing the name correctly!

- Refocus and clarify vague questions. Some interviewers are inexperienced and ill at ease in the role. Occasionally, you may have to ask your own question to understand what was asked, "By _____ do you mean _____?"

- Aim your answers at the key characteristics interviewers seek: expertise and competence, motivation, interpersonal skills, decision-making skills, enthusiasm for the job, and a pleasing personality. Employers are looking for these skills and traits.

- Stay focused on your strengths. Don't reveal weaknesses, even if you think they make you look human. You won't be hired for your weaknesses, only for your strengths.

- Use good English and enunciate clearly. Remember, you will be judged by how you communicate. Avoid slurred words like "gonna" and "din't," as well as slangy expressions like "yeah" and overuse of "like."

- Eliminate verbal static ("ah," "and ah," "uhm"). Make a tape recording as you practice answering expected interview questions. Is it filled with verbal static?

- Consider closing out some of your responses with "Does that answer your question?" or "Would you like me to elaborate on any particular experience?"

All-Time Favorite Questions With Selected Answers

The following questions represent those frequently asked of recent graduates and other job seekers. You'll also find a section of questions for you to ask when it is your turn. The interview questions are divided into groups. In each group the first question is answered. As you read the remaining questions, think about how you could respond most effectively.

Questions to Get Acquainted

1. Tell me about yourself. Experts agree that you must keep this answer short (1 to 2 minutes tops) but on target. Try practicing this formula:

   "My name is _____. I have completed a _____ degree with a major in _____. Recently I worked for _____ as a _____. Before that I worked for _____ as a _____. My strengths are _____ (interpersonal) and _____ (technical)."

   Try rehearsing your response in 30-second segments devoted to your education, your work experience, and your qualities/skills. Some candidates end with, *Now that I've told you about myself, can you tell me a little more about the position?*

2. What was your college major and why did you choose it?

3. If you had it to do over again, would you choose the same major? Why?

4. Tell me about your college and why you chose it.

5. Do you prefer to work by yourself or with others? Why?

6. What are your key strengths?

7. What are some things you do in your spare time? Hobbies? Sports?

8. Were you active in any extra-curricular activities in college?

9. What college professors did you like the most? The least? Why?

10. Have you changed your major in college? Why?

11. Are you willing to travel?

12. How did you happen to apply for this job?

13. What particular qualifications do you have for this job?

14. What courses prepared you for this job?

15. Do you consider yourself a team player? Describe your style as a team player.

Questions About Your Experience and Accomplishments

1. Why should we hire you when we have applicants with more experience or better credentials?

   In answering this question, remember that employers often hire people who present themselves well instead of others with better credentials. Emphasize your personal strengths that could be an advantage with this employer. Are you a hard worker? How can you demonstrate it? Have you had recent training? Some people have had more years of experience but actually have less knowledge because they have done the same thing over and over. Stress your experience using the latest methods and equipment. Emphasize that you are open to new ideas and learn quickly.

2. Tell me about your part-time jobs, internships, or other experience.

3. What were your major accomplishments in each of your past jobs?

4. Why did you change jobs?

5. What was a typical work day like?

6. What were your responsibilities at _____?

7. What job functions did you enjoy most? Least? Why?

8. Who was the toughest boss you ever worked for and why?

9. What were your major achievements in college?

10. What was your overall grade-point average? In your major?

Crystal Ball Gazing and Questions About the Future

1. Where do you expect to be five years from now?

   It's a sure kiss of death to respond that you'd like to have the interviewer's job! Instead, show an interest in the current job and in making a contribution to the organization. Talk about the levels of responsibility you'd like to achieve. One employment counselor suggests showing ambition but not committing to a specific job title. Suggest that you will have learned enough to have progressed to a position where you will continue to grow.

2. If you got this position, what would you do to be sure you fit in?

3. What if your supervisor gave you an assignment and then left town for two weeks. What would you do?

4. This is a large (or small) organization. Do you think that you'd like that environment?

5. You are aware that a coworker is falsifying data. What would you do?

6. Your supervisor is dissatisfied with your work. You think it is acceptable. How would you resolve the conflict?

7. After completing a job, how would you evaluate it?

8. What does dependability mean to you?

9. Describe someone whom you consider to be an excellent communicator. Explain your choice.

10. Do you plan to continue your education?

Questions to Make You Squirm

1. What are your key weaknesses?

   It's amazing how many candidates knock themselves out of the competition by answering this question poorly. Actually, you have many choices. You can present a strength as a weakness ("Some people complain that I'm a workaholic or too attentive to details"). You can mention a corrected weakness ("I found that I really needed to learn about the Internet, so I took a course. . ."). You could cite an unrelated skill ("I really need to brush up my Spanish"). You can cite a learning objective ("One of my long-term goals is to learn more about international management. Does your company have any plans to expand overseas?") Another possibility is to reaffirm your qualifications ("I have no weaknesses that affect my ability to do this job").

2. If you could change one thing about your personality, what would it be and why?

3. If I met some of your college chums, what do you think they would say about you?

4. What would your former boss say about you?

5. What do you want the most from your job? Money? Security? Power?

6. How do you handle authority? Criticism?

7. How did you prepare for this interview?

8. Do you feel you achieved the best grade-point average of which you were capable in college?

9. Do you ever lose your temper?

10. To what extent do you use liquor?

11. Have you ever used drugs?

12. Relate an incident when you faced an ethical dilemma. How did you react? How did you feel?

13. How long do you think this position will be challenging to you?

14. If your supervisor told you to do something a certain way, and you knew that way was dead wrong, what would you do?

15. When you are supervising people, how do you motivate them?

Questions About Money

1. How much money are you looking for?

   One way to handle salary questions is to ask politely to defer the discussion until it's clear that a job will be offered to you. ("I'm sure when the time comes, we'll be able to work out a fair compensation package. Right now, I'd rather focus on whether we have a match.") Another possible response is to reply candidly that you can't know what to ask until you know more about the position and the company. If you continue to be pressed for a dollar figure, give a salary range. Be sure to do research before the interview so that you know what similar jobs are paying. For example, check salary information on the Web at <www.salary.com>.

2. How much are you presently earning?

3. How did you finance your education?

4. Have you saved any money?

5. How much money do you expect to earn at age _____?

Questions for You to Ask

At some point in the interview, you will be asked if you have any questions. Your questions should not only help you gain information, but they should impress the interviewer with your thoughtfulness and interest in the position. Remember, though, that this interview is a two-way street. You must be happy with the prospect of working for this organization. You want a position for which your skills and personality are matched. Use this opportunity to find out whether this job is right for you.

1. What will my duties be (if not already discussed)?

2. Tell me what it's like working here in terms of the people, management practices, work loads, expected performance, and rewards.

3. Why is this position open? Did the person who held it previously leave?

4. What training programs are available from this organization? What specific training will be given for this position?

5. What are the possibilities for promotion from this position?

6. Who would be my immediate supervisor?

7. What is the organizational structure, and where does this position fit in?

8. Is travel required in this position?

9. What are housing conditions in the surrounding area?

10. Assuming my work is excellent, where do you see me in five years?

11. How long do employees generally stay with this organization?

12. What are the major challenges for a person in this position?

13. What can I do to make myself more employable to you?

14. What is the salary for this position?

15. When will I hear from you regarding further action on my application?

Fielding Illegal Questions

Because federal laws prohibit discrimination, interviewers may not ask questions like those in the following list. Nevertheless, you may face an inexperienced or unscrupulous interviewer who does ask some of these questions. How should you react? If you find the question harmless and if you want the job, go ahead and answer it. If you think that answering it would damage your chance to be hired, try to deflect the question tactfully with a response such as, "Could you tell me how my marital status relates to the responsibilities of this position?" Another option, of course, is to respond to any illegal question by confronting the interviewer and threatening a lawsuit. However, you could not expect to be hired under these circumstances. You might wish to reconsider working for an organization that sanctions such procedures.

Here are some illegal questions that you may or may not wish to answer.

1. Are you married, divorced, separated, or single?

2. Do you have any disabilities that would prevent you from doing this job? (But it is legal to ask "Can you carry a 50-pound sack up a 10-foot ladder five times daily?")

3. What is your corrected vision? (But it is legal to ask "Do you have 20/20 corrected vision?")

4. Does stress ever affect your ability to be productive? (But it is legal to ask "How well can you handle stress?")

5. How much alcohol do you drink per week? (But it is legal to ask "Do you drink alcohol?")

6. Have you ever been arrested? (But it is legal to ask "Have you ever been convicted of a crime?")

7. How old are you? What is your date of birth? (But it is legal to ask "Are you 18 years old or older?")

8. Of what country are you a citizen? (But it is legal to ask "Are you a citizen of the U.S.?")

9. What is your maiden name? (But it is legal to ask "What is your full name?")

10. What is your religious preference?

11. Do you have children?

12. Are you practicing birth control?

13. Are you living with anyone?

14. Do you own or rent your home?

15. How much do you weigh? How tall are you?

Interview Don'ts

No one is perfect in an interview. You can, however, avert sure disaster by avoiding certain topics and behaviors such as the following.

- Don't ask for the job. It's naive, undignified, and unprofessional. Wait to see how the interview develops.

- Don't trash your previous employer, supervisors, or colleagues. The tendency is for interviewers to wonder whether you would speak about their companies similarly.

- Don't be a threat to the interviewer. Avoid suggesting directly or indirectly that your goal is to become head honcho, a path that might include the interviewer's job.

- Don't try to memorize question answers. Your responses will sound "canned."

- Don't be late or too early for your appointment.

- Don't discuss controversial subjects, and don't use profanity.

- Don't smoke unless the interviewer smokes.

- Don't emphasize salary or benefits. If the interview goes well and these subjects have not been addressed, you may mention them toward the end of the interview.

- Don't be negative about yourself or others. Never dwell on your liabilities.

- Don't interrupt.

- Don't accept a job immediately after getting an offer.

- Don't accept an offer until you have completed all your interviews.

CAREER APPLICATION

1. Assume you have sent out your résumé to many companies. What information should you keep near your telephone and why?

2. Your first interview is with a small local company. What kind of information should you seek about this company and where could you expect to find it?

3. Name at least two ways in which you can practice for the interview and receive feedback on your performance.

4. What nonverbal messages do you think your appearance and demeanor send? How could you make sure your nonverbal messages are working for you?

5. Why is it important to make frequent eye contact with an interviewer?

6. What is your greatest fear of what you might do or what might happen to you during an employment interview? How can you overcome your fears?

7. Should you be candid with an interviewer when asked about your weaknesses?

8. How can you clarify vague questions?

9. Select three get-acquainted questions. Write each question on a separate sheet and then write an answer to it.

10. Select three crystal-ball and future questions. Write each question on a separate sheet and then answer it.

11. Select three *squirm* questions. Write each question on a separate sheet and then answer it.

12. Select two money questions. Write each question on a separate sheet and answer it.

13. Select three questions for you to ask. Write each on a separate sheet and answer it.

14. Select three illegal questions. Write each question on a separate sheet and then answer it.

15. Why is it important not to accept a job immediately after getting an offer?

Appendix A

160 FREQUENTLY MISSPELLED WORDS

absence	desirable	independent	prominent
accommodate	destroy	indispensable	qualify
achieve	development	interrupt	quantity
acknowledgment	disappoint	irrelevant	questionnaire
across	dissatisfied	itinerary	receipt
adequate	division	judgment	receive
advisable	efficient	knowledgeable	recognize
analyze	embarrass	legitimate	recommendation
annually	emphasis	library	referred
appointment	emphasize	license	regarding
argument	employee	maintenance	remittance
automatically	envelope	manageable	representative
bankruptcy	equipped	manufacturer	restaurant
becoming	especially	mileage	schedule
beneficial	evidently	miscellaneous	secretary
budget	exaggerate	mortgage	separate
business	excellent	necessary	similar
calendar	exempt	nevertheless	sincerely
canceled	existence	ninety	software
catalog	extraordinary	ninth	succeed
changeable	familiar	noticeable	sufficient
column	fascinate	occasionally	supervisor
committee	feasible	occurred	surprise
congratulate	February	offered	tenant
conscience	fiscal	omission	therefore
conscious	foreign	omitted	thorough
consecutive	forty	opportunity	though
consensus	fourth	opposite	through
consistent	friend	ordinarily	truly
control	genuine	paid	undoubtedly
convenient	government	pamphlet	unnecessarily
correspondence	grammar	permanent	usable
courteous	grateful	permitted	usage
criticize	guarantee	pleasant	using
decision	harass	practical	usually
deductible	height	prevalent	valuable
defendant	hoping	privilege	volume
definitely	immediate	probably	weekday
dependent	incidentally	procedure	writing
describe	incredible	profited	yield

CONFUSING WORDS

accede:	to agree or consent	*conscience:*	regard for fairness
exceed:	over a limit	*conscious:*	aware
accept:	to receive	*council:*	governing body
except:	to exclude	*counsel:*	to give advice; advice
	(prep) but	*credible:*	believable
adverse:	unfavorable, antagonistic	*creditable*	good enough for praise or
averse:	unwilling, opposed to		esteem; reliable
advice:	suggestion, opinion	*desert:*	(n) arid land
advise:	to counsel or recommend		(v) to abandon
affect:	to influence	*dessert:*	sweet food
effect:	(n) outcome, result	*device:*	invention or mechanism
	(v) to bring about, to create	*devise:*	to design or arrange
all ready:	prepared	*disburse:*	to pay out
already:	by this time	*disperse:*	to scatter widely
all right:	satisfactory	*elicit:*	to draw out
alright:	[unacceptable variant spelling]	*illicit:*	unlawful
altar:	structure for worship	*envelop:*	(v) to wrap, surround, or
alter:	to change		conceal
appraise:	to estimate	*envelope:*	(n) a container for a written
apprise:	to inform		message
ascent:	(n) rising or going up	*every day:*	each single day
assent:	(v) to agree or consent	*everyday:*	ordinary
assure:	to promise	*farther:*	a greater distance
ensure:	to make certain	*further:*	additional
insure:	to protect from loss	*flair:*	natural talent, aptitude
ascent:	rising, going up	*flare:*	to blaze up or spread out
assent:	agree or consent	*formally:*	in a formal manner
capital:	(n) city that is seat of goverment;	*formerly:*	in the past
	wealth of an individual	*grate:*	(v) to reduce to small particles;
	(adj) foremost in importance;		to cause irritation
	punishable by death		(n) a frame of crossed bars
capitol:	building used by state lawmakers		blocking a passage
cereal:	breakfast food	*great:*	(adj) large in size; numerous;
serial:	arranged in sequence		eminent or distinguished
cite:	to quote; to summon	*hole:*	an opening
site:	location	*whole:*	complete
sight:	(n) a view	*imply:*	to suggest indirectly
	(v) to see	*infer:*	to reach a conclusion
coarse:	rough texture	*lean:*	(v) to rest against; to incline
course:	a route; part of a meal; a unit		toward
	of learning		(adj) not fat
complement:	that which completes	*lien:*	(n) a legal right or claim to
compliment:	to praise or flatter		property

liable:	legally responsible	*reality:*	that which is real
libel:	damaging written statement	*realty:*	real estate
loose:	not fastened	*stationary:*	immovable
lose:	to misplace	*stationery:*	writing material
miner:	person working in a mine	*than:*	conjunction showing comparison
minor:	a lesser item; person under age	*then:*	adverb meaning "at that time"
patience:	calm perseverance	*their:*	possessive form of they
patients:	people receiving medical treatment	*there:*	at that place or point
persecute:	to oppress	*they're:*	contraction of they are
prosecute:	to sue	*to:*	a preposition; the sign of the infinitive
personal:	private, individual		
personnel:	employees	*too:*	an adverb meaning "also" or "to an excessive extent"
plaintiff:	a party to a lawsuit		
plaintive:	mournful	*two:*	a number
populace:	(n) the masses; population of a place	*vary:*	to change
		very:	extremely
populous:	(adj) densely populated	*waiver:*	abandonment of a claim
precede:	to go before	*waver:*	to shake or fluctuate
proceed:	to continue	*weather:*	(n) the state of the atmosphere (v) to bear up against
precedence:	priority		
precedents:	events used as an example	*whether:*	an introduction to alternatives
principal:	(n) capital sum; school official (adj) chief		
principle:	rule of action		

Appendix B
Solutions

CHAPTER 1

Chapter Review

1. T
2. F   Global competition and team-based projects are having a significant impact on the workplace.
3. T
4. F   Communication is successful when the receiver understands the idea as the sender intended it.
5. F   Feedback helps senders know that the message was received and understood.
6. T
7. T
8. F   To improve the flow of information, organizations formulate policies to encourage regular open communication, suggest means for achieving it, and spell out responsibilities.
9. T
10. T

Multiple Choice

11. c
12. d
13. b
14. a

Short Answer

15. Obstacles to interpersonal communication:
    a. Bypassing
    b. Frame of reference
    c. Lack of language skill
    d. Distractions

16. Technologies that have speeded up the flow of communication include e-mail, instant messaging (IM), text messaging, voice mail, cell phones, and wireless networks ("Wi-Fi").

17. Steps in the communication process:
    a. Sender has idea.
    b. Sender encodes idea in message.
    c. Message travels over channel.
    d. Receiver decodes message.
    e. Feedback travels to sender.

18. Ways to improve the upward flow of communication:
    a. Hiring communication coaches to train employees.
    b. Asking employees to report customer complaints.
    c. Encouraging regular meetings with staff.
    d. Providing a trusting, nonthreatening environment in which employees can comfortably share their observations and ideas with management.
    e. Offering incentive programs that encourage employees to collect and share valuable feedback.

19. Three disadvantages of oral communication are that it produces no written record, sometimes wastes time, and may be inconvenient.

20. Five questions to ask when facing an ethical dilemma:
    a. Is the action you are considering legal?
    b. How would you see the problem if you were on the opposite side?
    c. What are alternate solutions?
    d. Can you discuss the problem with someone whose advice you trust?
    e. How would you feel if your family, friends, employer, or coworkers learned of your action?

Matching

21. b
22. c
23. k
24. g
25. j
26. i
27. e
28. h
29. a
30. d

Spelling Pretest

31.   calendar
32.   consensus
33.   defendant
34.   exaggerate
35.   indispensable
36.   knowledgeable
37.   permanent
38.   recommendation

Career Track Spelling

39.   paid
40.   attorneys
41.   surprise, representative
42.   accidentally, writing
43.   deceive, definitely
44.   congratulation, incredible
45.   industrious
46.   companies, irrelevant
47.   occurred, government
48.   beige, serviceable, weekday

Career Track Vocabulary

49.   d
50.   f
51.   a
52.   c
53.   b
54.   e
55.   c
56.   b
57.   a
58.   c

59.   b
60.   c
61.   a
62.   b
63.   adverse
64.   advice
65.   accede
66.   averse
67.   advise
68.   exceed

CHAPTER 2

Chapter Review

1. T
2. T
3. F   During the storming phase, a good leader should set limits, control the chaos, and offer suggestions.
4. F   The three types of roles are task, relationship, and dysfunctional.
5. T
6. F   Striving for team diversity in terms of gender, background, experience, and training is the most effective way to avoid groupthink.
7. T
8. T
9. F   Meetings consist of three or more individuals.
10. F   Tools include audioconferencing, Web conferencing, screen sharing, chat servers, instant messaging, folder sharing, intranets, message boards, and e-mail. Hot-desking is not a collaboration tool.

Fill in the Blank

Team Skills

11. group
12. interdependently
13. dysfunctional
14. norming
15. unresolved
16. groupthink
17. consensus
18. leadership
19. ground rules
20. deadlines

Meetings and Collaboration Technologies

21. face-to-face
22. ideas
23. problem solving
24. agenda
25. background
26. dysfunctional
27. understanding
28. few days
29. collaboration technology
30. media
31. unrestricted
32. sales transactions

Short Answer

33. Characteristics of self-directed teams:
     a. Clearly stated goals
     b. Autonomy
     c. Decision-making authority
     d. Frequent communication
     e. Ongoing training

34. Kinds of positive group task roles:
    a. Initiator
    b. Information seeker/information giver
    c. Opinion giver/opinion seeker
    d. Direction giver
    e. Summarizer
    f. Diagnoser
    g. Energizer
    h. Gatekeeper
    i. Reality tester

35. Kinds of positive group relationship roles:
    a. Participation encourager
    b. Harmonizer/tension reliever
    c. Evaluator of emotional climate
    d. Praise giver
    e. Empathic listener

36. Ethical responsibilities of group members and leaders:
    a. Determine to do your best.
    b. Decide to behave with the group's good in mind.
    c. Make a commitment to fair play.
    d. Expect to give and receive a fair hearing.
    e. Be willing to take on a participant/analyst role.
    f. As a leader, be ready to model appropriate team behavior.

Matching

37.	f		42.	c
38.	i		43.	d
39.	g		44.	k
40.	a		45.	j
41.	b		46.	e

Career Track Spelling

47. absence
48. achieve
49. C
50. recommendation
51. personnel
52. sufficient
53. omitted
54. C
55. occasionally
56. judgment

Career Track Vocabulary

57.	c		67.	a
58.	f		68.	a
59.	a		69.	c
60.	e		70.	a
61.	b		71.	all ready
62.	d		72.	altar
63.	b		73.	effect
64.	a		74.	already
65.	c		75.	affect
66.	c		76.	alter

C.L.U.E. Checkpoint

77.   RO . . . to hit; get them . . . *OR* . . . to hit, and get . . .
78.   CS . . . cards; however, they . . .
79.   FG . . . hoped . . .
80.   RO . . . problem; he asked . . . *OR* . . . problem. He asked . . .
81.   CS . . . want; you ask . . .
82.   CS . . . employees; however, . . .
83.   FG . . . guidance, he . . .
84.   CS . . . resort; however, . . .
85.   C
86.   CS . . . deadlines; then . . .

CHAPTER 3

Chapter Review

1. T
2. F   Experts say that we listen at only 25 percent efficiency; they say that we ignore, forget, distort, or misunderstand 75 percent of everything we hear.
3. F   As an entry-level employee, while you will be concerned about listening to colleagues and team members, you will be most concerned about listening to your superiors.
4. T
5. F   Listening takes place in four stages: perception, interpretation, evaluation, and action.
6. F   Listening to friends is challenging because friends tend to interrupt, jump to conclusions, and take each other for granted.
7. T
8. F   When verbal and nonverbal messages are contradictory, listeners believe and act on the nonverbal message.
9. T
10. F   The way you look telegraphs an instant nonverbal message about you, and viewers make quick judgments about your status, credibility, personality, and potential.

Fill in the Blank

Listening

11. worker
12. explanations
13. reflecting
14. opinions
15. social
16. evaluation
17. reviewing
18. distractions
19. assertions
20. interrupting

Nonverbal Messages

21. five
22. spoken
23. distress
24. submissiveness
25. palm
26. attitudes
27. territory
28. permanent
29. style
30. cues

Short Answer

31. Types of workplace listening:
    a. Listening to superiors
    b. Listening to colleagues and teammates
    c. Listening to customers

32. Practices of trained listeners that improve customer relations:
    a. Defer judgment; listen for the customer's feelings and assess the situation.
    b. Pay most attention to content, not to appearances, form, or other surface issues.
    c. Listen completely, trying to really understand every nuance.
    d. Listen primarily for the main idea and avoid replying to everything, especially sidetracking issues.
    e. Do one thing at a time, realizing that listening is a full-time job.
    f. Control your anger, refusing to allow your emotions to govern.
    g. Be silent for a few seconds after a customer finishes to ensure the thought is completed.
    h. Give affirming statements and invite additional comments.

33. Common mental listening barriers:
    a. Inattention
    b. Prejudgment
    c. Frame of reference
    d. Closed-mindedness
    e. Pseudolistening

34. Recommendations to improve your listening effectiveness:
    a. Stop talking.
    b. Work hard at listening.
    c. Block out competing thoughts.
    d. Control the listening environment.
    e. Maintain an open mind.
    f. Paraphrase the speaker's ideas.
    g. Listen between the lines.
    h. Distinguish between facts and opinions.
    i. Capitalize on lag time.
    j. Use memory devices.
    k. Take selective notes.

35. Techniques to improve your nonverbal communication skills:
    a. Improve your decoding skills.
    b. Probe for more information.
    c. Avoid assigning nonverbal meanings out of context.
    d. Associate with people from diverse cultures.
    e. Appreciate the power of appearance.
    f. Observe yourself on videotape.
    g. Enlist friends and family.

Matching

36.	d		41.	c
37.	e		42.	h
38.	f		43.	b
39.	g		44.	k
40.	a		45.	i

Career Track Spelling

46. prominent
47. C
48. existence
49. excellent
50. bankruptcy
51. privilege
52. immediate
53. succeed
54. consistent
55. control, dependent

Career Track Vocabulary

56. b
57. e
58. a
59. f
60. d
61. c
62. a
63. c
64. b
65. a
66. c
67. b
68. b
69. a
70. ascent
71. ensure
72. insure
73. apprise
74. assent
75. appraise
76. assure

C.L.U.E. Checkpoint

77. The president of **Data Systems, Inc.**, received his bachelor's degree from **Pepperdine University**.

78. When **President Bush** visited **Ireland**, the crowds lined the streets.

79. At the national **YMCA** convention, students from all parts of the nation exchanged stories about their programs.

80. Attending the conference were **Vice President Atwood** and **President Wilkerson**.

81. Our finance class took a field trip to see the **New York Stock Exchange** in **Manhattan**.

82. Richard enrolled in **Management** 304, **Computer Science** 205, and marketing.

83. Our vacation included **Shenandoah National Park** in the **Blue Ridge Mountains**.

84. Send the **Xerox** copies to **Kimberly Gorman, Marketing Manager, Globex Incorporated**, 769 **Valencia Street**, **San Francisco**, CA 94010, as soon as possible.

85. The **Pacific Design Center** featured **French** prints, **Mexican** pottery, and **Asian** fabrics.

86. Until the promotion of her first book, *Rise of the Meritocracy*, Lucy Stoppard had never traveled outside her native **Chicago**.

CHAPTER 4

Chapter Review

1. T
2. F   The most important factor in the rise of the global market is the development of new transportation and information technologies.
3. T
4. F   Practices are outward symbols of deeper values that are invisible.
5. F   Context is perhaps the most important cultural dimension, but it is difficult to define.
6. T
7. T
8. F   Humor doesn't translate well, and using it in written messages may cause significant problems or misunderstanding.
9. T
10. F   While diversity can be a positive force and help companies succeed, if mismanaged, it can become a tremendous drain on a company's time and resources.

Fill in the Blank

Intercultural Communication

11. misunderstandings
12. adapt
13. country-specific
14. society
15. self-identity
16. prejudice
17. action oriented
18. evasiveness
19. ethnocentrism
20. empathy

Dimensions of Culture and Intercultural Sensitivity

21. face
22. differ
23. comprehension
24. gestures
25. nonverbal
26. grammar
27. negative
28. public
29. treaty
30. diversity

Short Answer

31. Below are lists of three high-context and three low-context cultures and their characteristics.

High-context cultures

1. Japanese
2. Chinese
3. Arab

Low-context cultures

1. German
2. North American
3. Scandinavian

Characteristics of high-context cultures

1. Prefer indirect verbal interaction.
2. Tend to understand meanings embedded at many sociocultural levels.
3. Generally are more proficient in reading nonverbal cues.
4. Value group membership.
5. Rely more on context and feeling.
6. Employ spiral logic.
7. Talk around point; avoid saying no.
8. Communicate in simple, ambiguous, noncontexted messages.
9. Understand visual messages readily.

Characteristics of low-context cultures

1. Tend to prefer direct verbal interaction.
2. Tend to understand meaning at one level only.
3. Generally are less proficient in reading nonverbal cues.
4. Value individualism.
5. Rely more on logic.
6. Employ linear logic.
7. Say no directly.
8. Communicate in highly structured messages that provide details and stress literal meanings.

32. Suggestions that may be helpful for situations in which one or more of the communicators may be using English as a second language:
    a. Learn foreign phrases.
    b. Use simple English.
    c. Speak slowly and enunciate clearly.
    d. Observe eye messages.
    e. Encourage accurate feedback.
    f. Check frequently for comprehension.
    g. Accept blame.
    h. Listen without interrupting.
    i. Remember to smile.
    j. Follow up in writing.

33. Suggestions for helping business communicators improve intercultural proficiency and communication:
    a. Study your own culture.
    b. Learn about other cultures.
    c. Curb ethnocentrism.
    d. Avoid judgmentalism.
    e. Seek common ground.
    f. Observe nonverbal cues in your own culture.
    g. Use plain English.
    h. Encourage accurate feedback.
    i. Adapt to local preferences.

34. Tips for improving communication among diverse workplace audiences:
  a. Seek training.
  b. Understand the value of differences.
  c. Don't expect conformity.
  d. Learn about your cultural self.
  e. Make fewer assumptions.
  f. Build on similarities.

Matching

35. e
36. c
37. h
38. a
39. k

40. f
41. d
42. b
43. i
44. g

Career Track Spelling

45. employee
46. committee, deductible
47. grammar
48. mileage, sufficient
49. forty
50. adequate, throughout
51. budget, harassment
52. irrelevant, efficient
53. permanent, fascinate
54. ninety

Career Track Vocabulary

55. c
56. a
57. e
58. b
59. d
60. f
61. a
62. c
63. c
64. a
65. b

66. c
67. b
68. b
69. cereal
70. cite
71. sight
72. site
73. Capitol
74. serial
75. capital
76. capitol

C.L.U.E. Checkpoint

77. When the **Space Shuttle Columbia** burned up on reentry and exploded, many skeptics doubted whether **NASA** could survive.

78. Ginger Putnam, a systems programmer in our **Accounting Department**, drinks **Diet Coke** all day.

79. Axelrod's book on **Queen Elizabeth I** combines history with twenty-**first century** business concepts.

80. In **Barnes and Noble** she bought a book called *How to Buy a House, Condo, or Co-op*.

81. James Dale, president of **Quaker Oats Company**, discussed **Gatorade**, its popular sports drink.

82. Please complete **Form 1040** and send it to the **Internal Revenue Service** before **April** 15.

83. Our **Student Fees and Admissions Committee** will meet in **Room 12** on the east side of **Douglas Campus Center**.

84. The city of **New York** continues to be the heart of our country's financial operations, even after the tragic events of **September** 11.

85. Easterners and **Midwesterners** often travel south to **Florida** to spend their winters.

86. Did you see the **Toshiba** computer that **Vice President Rose** bought for his trip to **Europe**?

CHAPTER 5

Chapter Review

1. F   Business writing differs from academic writing: your goals are to solve problems, convey information, express ideas clearly and concisely, and view issues from a reader's rather than writer's perspective.
2. T
3. F   In most projects writers schedule about 25 percent of the time for writing.
4. F   Collaboration in writing is especially important for big tasks, items with *short* deadlines, and team projects that require a variety of expertise.
5. T
6. F   Good writers weigh a number of factors such as the importance of a message, the cost of the channel, amount and speed of feedback required, necessity of a permanent record, and degree of formality required.
7. T
8. F   When writing, you should consider both primary and secondary audiences.
9. F   A business writer shouldn't try to dazzle readers with his or her extensive knowledge, powerful vocabulary, or graceful phrasing. The goal in business writing is to *express* rather than *impress*.
10. T

Fill in the Blank

*Applying a
Writing Process*

11. reader oriented
12. recursive
13. collaborative
14. writing
15. track changes
16. inform
17. channel
18. report or proposal
19. profiling

*Adapting to the
Task and Audience*

20. tone
21. benefits
22. second
23. nonverbal
24. sender
25. gender
26. blame
27. familiar
28. jargon

*Adapting to Legal
Responsibilities*

29. language
30. marketing
31. highlighting
32. promissory

Short Answer

33. a. Voice mail message: When you wish to leave important or routine information that the receiver can respond to when convenient.

    b. E-mail: When you need feedback but not immediately. The lack of security makes it problematic for personal, emotional, or private messages; however, it is effective for communicating with a large, dispersed audience.

    c. Video- or teleconference: When group consensus and interaction are important but members are geographically dispersed.

    d. Memo: When you want a written record to clearly explain policies, discuss procedures, or collect information within an organization.

    e. Letter: When you need a written record of correspondence with customers, the government, suppliers, or others outside an organization.

34. Questions that help you profile your primary audience:

    a. Who is my primary reader or listener?

    b. What is my personal and professional relationship with this person?

    c. What position does the individual hold in the organization?

    d. How much does this person know about the subject?

    e. What do I know about this person's education, beliefs, culture, and attitudes?

    f. Should I expect a neutral, positive, or negative response to my message?

35. Kinds of bias and an example of each:

    a. Gender bias: *mankind*

    b. Racial or ethnic bias: *Hispanic lawyer*

    c. Age bias: *slow-moving old man*

    d. Disability: *crippled by*

Reader Benefits and "You" View

36. So that you may receive your monthly newsletter on time, please complete the enclosed card.

37. I would like to talk with you about the ways in which my education and training could be put to work for General Biofilm as you expand your company's research division.

38. To ensure that you have the information you need to make an informed decision, we publish the actual manufacturer's price along with our retail price.

Language Bias

39. Although Jim uses a wheelchair, he travels to all functions easily.

40. New subscribers may cancel their subscriptions within two weeks.

41. We filled the position with Juanita Sanchez, who just graduated from the state university.

Positive Expression

42. We will ship the MP3 recorder you ordered on March 1.

43. Thank you for your letter about our dining facility; we appreciate any feedback that enables us to find ways to improve our customers' experiences.

44. Your letter arrived in our New York office on May 5.

Courteous Expression

45. To enroll in our program, please complete the enclosed application.

46. To load paper in the copier, please read the instructions on page 10 of the manual, which you'll find hanging on the right side of the machine.

47. Your policy covers drivers who are 21 and older.

Familiar Words

48. Please ask the human resources manager what the position pays.

49. Before our meeting today, I will ask Jason to provide details about some of the recommendations in his report.

Career Track Spelling

50. across
51. C
52. exempt
53. miscellaneous
54. paid
55. February
56. permanent
57. recognized
58. envelopes
59. grateful

Career Track Vocabulary

60. c
61. a
62. e
63. f
64. b
65. d
66. b
67. a
68. c
69. a
70. c
71. b
72. b
73. b

74. counsel
75. compliment
76. course
77. coarse
78. complement
79. council

C.L.U.E. Checkpoint

80. **Fourteen hundred** people in **four** different counties have already signed the recall petition.

81. **Nine** employees have signed up to attend the training session at 1 p.m.

82. On **January 15** we will advertise **two** job openings.

83. Marianne bought three gifts; **one** cost **$10**, and the other two cost $15.95.

84. At the age of **twenty-one**, Gordon started a business with an investment of **$10,000**.

85. Take the second street on the right, then travel **nine** miles before turning right at Bonvale Drive. Our office's address is 420 Bonvale; we're the **third** building on the left.

86. Our sales force of **nine** representatives serves 900 accounts in **three** countries.

87. The unemployment rate was **5.6** percent for the six-month period.

88. Your loan is at 9 **percent** for **60** days and is payable on March **12**.

89. Our **three** branch offices, with a total of **96** workers, need to add six computers and three printers.

Super C.L.U.E. Review

90. **Whopper's** new **Double Bacon Burger** contains **810** calories and costs **$3.49**.

91. After Burger King advertised its new creation, an animal rights group began a **two-month** protest to end meat and dairy consumption, fishing, hunting, and trapping.

92. The **American Association for Training and Development** estimates that **5** percent of the **nation's** employers will annually spend **$30 billion** on employee training.

93. A rule of thumb for determining office-space needs is **150** to **200** square feet per employee, plus **15** percent for traffic flow.

94. If you propose work related to our **21** offices in **Europe** or **Asia**, expect to take center stage **occasionally**.

95. The **manager's** latest policy had a positive **effect** on the production **line's** performance.

96. Once a week, I **receive** several notes from **President** Jones, whose office is in Toronto.

97. Centron **Oil Company**, with headquarters in western **Texas**, hopes to **exceed its** past record of **10,000** gallons in a day.

98. **One hundred ten companies** formerly located in the **World Trade Center** had to relocate.

99. All visitors to Boston should take a walk along the **Charles River**; they should also take the time to visit the **Museum of Fine Arts, one** of the **country's** finest.

CHAPTER 6

Chapter Review

1. T
2. F   Long reports and complex business problems generally require formal research methods.
3. F   Brainstorming is a proven method of generating ideas.
4. T
5. F   The hardest part of creating an outline is grouping ideas into components and categories.
6. T
7. F   The direct pattern is most effective for receptive audiences.
8. F   The API recommends limiting sentences to *20 words or less* for effective communication.
9. T
10. T

Multiple Choice

11.	a		19.	d
12.	a		20.	d
13.	d		21.	c
14.	d		22.	b
15.	b		23.	a
16.	a		24.	a
17.	a		25.	b
18.	c		26.	d

Sentence Elements

27. IC; subject = you, verb = should approach

28. DC; subject = manager, verb = reviewed

29. DC; subject = candidate, verbs = is prepared, has done

30. P [phrases do not have subjects and verbs]

31. IC; subject = employers, verb = are concerned

Sentence Length

32.   Questions about career advancement present a delicate problem. On one hand, you need this information to make an informed career choice. On the other hand, you risk alienating an employer who does not want to hire an unrealistically ambitious college graduate for the average entry-level position. As a result, some recruiters warn against asking straight out how soon you can be considered for a promotion.

33.   After long negotiations the museum persuaded the artist to show her early drawings. She also agreed to display three sculptures, two paintings, and several sketches. As a result, this show will be the first in North America to display works from all of her periods over the past 40 years.

Active and Passive Voice

34.   Please submit your vacation request by this Friday.

35.   Bodke Construction Company submitted initial figures for the bid before the June 1 deadline.

36.   Procter & Gamble designed the survey to capture emotional reactions of women under 50.

37.   The report was submitted to Congress late last night by the Office of Management and Budget.

38.   A warning about the use of this pesticide was first issued 15 months ago.

39.   Because the CEO was ill, the keynote address was given by the vice president.

Misplaced Modifiers

40.   As assistant editor, you will be interviewing executives.

41.   During surgery doctors discovered his ankle had been fractured in five places.

42.   To apply for a job, you must submit a résumé.

43.   To be successful in responding to employee problems, management needs good listening skills.

44.   Ignoring the warning on the screen, Palmer turned his computer off.

Transitional Expressions

45.   We tailor our service efforts specifically to individual customer needs. Consequently, we have seen the volume at our plants grow. Moreover, our profitability has increased, and we expect even better results in the future.

46.   Because no business can anticipate every customer's needs, we keep our hotel management staff on duty 24 hours a day. In this way, customers always have someone of authority available.

47.   Your responsibility is to listen to customers and hear what they are saying. In addition, you are responsible for making them feel that their concerns are your concerns. Your responsibility also includes taking care of their concerns to their satisfaction.

Career Track Spelling

48.   omission
49.   unnecessarily
50.   calendars, February
51.   supervisor
52.   automatically
53.   pamphlets
54.   budget
55.   government
56.   separate
57.   mortgages

Career Track Vocabulary

58.   d
59.   c
60.   f
61.   b
62.   a
63.   e
64.   b
65.   a
66.   c
67.   b
68.   a

69.   c
70.   b
71.   a
72.   credible
73.   devise
74.   creditable
75.   conscious
76.   device
77.   dessert
78.   desert
79.   conscience

C.L.U.E. Checkpoint

80.   When she enrolled at Midwestern **University**, Tina was unsure of a major.

81.   When proofreading for problems in **grammar**, check to see whether the pronouns agree with their antecedents.

82.   After writing a dynamite **résumé**, he sent it to 11 companies on his list.

83.   Government in this country is intended to be of the **people**, by the **people**, and for the people.

84.   Mike researched 15 companies in the **Midwest**, and he finally found one that needed someone with a background in robotics.

85.   In the spring of this **year**, Unitech received hundreds of résumés.

86. A cover letter is meant to introduce your résumé and to help you secure a personal interview. [No comma is necessary before *and* because it does not introduce an independent clause.]

87. She submitted a résumé to eight companies and began thinking about **friends, relatives,** and acquaintances to serve as a network in her job search. [No comma is necessary after *companies* because it is not followed by an independent clause.]

88. A few companies send recruiters to college campuses in the **fall,** but many more send representatives and conduct interviews in the spring.

89. When you expect an audience will be receptive to the **message,** use the direct pattern.

Super C.L.U.E. Review

90. **Approximately 20** to **30** percent of all companies must restructure to reduce **errors, delays,** and returns.

91. When **Coca-Cola** and **Pepsi** compete in **Asia,** they spend hundreds of thousands of dollars in marketing efforts.

92. Employees are encouraged to ask **questions,** and these questions become a valuable source of feedback to management.

93. **Thirty-four percent** of the **1,200** job applicants in one study falsified information on their résumés.

94. When GM began selling **Daewoo** cars under the **Chevrolet brand,** it hoped to overcome negative perceptions in **Europe.**

95. Our human resources manager schedules and attends all job **interviews,** but the hiring managers make all final selections.

96. The house was **appraised** at **$125,000; however,** we felt its actual worth was at least **20** percent more.

97. We **recommend** that **15** realtors visit the property at **10** a.m. and that the remaining **23** inspect it between 3:30 and **5** p.m.

98. When the recruiter visited **Indiana State University,** she was **conscious** of increased campus interest in ethics.

99. If you caused the accident and have liability insurance with **State Farm,** expect the company to pay for the damages you caused and any medical expenses arising from your **negligence.**

CHAPTER 7

Chapter Review

1.   F   Revising means improving the content and sentence structure of your message. Proofreading involves other aspects.
2.   T
3.   F   Clarity is enhanced by language that sounds like conversation.
4.   T
5.   F   Although familiar phrases roll off the tongue easily, they often contain expendable parts. Clear communication eliminates empty words.
6.   F   To revise for vigor and directness, transform noun phrases into verbs.
7.   T
8.   F   Although graphic techniques such as underlining and using all capital letters do improve readability, they must be used with care because some readers will feel that you are shouting at them.
9.   F   When proofreading computer messages on a screen, using the down arrow to reveal one line at a time is a good strategy; a safer method is to read from a printed copy.
10.   T

Fill in the Blank

Revising Messages
11. first draft
12. impress
13. redundant
14. concise
15. parallelism
16. bulleted
17. heading
18. readability
19. recognize

Proofreading and Evaluating Messages
20. numbers
21. time
22. two
23. words
24. spelling

Multiple Choice

25. c
26. c
27. a
28. b
29. b

30. a
31. c
32. d
33. a
34. c

Short Answer

35.   Four strategies to help readers anticipate and comprehend ideas quickly:
    a.   Parallelism, which involves balanced writing.
    b.   Lists and bullets, which facilitate quick comprehension.
    c.   Headings, which make important points more visible.
    d.   Other highlighting techniques to improve readability.

36.   Items that proofreaders should check carefully are spelling, grammar, punctuation, names and numbers, and format.

Clarity

37.   As you recommended, we will look at our personnel policy to see whether it should be changed.

38.   If we have doubts about purchasing new computers, we should investigate our current computer use.

39.   Your employees will benefit if you explain the company's new e-mail guidelines to them.

40.   We suggest that you get the department head's approval before beginning the project.

41.   We are pleased to welcome you as a new customer.

Conciseness

42.   Seventeen new vehicles need to be priced before we can sell them.

43.   Because the statement seemed wrong, I sent a $200 check.

44.   Mattel and Fisher-Price merged their toy lines.

45.   I believe we cannot reduce our inventory until we lower prices.

46.   Until we can locate all duplicate addresses, avoid mass mailings.

47.   Although only one van is available, response to the employee van pooling program is remarkable.

48.   The survey of applicants for private parking spaces determined that over 66 percent do not believe that parking is a problem.

49.   Vendors may not fully [*Or completely*] understand our difficulty.

50.   Applications for entry-level positions will be accepted later.

51.   Careful revision eliminates many words.

Vigor

52.   Three staff members are trying to locate your order.

53.   We've enclosed the contract that we have prepared for you.

54.   Please consider our latest proposal, even though it conflicts with our original goals.

55.   If I may help, please call me at (212) 499-3029.

Parallelism

56.   As a successful entrepreneur, I wrote a business plan, analyzed cash flow, designed promotional materials, and marketed the business.

57.   Researchers examined data concerning our employees' income, health, and stress.

58.   Ensuring equal opportunities and eliminating age discrimination are our goals.

59.   Employers can avoid complaints of discrimination if they ask each applicant the same questions, limit questions to job-related topics, and use trained interviewers.

60.   In my last job I set up a log of all incoming materials, inspected the contents, documented the findings, and reported the results to the shipping department.

Career Track Spelling

61.	C	66.	ninety
62.	referred	67.	incidentally
63.	practical	68.	maintenance
64.	occurred	69.	foreign
65.	calendar	70.	usage

Career Track Vocabulary

71.	f	81.	a
72.	a	82.	b
73.	b	83.	c
74.	e	84.	b
75.	c	85.	disburse
76.	d	86.	elicit
77.	b	87.	illicit
78.	a	88.	envelop
79.	b	89.	disperse
80.	c		

C.L.U.E. Checkpoint

90.   Send the material to Harlan D. **Miller,** 20 Hawthorne **Street, Boston,** MA **02114,** as soon as possible.

91.   Our manager is from **Raleigh,** North Carolina.

92.   Joan **Winkoff,** who is one of the executives attending the **conference,** plans to leave **Thursday,** June 5.

93.   Business at our Allentown **branch,** which was opened last **February,** has boosted company profits considerably.

94.   In the **meantime,** please list David Smith as a **contract,** not a **permanent,** employee.

Super C.L.U.E. Review

95.   Among the topics discussed at the staff meeting held on **April 5, 2004,** were **schedules, deadlines,** and suppliers.

96.   Eric Sims, one of the four company **founders,** invested **capital** of just under **$30,000.**

97.   **Companies** now include disclaimers saying that the employee policy manual is not a **contract,** that policies may be changed or **withdrawn,** and that the individual and the company may **separate** at any time for any reason.

98.   Our new policy **manual,** which was adapted from an industry **publication,** is **26** pages long.

99.   We hired Dr. **Nocaponte,** who is known for his expertise in tropical **diseases,** as a consultant for the upcoming project in **Mexico,** which begins on June **10,** at a monthly rate of **$2,300.**

100. In today's fast-paced global **marketplace,** companies that can move products through the development process fastest enjoy a cost advantage through increased **efficiency.**

Career Application

Current date

Ms. Michele Taylor
Abonte Guaranty Company
3401 Providence Avenue
New York, NY 10001

Dear Michele:

Two agents' packages will be sent to you on October 6. Because you need these immediately, we are using Federal Express.

We are able to offer new agents a 60/40 commission split. Two new agreement forms show this commission ratio. When you sign new agents, have them fill in both forms.

When you send me an executed agency agreement, please tell me what agency package was assigned to the agent. We need this information to distribute commissions properly.

Call me if you have any questions.

Very truly yours,

*All solutions illustrate one way the problem could be solved. Other good solutions are also possible.

CHAPTER 8

Chapter Review

1. T
2. F   A phone call or a face-to-face visit would work better.
3. T
4. F   Most e-mail is used to cover *nonsensitive* information.
5. F   When typing the body of an e-mail message, use standard caps and lowercase characters—never all uppercase or lowercase characters.
6. T
7. F   Information and procedure messages generally flow downward.
8. T
9. F   When responding to requests, be direct.
10. T

Fill in the Blank

Routine Memos and E-mail Messages

11. goals
12. abilities
13. text
14. subject
15. topic
16. lists
17. summary
18. closings

Using E-mail and Memos Effectively

19. letter
20. channel
21. private
22. compose
23. delete
24. scan
25. thread
26. cultural
27. procedure
28. requests

Multiple Choice

29. b
30. c
31. d

32. a
33. a
34. b

Short Answer

35. Questions you should ask yourself before writing an e-mail or memo:
    a. Do I really need to write this e-mail or memo?
    b. Should I send an e-mail or a hard copy memo?
    c. Why am I writing?
    d. How will the reader react?
    e. How can I save my reader's time?

36. Messages should generally end with action information including dates and deadlines, a summary, or a closing thought.

37. Key issues to consider to help you get off to a good start in using e-mail smartly and safely:
    a. Consider composing offline.
    b. Get the address right.
    c. Avoid misleading subject lines.
    d. Apply the top-of-the-screen test.

38. Rules of polite online interaction involving e-mail:
    a. Limit any tendency to send blanket copies.
    b. Never send "spam."
    c. Consider using identifying labels.
    d. Use capital letters for emphasis or for titles.
    e. Don't forward without permission.
    f. Reduce attachments.

39. Items to be included in a confirmation memo or e-mail:
    a. Names and titles of involved individuals
    b. Concise statement of major issues or points
    c. Request for feedback regarding unclear or inaccurate points

Career Track Spelling

40.	fourth	46.	C
41.	nevertheless	47.	extraordinary
42.	indispensable	48.	noticeable
43.	questionnaire	49.	column
44.	argument	50.	C
45.	consistent		

Career Track Vocabulary

51.	f		61.	c
52.	c		62.	c
53.	a		63.	a
54.	e		64.	flair
55.	b		65.	every day
56.	d		66.	further
57.	b		67.	flare
58.	c		68.	farther
59.	a		69.	everyday
60.	a			

C.L.U.E. Checkpoint

70. Kristin prepared a chronological **résumé;** Michael preferred a functional résumé.

71. Travis was determined to become a **C.P.A.; consequently,** he majored in accounting.

72. Although hotel managers say that customers' needs are met nearly all the **time,** only 40 percent of travelers agree. [Don't use a semicolon after a dependent clause.]

73. General Electric interviewed marketing candidates from [delete colon] Central Michigan University, Ohio University, and Texas Tech. [Omit colon. No punctuation is required when a list follows a preposition.]

74. Nominees for president included [delete colon] Jacki Ames, **Miami;** Thomas Hart, **Atlanta;** and Tamala Wilson, Tampa. [Omit colon. No punctuation is required when a list is introduced by a verb.]

Super C.L.U.E. Review

75. After we investigate the matter **further,** we hope to develop a set of **everyday** procedures that all **employees** can follow.

76. Underinflation reduces the life of a **tire;** overinflation may cause a blowout.

77. Some people thought that technology would mean they would be doing less writing on the **job; however,** just the opposite has **occurred.**

78. Recruiters were looking for three **principal qualities:** initiative, reliability, and enthusiasm.

79. The American **Bar** Association elected Dennis **R. R**adiman, **president;** Harriet Lee-Thomas, **vice president;** and **E. M.** Miles, secretary.

80. All the Mexican restaurants were **farther** away than we **realized; therefore,** we decided to have our staff lunch at a nearby **T**hai restaurant.

81. We are **grateful** that **24** companies submitted **bids; unfortunately,** only **3** will be selected. [Use the figure *3* instead of *three* because it relates to the previous figure, *24*.]

82. Reports from [delete colon] **Ms.** S**ampson, Mr.** T**omas,** and **Mrs.** J**ay** are **overdue**.

83. All employees will **personally receive** copies of their performance **evaluations,** which the **p**resident said would be the primary basis for promotion.

84. Our manager gives many oral **compliments** to deserving **workers; however,** the praise would be more lasting if written in notes or reports.

Career Application: Critical Thinking Questions

85. Although all employees are the primary audience, you should be aware that anything you write for your boss will become part of her evaluation of your skills.

86. Because you know that employees tend to undervalue this information, you'll want to emphasize its importance—particularly the limited open enrollment period.

87. Your boss will be most interested in how clearly you cover all the main points.

88. The purpose of the memo is to announce the open enrollment period. You want employees to read the enrollment package, decide if they want to make changes, and return the application by November 29.

89. You will have to check with other representatives to set up a schedule of times for counseling employees. You would probably also read all of the enrollment package carefully so that you could anticipate areas that might need clarification.

90. This memo delivers important, yet nonsensitive, routine information. Hence, develop it directly. Employees will not be upset by this information.

91. A possible opening sentence: Please examine the enclosed open enrollment package so that you may make any changes before November 29.

92. Dental coverage, life insurance options, and medical coverage.

93. Use itemization techniques to improve readability of the three changes in coverage, as well as the times for answering questions.

94. The closing should tell employees what to turn in, where to do it, and when to do so.

Career Application

DATE: Current

TO: Staff Members

FROM: Pauline M. Wu, Director, Human Resources

SUBJECT: OPEN ENROLLMENT FOR BENEFIT PROGRAMS

Please examine the enclosed open enrollment package so that you may make any changes before November 29.

Your decisions about coverage are very important because they affect your well-being and that of your family. You'll want to study the choices carefully, since your decisions will remain in effect until the next open enrollment period one year from now.

Although most of the program is unchanged, we have made the following improvements:

- Dental coverage has been expanded; you now have two carriers from which to choose.
- Life insurance options increase coverage for family members.
- Medical coverage now includes a basic plan and a prudent buyer plan.

Representatives from Human Resources will be available to answer your questions in the East Lounge at the following times:

Tuesday, November 19	3 p.m. to 5 p.m.
Wednesday, November 20	7 a.m. to 9 a.m.
Friday, November 22	11 a.m. to 1 p.m.

Remember, this is the only time you may make changes in your benefits package, other than a qualified change in family status.

For employees making changes, complete the enclosed form and return it to Human Resources by November 29.

Enclosure

CHAPTER 9

Chapter Review

1. F   Letters are a primary channel of communication for delivering messages outside an organization.
2. F   Business letters are important when a permanent record is required, when formality is necessary, and when a message is sensitive and requires an organized, well-considered presentation.
3. T
4. F   Use the direct strategy for routine, everyday messages.
5. T
6. T
7. F   When sending a direct reply, knowledgeable business communicators often use a subject line to refer to earlier correspondence so that in the first sentence, they are free to address the main idea.
8. T
9. T
10. F   Although ready-made cards have their uses, personal notes are far more effective when expressing thanks.

Fill in the Blank

Using the Writing Process
11. customers
12. visualizing
13. main idea
14. action
15. correct form
16. paragraph
17. questions
18. goodwill
19. block

Writing Routine Letters
20. costs
21. information
22. justification
23. appreciation
24. payment
25. claim
26. logically
27. adjustment
28. employers
29. foreign
30. customs

Multiple Choice

31. d
32. c
33. c
34. a

35. b
36. c
37. c
38. b

39. b
40. c
41. c
42. d

Short Answer

43.   Strategies for writing a direct claim letter:
    a.   Begin with the purpose.
    b.   Explain objectively.
    c.   End by requesting action.

44.   Goals of adjustment letters:
    a.   Rectifying the wrong, if one exists.
    b.   Regaining the customer's confidence.
    c.   Promoting further business.

45.   Don'ts to consider when writing adjustment letters:
    a.   Don't use negative words.
    b.   Don't blame customers.
    c.   Don't blame individuals or departments within your organization.
    d.   Don't make unrealistic promises.

46.   Cautions that writers of recommendations should heed:
    a.   Respond only to written requests.
    b.   State that their remarks are confidential.
    c.   Provide only job-related information.
    d.   Avoid vague or ambiguous statements.
    e.   Apply specific evidence for any negatives.
    f.   Stick to the truth.

47.   Tips for writing effective letters of recommendation:
    a.   Identify the purpose and confidentiality of the message.
    b.   Establish your relationship with the applicant.
    c.   Describe the length of employment and job duties, if relevant.
    d.   Provide specific examples of the applicant's professional and personal skills.
    e.   Compare the applicant with others in his or her field.
    f.   Offer an overall rating of the applicant.
    g.   Summarize the significant attributes of the applicant.
    h.   Draw a conclusion regarding the recommendation.

48.   The five *S*'s in writing goodwill messages:
    a.   Selfless
    b.   Specific
    c.   Sincere
    d.   Spontaneous
    e.   Short

Career Track Spelling

49. ordinarily
50. legitimate
51. valuable
52. conscious
53. division

54. tenant
55. feasible
56. profited
57. C
58. offered

Career Track Vocabulary

59. c
60. a
61. b
62. e
63. f
64. d
65. b
66. c
67. a
68. c

69. a
70. a
71. a
72. c
73. whole
74. grate
75. formally
76. formerly
77. great
78. hole

C.L.U.E. Checkpoint

79. Ms. **Wilson's** staff is responsible for all accounts receivable contracted by customers purchasing electronics parts.

80. In less than a **year's** time, both **attorneys'** offices were moved.

81. Luke would appreciate **your** answering his telephone while he is gone.

82. Three **months'** interest on the two notes will be due February 1.

83. After a **month's** delay, Lucy **Johnson's** car registration finally arrived.

Super C.L.U.E. Review

84. Although I **referred** to Figure 12 on page **4,** I was **disappointed** when I could not find Paul **Stanley's** sales figures.

85. The **union's** officers **sincerely** hope that employees will **accede** to **management's** latest wage proposals.

86. A key factor to be observed in our hiring program [delete comma] is that all **candidates'** references must be checked thoroughly.

87. Everyone has noticed **Misty's flair** for **words; therefore,** she is being promoted to our Editorial **D**epartment. [Remember to capitalize names of departments within your organization.]

88. Because of her recent **accident,** Mrs. **Wilson's** insurance premium will be increased **$112** for every six-month billing period.

89. **Today's** weather is much better than **yesterday's; consequently,** we'll work outside.

90. Ted **Bowman,** the new marketing **manager, offered nine** different suggestions for targeting potential customers.

91. We are hoping that **Ted's** suggestions are **feasible** [delete comma] and that they will **succeed** in turning around our sales decline.

92. Both **companies'** offices will open at **8 a.m.; however,** only the **Atlantic** branch will offer full counter service until **5 p.m.**

93. **Zachary's** spring schedule includes the following **courses:** English, history, and business law.

Career Application: Critical Thinking Questions

94. The format of the letter should be either block or modified block rather than the combination shown. For block style, start each line at the left. For modified block style, move the closing lines to the center and block the paragraphs.

95. A negative tone is created by such expressions as *you complain, misunderstanding, you claim, you must be aware,* and *we can't prevent you.*

96. The letter should be organized directly because the reader will be pleased with its message. It is now organized indirectly with explanations preceding the good news.

97. In an adjustment letter the writer's three goals are to (a) rectify the wrong, if one exists, (b) regain the confidence of the customer, and (c) promote further business.

98. The good news is that the problem has been solved and that the double mailing will cease.

99. In this instance the writer should explain why the double mailing occurred, since little liability exists. However, if an explanation might place an organization at risk, that explanation should be avoided.

100. This letter should end with a forward-looking, pleasant statement.

Career Application

Current date

Mrs. Thomas Dobbin
2950 King Street
Alexandria, VA 22313

Dear Mrs. Dobbin:

You're right! Instead of starting a new subscription we should have extended your current subscription to *Home Computing*. Beginning in January, you will receive issues for 14 additional months—a bonus of two free months.

Apparently, when you ordered magazines through your son's school program, your name was recorded as Patricia R. Dobbin. Your current subscription is listed under Mrs. Thomas Dobbin. Therefore, our computers started a new account for you. That's why you are receiving two issues each month.

You may receive one or two more double issues, but you're not being charged for them. Please share these magazines with your friends or neighbors. Although you ordered 12 months of *Home Computing,* we're giving you 14 months—just to let you know how important your satisfaction is to us.

Sincerely,

Roger W. Hobart
Circulation Manager

CHAPTER 10

Chapter Review

1. T
2. F   The first step is to determine the purpose, which establishes the strategy of a message.
3. T
4. F   Using persuasion in an attempt to deceive is considered *unethical* behavior.
5. T
6. F   Instructions or directives moving downward from superiors to subordinates usually require little persuasion.
7. T
8. F   The primary goal in writing a sales message is to get someone to devote a few moments of attention to it.
9. F   The final paragraph of the sales message carries the punch line.
10. T

Fill in the Blank

	Persuasive Messages				*Sales Messages*		
11.	persuasion	16.	action	21.	electronic	26.	competitor
12.	given	17.	direct	22.	letter	27.	benefits
13.	attention	18.	indirect	23.	target	28.	desire
14.	needs	19.	logical	24.	stimulating	29.	act
15.	resistance	20.	agreement	25.	appeals	30.	postscript

Multiple Choice

31.	b	36.	a
32.	d	37.	b
33.	c	38.	d
34.	a	39.	d
35.	c	40.	c

Short Answer

41. Four questions that will help you adapt a persuasive or sales request to a receiver:
    a. Why should I (the receiver)?
    b. What's in it for me (the receiver)?
    c. What's in it for you (the sender)?
    d. Who cares?

42. The four parts of the indirect pattern for persuasive or sales messages:
    a. Gain attention.
    b. Build interest.
    c. Reduce resistance.
    d. Motivate action.

43. Techniques that gain attention in opening a persuasive request:
    a. Problem description
    b. Unexpected statement
    c. Reader benefit
    d. Compliment
    e. Related fact
    f. Stimulating question

44. Devices that build interest in a persuasive request:
    a. Facts, statistics
    b. Expert opinion
    c. Direct benefits
    d. Examples
    e. Related fact
    f. Indirect benefits

45. Techniques for gaining attention in the opening of a sales message:
    a. Offer
    b. Promise
    c. Question
    d. Quotation or proverb
    e. Product feature
    f. Testimonial
    g. Startling statement
    h. Personalized action setting

46. Techniques for overcoming resistance and proving the credibility of a product:
    a. Testimonials
    b. Names of satisfied users
    c. Money-back guarantee or warranty
    d. Free trial or sample
    e. Performance tests, pools, awards

Career Track Spelling

47. criticize
48. knowledgeable
49. bankruptcy
50. friend
51. fiscal
52. necessary
53. qualify
54. business, noticeable
55. opportunity
56. adequate

Career Track Vocabulary

57.	b	67.	c
58.	f	68.	a
59.	e	69.	c
60.	c	70.	b
61.	a	71.	libel
62.	d	72.	lien
63.	c	73.	liable
64.	b	74.	lean
65.	b	75.	infer
66.	c	76.	imply

C.L.U.E. Checkpoint

77. (Direct quotation) **"Someone** who never asks **anything,"** said Malcolm **Forbes, "either** knows everything or knows **nothing."**

78. Could you please send a corrected statement of my credit **account.** [Don't use a question mark for this polite request.]

79. (De-emphasize) Directions for assembly (**see** page **15**) are quite simple.

80. (Emphasize) Only two possible **dates**—May 5 and June **6**—are available for a team videoconference.

81. Learning, earning, and **yearning**—these are natural pursuits for most of us.

82. Our next conference is scheduled for Monday at 3 **p.m.,** isn't **it?**

83. In *Business Week* I saw an article titled **"Outsourcing: A Look** at the **Facts."**

84. A business office filled with cubicles is often called a **"cube farm."**

85. (Emphasize) Two of our **researchers**—Emily Smith and José **Real**—resigned yesterday.

86. (De-emphasize) Three employees in our Marketing Department (**David,** Debbie, and **Joy**) were responsible for all product promotional materials.

Super C.L.U.E. Review

87. The treasurer will **disburse** all excess dues **collected,** won't **she?**

88. You may cancel your calling plan (**see** page 3 of your customer **agreement**) within **15** days of **accepting.**

89. The two **recruiters'** remarks seemed to **imply** that they were most interested in **candidates** with computer and accounting skills.

90. (De-emphasize) The major functions of a manager (**planning, directing,** and **controlling**) will be covered in **Management 301.**

91. Any letter sent to the **bank's** customers must have a professional **appearance; otherwise, its** message may be disregarded.

92. **Forty** people enrolled in the **class; however,** only 32 actually appeared at 7 **p.m.**

93. (Direct quotation) **"When** you are **right,"** said Martin Luther King, Jr., **"you** cannot be too **radical;** when you are **wrong,** you cannot be too **conservative."**

94. (Emphasize) States with the best export assistance programs—**California,** Illinois, Minnesota, and **Maryland**—offer seminars and conferences.

95. When we promote our **inventory** reduction **sale** in **June,** you'll find the **year's** best prices. [Delete the quotation marks.]

96. (Emphasize) Each of these **cities—Rochester, Albany,** and **Purchase**—has substantial taxes **already** in **effect.**

Career Application: Critical Thinking Questions

97. The primary audience for this adjustment request is a representative of Copy World, and the chances are that this person has nothing to do with the pain Tracy has suffered. Moreover, this person has feelings and won't like being the target of angry words. In reality, it's probably unnecessary to try to establish who is to blame.

98. The purpose of this letter should not be to vent anger or point fingers. Tracy's letter is so unfocused that it's difficult to tell exactly what she wants done. A better letter would concentrate on an action that would solve the problem. Apparently, she wants to purchase two Model S-55 copiers (at $13,500 each), but she wants Copy World to accept her four CopyMaster Model S-5 copiers (original cost $2,500 each or $10,000) in trade. And she wants $8,000 trade-in on the four returned copiers.

99. Copy World may resist this request, since its representative has already said that Copy World must take 50 percent depreciation on the four used copiers. At 50 percent depreciation, Copy World would be offering only $5,000 for the returned copiers.

100. Three arguments that Tracy could make to reduce resistance:
     - The S-5 machines were used only a short time, and they can be resold easily.
     - Copy World will be making a sizable profit on the sale of two top-of-the-line, Model S-55 copiers.
     - Copy World service technicians will no longer have to make trips to service the overworked four S-5 models.

101. Tracy would be wise to keep her cool and say something about purchasing these copiers in good faith on the advice of Copy World's salesperson. And she should emphasize that it is Copy World's responsibility to help provide the proper model for a company's needs. Probably one of the most successful appeals to any company is that of maintaining its good reputation.

102. A day-by-day chronology of her copier troubles would bore the reader, causing that person to merely skim over it. Instead, Tracy should use objective language and tell the story briefly. If she has a repair record, she should enclose it.

103. If Tracy opens directly with her request, she risks the chance of an immediate refusal. The reader may never learn what reasons prompted the request. Her letter will be stronger if she starts indirectly with explanations and logical reasoning.

104. Four possible ways to open a claim letter are with (a) sincere praise, (b) an objective statement of the problem, (c) a point of agreement, or (d) a quick review of what has been done to resolve the problem. Probably for this situation a concise statement of the problem would be most effective.

105. Tracy's closing doesn't request any specific action. The reader has to guess what Tracy wants done. A better closing would spell out exactly what would please Tracy.

106. One way to make it easy for Copy World to respond would be to state exactly what action is to be taken and to ask the reader to initial the letter to show approval. Tracy could offer to work out the details with the local salesperson. Enclosing a preaddressed envelope would make the agreement even easier to conclude.

Now that you've done the preparation for writing this adjustment request, write your version on a separate sheet of paper (preferably at your computer). Use your own name or use Tracy's. Then compare your version with the version that follows. Don't expect yours to look exactly like our version. Yours may be better!

Career Application

Current date

Mr. James Ferraro
Vice President, Sales
Copy World
2510 East Pine Street
Tulsa, OK 74160-2510

Dear Mr. Ferraro:

The four CopyMaster Model S-5 photocopiers that we purchased three months ago are inadequate for our volume of copying.

Although we told your salesperson, Kevin Woo, that we averaged 3,000 copies a day, he recommended the Model S-5. This model appears to be the wrong choice for our heavy use, and we're disappointed in its performance. Therefore, we'd like to trade in our four S-5 copiers (about $2,500 each as shown on the enclosed invoice) on the purchase of two Model S-55 copiers (about $13,500 each).

When I discussed this possibility with your district manager, Keith Sumner, he said that we would be charged 50 percent depreciation if we traded in the four S-5 copiers. That amounts to $5,000, a considerable sum for three months of copier use. We think a depreciation rate of 20 percent is more reasonable. Your company would profit in three ways:

1. The S-5 machines were used a short time, and they can be resold easily.

2. You'll be making a sizable profit when we purchase two Model S-55 copiers.

3. Your service technicians will save time by making fewer trips to repair our overworked S-5 machines.

We purchased the Model S-5 copiers in good faith on the recommendation of your salesperson. It is your responsibility to help us secure the proper model for our needs.

Please approve my request to trade in four CopyMaster Model S-5s for a value of $8,000 (allowing for 20 percent depreciation) toward the purchase of two CopyMaster Model S-5s. Just initial this letter showing your approval, and return it to me in the enclosed envelope. I'll work out the details of the new purchase with your salesperson.

Sincerely yours,

Tracy W. Quincy
Manager

Enclosure

CHAPTER 11

Chapter Review

1. F   Organizing bad-news messages indirectly increases the chances that the reader will be aware of the reasons for the bad news and more likely to accept it, but it doesn't guarantee it.
2. T
3. F   Bad-news messages require more preparation than most other messages.
4. F   The most important part of a bad-news letter is the discussion of reasons.
5. T
6. T
7. F   When situations involve sending information to many unhappy customers, companies may need to write personalized form letters.
8. F   Sometimes your company is at fault, in which case an apology is generally in order.
9. T
10. F   Americans prefer to present bad news indirectly.

Fill in the Blank

11.	accepts		16.	praise
12.	slander		17.	problem
13.	subordinate		18.	blame
14.	compromise		19.	reasons-first
15.	reader		20.	refusal

Multiple Choice

21.	a		26.	a
22.	d		27.	b
23.	d		28.	d
24.	c		29.	b
25.	c		30.	b

Short Answer

31. The four parts of the indirect pattern for revealing bad news:
    a. Buffer—a neutral or positive opening that does not reveal the bad news.
    b. Reasons—an explanation of the causes for the bad news, offered before disclosing it.
    c. Bad news—clear but understated announcement of the bad news; it may include an alternative or a compromise.
    d. Closing—a personalized, forward-looking, pleasant statement.

32. Specific causes of legal problems:
    a. Abusive language, such as *You deadbeat, crook, or quack.*
    b. Careless language, such as suggesting a workplace is dangerous or making a joking threat against a coworker.
    c. The good-guy syndrome, such as saying that poor work is satisfactory just to avoid confronting a person.

33. Possibilities for buffers in a bad-news message:
    a. Start with the best part of the news.
    b. Offer a sincere compliment regarding accomplishments or efforts.
    c. Show appreciation; offer thanks.
    d. Show agreement with the reader on some issue.
    e. Provide solid facts.
    f. Indicate that you understand the problem.

34. Techniques for cushioning bad news:
    a. Position the bad news strategically. Sandwich it between other sentences. Avoid high visibility spots.
    b. Use the passive voice (*Parking is not permitted . . .*).
    c. Accentuate the positive *(Parking is permitted in . . .).*
    d. Imply the refusal (*Although our funds are tied up this year, perhaps next year . . .*).
    e. Suggest a compromise or an alternative (*Although my schedule is full, my colleague may be able to speak . . .*).

35. Ways to close a bad-news message:
    a. Look forward to future relations or business.
    b. Offer your good wishes.
    c. Refer to free coupons, samples, or gifts.
    d. Employ resale or sales promotion.

36. Written messages are important (1) when personal contact is impossible, (2) to establish a record of the incident, (3) to formally confirm follow-up procedures, and (4) to promote good relations.

37. To avoid saying *no,* Asians might respond with silence or counter with a question. They might also change the subject or tell a white lie. Sometimes they might respond with a qualified *yes,* which should be recognized as *no.*

Career Track Spelling

38. changeable
39. legitimate
40. Usually
41. dissatisfied
42. C

43. prominent
44. unnecessarily
45. C
46. permitted
47. exempt

Career Track Vocabulary

48.	d	58.	c
49.	c	59.	b
50.	f	60.	b
51.	a	61.	a
52.	b	62.	patients
53.	e	63.	minor
54.	c	64.	patience
55.	a	65.	lose
56.	a	66.	miner
57.	b	67.	loose

C.L.U.E. Checkpoint

68. If I **were** you, I would have **brought** a backup for our presentation slides.

69. Craig must have **known** the salary, or he would never have **taken** the job.

70. When I **saw** Jan's letter, I immediately gave her a call.

71. I wish I **were** finished with my degree so that I could have **gone** to work at LaserTech.

72. Many computer users wished they had **chosen** a different printer.

Super C.L.U.E. Review

73. If Courtney **were manager,** I'm convinced she would have more **patience** with employees.

74. We **paid** every credit card bill when it **arrived; however,** we still **received** late charges.

75. If the package had **come earlier,** we could have finished by **5 p.m.**

76. The *Herald Post Dispatch,* our local **newspaper, surprised** me with an article titled **"How to** Keep Employees **Safe."**

77. C

78. John should have **known** that our **competitors'** products would be featured at the Denver **Home** and **Garden Show.**

79. If I **were you,** I would schedule the conference for one of these **cities: Atlanta, Memphis,** or Nashville.

80. We **chose** the Madison **Hotel** because it can **accommodate 200** convention guests [omit comma] and has parking facilities for **100** cars.

81. The **CEO's** management book was **written** long before a publisher **accepted** it.

82. When she **came** to our office **yesterday,** she **brought** a **whole** box of printer cartridges.

Career Application: Critical Thinking Questions

83.   Although this bad news is not earth-shattering, it still represents a disappointment to the reader. Therefore, the indirect approach would be worth the effort.

84.   Your buffer might include both appreciation for being asked and perhaps acknowledgment of Sherry's role of leadership in this campus honorary organization. If you don't compliment her in the beginning, you'll probably want to include praise later in the letter.

85.   Following the buffer you should explain why you cannot accept the invitation on the date selected.

86.   For this situation the bad news probably need not be stated bluntly ("I cannot accept your invitation"). The reader will doubtless infer the refusal because you are busy elsewhere on the same day.

87.   The compromise, of course, is offering a substitute speaker. This compromise should be presented after the implied refusal.

88.   The closing should end pleasantly without referring to the bad news or without an apology (you have done nothing for which you should apologize). This might be a good place to compliment Sherry for her success in this organization. You might volunteer for future programs.

Career Application

Current date

Ms. Sherry A. Lopez
President, Alpha Gamma Sigma
1150 Del Ray Avenue
Miami, FL 33178

Dear Sherry:

It's good to learn that Miami-Dade has an active student business honorary, and I appreciate your invitation to speak at its February meeting on the topic of careers in public accounting.

On February 17, the day of your meeting, I will be in Lake Worth representing our firm at a three-day seminar about recent changes in tax laws related to corporations. Since many of our clients file corporate tax returns, this seminar is particularly important to my organization and my clients.

Our local Miami CPA organization has a list of speakers who are prepared to make presentations on various topics. In consulting this list, I found that Paul Rosenberg, a Miami CPA with 14 years of experience, is our expert on careers in accountancy and preparation for the CPA examination. I checked with him and found that he could address your organization if you will call him before January 28. His telephone number is 390-1930.

I'm very pleased that you have taken a leadership role in your campus business honorary, Sherry, and you may be sure that you can call on me for any future assistance in developing appropriate programs.

Sincerely,

Nelson R. Raymond

CHAPTER 12

Chapter Review

1. T
2. F Reports organized in the indirect pattern usually begin with an introduction or description of the problem, followed by facts and interpretations from the writer.
3. F Concentrating solely on a primary reader is a major mistake because many other people may read the report.
4. T
5. F The newspaper article is an example of *secondary* data.
6. T
7. F Open-ended questions do not provide quantifiable data. The most effective questions are those that provide quantifiable data: check-off, multiple-choice, yes-no, and scale (rank-order) questions.
8. T
9. T
10. F Line charts enable you to show changes over time, thus indicating trends.

Fill in the Blank

Report Basics

11. informational
12. analytical
13. indirect
14. letter
15. memo
16. problem
17. purpose
18. limitations
19. factoring
20. strategy

Gathering Report Information

21. secondary
22. periodicals
23. database
24. commercial
25. search
26. Boolean
27. accuracy
28. survey
29. designs
30. observation

Illustrating and Documenting Data

31. documentation
32. plagiarism
33. paraphrase
34. bibliographies
35. emphasize
36. trends
37. bar charts
38. percentages
39. flow charts
40. budget

Short Answer

41. A formal writing style is found in theses, research studies, and controversial or complex reports. It gives the impression of objectivity, accuracy, professionalism, and fairness. It generally creates a distance between the writer and reader. A formal style omits first-person pronouns, contractions, humor, figures of speech, and editorializing. It uses passive-voice verbs, complex sentences, and long words.

    An informal writing style is found in short, routine reports for familiar audiences. This style conveys a feeling of warmth, personal involvement, and closeness. This style uses first-person pronouns, contractions, active-voice verbs, shorter sentences, familiar words, occasional humor, and some editorializing.

42. Primary, firsthand information comes from surveys, interviews, observation, and experimentation. Secondary information results from reading what others have experienced and observed. Principal sources of secondary data are books, periodicals, newspapers, encyclopedias, dictionaries, handbooks, and electronic databases.

43. Internet search tips and techniques:
    a. Use two or three search tools.
    b. Know your search tool.
    c. Understand case sensitivity.
    d. Use nouns as search words and up to six to eight words in a query.
    e. Combine keywords into phrases.
    f. Omit articles and prepositions.
    g. Use wild cards.
    h. Learn basic Boolean search strategies.

44. Strategies for preparing surveys:
    a. Select the survey population carefully.
    b. Explain why the survey is necessary.
    c. Consider incentives.
    d. Limit the number of questions.
    e. Use questions that produce quantifiable answers.
    f. Avoid leading or ambiguous questions.
    g. Make it easy for respondents to return the survey.
    h. Conduct a pilot study.

45. Kinds of material to document:
    a. Another person's ideas, opinions, examples, or theory
    b. Any facts, statistics, graphs, and drawings that are not common knowledge
    c. Quotations of another person's actual spoken or written words
    d. Paraphrases of another person's spoken or written words

Career Track Spelling

46. foreign
47. privilege
48. committee, thoroughly
49. C
50. schedule
51. analyze
52. indispensable
53. deductible
54. guarantee
55. evidently

Career Track Vocabulary

56.	f		66.	c
57.	c		67.	b
58.	a		68.	b
59.	b		69.	a
60.	e		70.	personal
61.	d		71.	precede
62.	a		72.	personnel
63.	c		73.	populous
64.	c		74.	proceed
65.	a		75.	populace

C.L.U.E. Checkpoint

76. The Council on Consumer Prices **has** taken a firm position. [*Council* is a collective noun; members of the Council seem unified.]

77. Neither Sofia nor Alysia **was** able to install a computer firewall. [Make the verb agree with the closer subject, *Alysia*.]

78. A revised list of customers' names and e-mail addresses **is** being sent today. [Make the verb agree with the true subject, *list*.]

79. Our president, along with the manager and three sales representatives, **is** flying to the meeting. [Make the verb agree with *president*.]

80. The tone and wording of each personnel message **are** important in creating goodwill. [*Tone* and *wording* are plural subjects.]

81. A group of players, coaches, and fans **is** booking a personal charter flight. [The subject is *group*, a singular noun.]

82. Each of the recently hired staff members **is** scheduled for a private performance review. [Make the verb agree with the singular subject, *each*.]

83. One of your duties, in addition to the tasks already outlined, **involves** budgeting department expenses. [The singular verb *involves* agrees with the singular subject *One*.]

84. The renovation and the landscaping, which cost over $200,000, **were** finished in June. [The subjects are *renovation* and *landscaping*.]

85. Legal experts say that the extent of the company's contract rights **is** murky. (The subject is *extent*.)

Super C.L.U.E. Review

86. An increase in our **company's** sales in the United States **has** prompted us to **assure** our stockholders that we plan to expand overseas.

87. Research and **development,** of **course, are** essential [delete period] **if** we plan to have new products available for global expansion.

88. Although we called several **bookstores,** neither of the **dictionaries is** available.

89. Either of the two applicants **is satisfactory; however,** our **Personnel Department** must check their references.

90. A set of guidelines to standardize input and output **has already** been submitted to our **Document Production Department.**

91. If stock prices **have sunk** to their lowest **point,** our broker will begin buying.

92. Something about these insurance claims **appears questionable; therefore,** I want the **whole** investigation reopened.

93. Anyone in the class action suit **is** eligible to make a **personal** claim.

94. Mr. Wilson asked a clerk to help him select a tie and shirt that **have complementary** colors.

95. Any one of the auditors **is** authorized to **proceed** with an **independent** investigation.

Career Application: Critical Thinking Questions

96. The audience for this data will be your boss. The information may become part of a final report that your boss submits to management to support his recommendation about lighting in the remodeled offices.

97. The data for computer workers in environments with indirect lighting would be most readable in a line chart. Line charts are especially good for showing changes in data over time.

98. Although the thought crosses your mind to emphasize all the data that support indirect lighting, you realize immediately that your boss is depending on you to present all the data you collect, whether it supports your own personal view or not. Moreover, you think that the facts would be most credible if they showed both positive and negative effects of indirect lighting. Presenting only one side of a picture (or what appears to be only one side) could suggest that you didn't do a thorough job of researching.

99. Indirect lighting seemed to cause a loss in productivity of 15 to 20 minutes per day. This information should be presented objectively, without emphasis or deemphasis.

100. Based on this information, you will probably recommend the use of indirect lighting. Most of the information indicates that workers in a controlled research study felt positive physical and mental effects as a result of indirect lighting.

101. Numbers of workers should be plotted vertically, perhaps in millions. Years from 1991 to 2005 should be plotted horizontally. The numbers should be rounded off to even millions or fractions thereof, such as .5 million, .75 million. For a half million, you would show a dot halfway up in the first box or increment.

Career Application

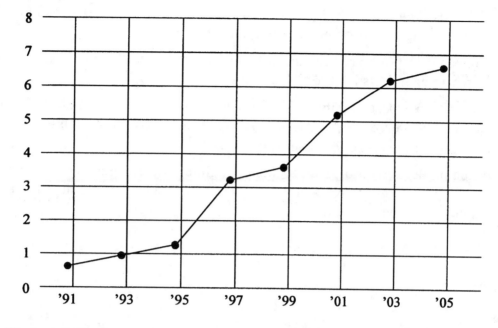

Computer Workers in Environments With Indirect Lighting, 1991 through 2005

Conclusions

Based on the research I have conducted, the following conclusions may be drawn about direct and indirect lighting for workers in computer environments:

1. Management and workers must think that indirect lighting is better than direct lighting, since the number of computer workers in indirect lighting environments has grown steadily from fewer than a half million workers to over 6.5 million in the past 14 years.

2. In a study of 200 computer workers conducted by Cornell University, indirect lighting had a positive effect on the performance, satisfaction, and visual health of participants.

3. Overall, 72 percent of the participants preferred indirect lighting to standard lighting, finding it more pleasant, more comfortable, and more likable.

4. Although workers in the study preferred indirect lighting, the lighting seemed to produce loss in production of 15 to 20 minutes per day. Apparently, indirect lighting causes workers to slow down or to make mistakes that reduce their overall productivity somewhat.

Recommendations

As a result of my research and analysis, I submit the following recommendations in regard to the installation of indirect lighting in computer environments:

1. The company, 21st Century Insurance, should install indirect lighting when it remodels offices where computers are used extensively.

2. Because we can expect slightly reduced productivity to accompany indirect lighting, I recommend that we treat this reduced productivity as a small price to pay for improving the health and happiness of our computer workers.

3. If reduced productivity as a result of indirect lighting seems significant, I recommend that we ask computer workers to search for ways to maintain or improve their productivity after indirect lighting is installed.

CHAPTER 13

Chapter Review

1. T
2. F   Cross-tabulation is a process that allows analysis of two or more variables.
3. F   The median represents the midpoint in a group of figures arranged from lowest to highest (or vice versa); the mode is the value that occurs most frequently.
4. T
5. F   Conclusions explain a problem; recommendations offer specific suggestions for solving the problem.
6. T
7. T
8. F   Investigative or informational reports deliver data for a specific situation without offering interpretation or recommendations.
9. F   The three typical analytical reports that answer business questions are justification/recommendation reports, feasibility reports, and yardstick reports.
10. T

Fill in the Blank

Interpreting and Organizing Data

11. answers
12. tables
13. mean
14. conclusions
15. commands
16. time
17. importance
18. transitions
19. ideas

Writing Reports

20. persuaded
21. management
22. customers
23. direct
24. conclusions
25. analytical
26. topic
27. internal
28. measures

Short Answer

29. Mean: 4   (The total, 32, divided by the total number of items, 8)
    Mode: 3   (The value most frequently represented)
    Median: 3   (The midpoint in the line of numbers)
    Range: 2 to 10

30. Tips for writing conclusions:
    a. Interpret and summarize the findings; tell what they mean.
    b. Relate the conclusions to the report problem.
    c. Limit the conclusions to the data presented; do not introduce new material.
    d. Number the conclusions and present them in parallel form.
    e. Be objective; avoid exaggerating or manipulating the data.
    f. Use consistent criteria in evaluating options.

31. Informational Reports
    I. Introduction/background
    II. Facts/findings
    III. Summary/conclusion

    Analytical Reports—*Direct* Pattern
    I. Introduction/problem
    II. Conclusion/recommendations
    III. Facts/findings
    IV. Discussion/analysis

    Analytical Reports—*Indirect* Pattern
    I. Introduction/problem
    II. Facts/findings
    III. Discussion/analysis
    IV. Conclusion/recommendations

32. Basic guidelines for creating effective headings:
    a. Use appropriate heading levels.
    b. Capitalize and underline carefully.
    c. Balance headings within levels.
    d. For short reports use first- or second-level headings.
    e. Include at least one heading per report page.
    f. Keep headings short but clear.

33. A progress report about the status of a company ride-sharing program might contain this information:
    a. A concise description of the purpose and nature of the ride-sharing program
    b. Background information, especially if the audience is unfamiliar with the program
    c. Description of all ride-sharing efforts thus far
    d. Explanation of current activities, including names of people, methods, and results thus far
    e. Description of any anticipated problems, along with possible solutions
    f. Discussion of future activities and date for completion of program, if an end date has been established.

34. Possible problem for a yardstick report: selection of new office printers. You might organize such a yardstick report as follows:
    a. Begin by describing the need for new printers.
    b. Explain the kinds of new printers available and what each could do.
    c. Decide what criteria are most important for your printers (speed, quality print, pricing, or service, for example).
    d. Discuss each printer choice in terms of the criteria established.
    e. Draw conclusions and recommend one printer.

Career Track Spelling

35. itinerary
36. affable
37. transferred
38. criterion
39. C

40. C
41. emphasize
42. existence
43. interrupt
44. miscellaneous

Career Track Vocabulary

45. e
46. d
47. c
48. f
49. b
50. a
51. b
52. c
53. a
54. c

55. a
56. b
57. b
58. b
59. plaintiff
60. prosecuted
61. precedents
62. persecuted
63. plaintive
64. precedence

C.L.U.E. Checkpoint

65. Although the manager and **I** are interested in this laptop, **its** price seems high.

66. The list of customers' names and addresses intended for her and **me** was delivered to Jeffrey and **him** by mistake.

67. Just between you and **me,** our C.P.A said that the company and **its** profits might be investigated.

68. All my luggage was found, but **yours** and **hers** are still missing.

69. Do you think it was **he** who sent the gift?

Super C.L.U.E. Review

70. At the last **department** meeting, the **manager** and **he** reminded all **newly hired employees** about the **importance** of submitting regular progress reports.

71. Her knowledge of computing and her genuine interest in people **are** what appealed to the recruiter and **me**. [The two subjects, *knowledge* and *interest,* require a plural verb, *are.*]

72. If anyone is **disappointed,** it will be **I; however,** I do not anticipate bad news. [Use the nominative pronoun *I* as a complement following the linking verb *be.*]

73. The body of the feasibility report and **its** footnotes are on **separate** pages.

74. Because we have no precedents for problems like **these,** Ms. Sheridan and **I** will seek **advice** from a management consultant.

75. All class members except Karen and **him** knew the assignment [omit comma] and were prepared with **their** reports when they were **due.**

76. Just between you and **me,** do you think it was **he** who complained?

77. If you will send the shipment to Tran or **me,** we will inspect **its** contents **thoroughly.** [Use a comma, not a semicolon, after the introductory clause.]

78. The itinerary for Jason and **him** included these **countries: Holland, France,** and **Germany.**

79. The use of concrete nouns and active verbs **is important if** you want to improve your writing. [No punctuation is necessary in joining the fragment to the sentence.]

Career Application: Critical Thinking Questions

80. The primary audience for Rick's report is his boss, John Zurawski. However, the report could possibly be distributed to other executives who are interested in the project. Rick would be wise to look beyond the immediate audience.

81. The tone of the report is informal, including many *I*'s and addressing the receiver by his first name. The word choice and punctuation are also casual (*lots of, tons of,* and overuse of exclamation marks). The tone could be improved by less dependence on *I.* In fact, Rick probably ought to check with his boss to learn how formal to be in both the progress and the final reports. Should his reports be written in first person (*I conducted research*) or third person (*Research was conducted* or *Research reveals that*)?

82. One reason the report is hard to read is its lack of headings. Moreover, the topic is broad and Rick was given little guidance. With many diverse items, a report is hard to organize. Yet Rick has already partially ordered his findings. But he has given his readers few cues to help them see that organization. Three cues that help readers are (a) introductions that preview what is to follow, (b) transitional words, and (c) headings. Graphic highlighting (lists and bulleted items) might also improve readability.

83. Progress reports might contain categories such as *Background, Work Completed, Work to Be Completed,* and *Anticipated Problems.* By using these functional heads, Rick could make the report much easier to read.

84. Rick forgets to indicate whether he is on schedule and when the final report will be completed.

Now prepare an outline to guide Rick in revising his progress report.

Chapter 13 - Outline Revision

Outline for Progress Report

I. Introduction
   A. Identify report specifically
   B. Describe purpose
   C. Preview how report is organized

II. Background
   A. Tell why report is necessary
   B. Describe methods for collecting data

III. Work completed
   A. Internal programs and recruitment
      1. Videotapes
      2. In-house seminars
      3. Intensive language and culture courses
      4. Emphasis on recruiting globally oriented young employees
   B. External programs
      1. Short- and long-term assignments abroad offered by six model companies
      2. Intensive programs at specialized schools

IV. Work to be completed
   A. Internal programs
      1. Evaluate training videos
      2. Interview consultant for in-house seminar
   B. External programs
      1. Evaluate literature from specialized schools
      2. Conduct telephone interviews with U.S. companies about their programs

V. Problems
   A. Not being able to reach busy executives for interviews
   B. Report will include only the data collected before deadline

VI. Completion
   A. Cutoff date for collection of data
   B. Date when final report will be submitted

CHAPTER 14

Chapter Review

1.	F	Proposals may be divided into two categories: solicited and unsolicited.
2.	T	
3.	T	
4.	F	An abstract is a brief summary of a proposal's highlights; a letter of transmittal describes how the writer learned about the problem or how the proposal will respond to it.
5.	T	
6.	F	Formal reports are similar to formal proposals in length, organization, and tone.
7.	F	Formal reports often have a degree of redundancy because they contain many parts that serve different purposes; it is quite common to have some of the same information in the letter of transmittal, the summary, and the introduction.
8.	T	
9.	F	The second phase of writing a report involves researching the data, organizing it into a logical presentation, and composing the first draft.
10.	F	When writing formal reports, generally avoid *I* and *we*.

Fill in the Blank

*Formal and
Informal Proposals*

11. proposal
12. request for proposal
13. staffing
14. credentials
15. contract
16. appendixes
17. online
18. mission
19. market

Formal Reports

20. investigation
21. tone
22. topic
23. scope
24. research findings
25. recommendations
26. bibliography
27. timetable
28. outline
29. formatting

Short Answer

30. Techniques for capturing the interest of the reader in the introduction to a proposal:
    a. Hint at extraordinary results with details to be revealed shortly.
    b. Promise low costs or speedy results.
    c. Mention a remarkable resource available exclusively to you.
    d. Identify a serious problem (worry item) and promise a solution.
    e. Specify a key issue or benefit that you believe is the heart of the proposal.

31. Your chief aim in a solicited proposal is to convince the reader that you understand the problem completely.

32. The budget is especially important because it represents a contract; you can't change its figures later.

33. Special components of formal proposals:
     a. *A copy of the RFP,* which may be included in the opening parts, primarily as a means of helping a large organization identify which of its RFPs is being addressed.
     b. *A letter of transmittal,* which addresses the person designated to receive the proposal or make the final decision, describes how the writer learned about the problem, or confirms that the proposal responds to the enclosed RFP.
     c. *An abstract or executive summary:* an abstract provides an overview of the proposal's highlights and is intended for a technical audience, while an executive summary reviews those highlights for a more general audience, usually managers.
     d. *A title page,* which usually includes the title of the proposal, name of client organization, RFP number or other announcement, date of submission, author's name, and/or the author's organization.
     e. *A table of contents,* which should include all headings and their beginning page numbers.
     f. *A list of figures,* which helps readers when proposals contain many tables or figures.
     g. *Appendixes,* which include ancillary material of interest to some readers.

34. Elements most commonly found in business plans:
     a. Letter of transmittal and/or executive summary with mission statement
     b. Table of contents
     c. Company description
     d. Product/service description
     e. Market analysis
     f. Operations and management
     g. Financial analysis
     h. Appendices

35. The executive summary of a formal report summarizes report findings, conclusions, and recommendations. The introduction covers the background, problem or purpose, significance, scope, and organization. The introduction may also include identification of the person authorizing the report, a literature review, sources and methods, and definitions of key terms.

36. A formal report should be proofread at least three times. Read once slowly for word meanings and content. Read a second time for spelling, punctuation, grammar, and other mechanical errors. Read a third time for formatting and consistency.

Career Track Spelling

37.	grammar	42.	mileage
38.	contingent	43.	C
39.	desirable	44.	committed
40.	feasible	45.	incredible
41.	opposite	46.	C

Career Track Vocabulary

47.	b	57.	c
48.	a	58.	a
49.	f	59.	c
50.	c	60.	a
51.	e	61.	stationery
52.	d	62.	principal
53.	b	63.	realty
54.	c	64.	principle
55.	b	65.	stationary
56.	a	66.	reality

C.L.U.E. Checkpoint 1

67. Please distribute the supplies to **whoever** ordered them. [*he/whoever ordered them. Whoever* functions as the subject of the verb *ordered*.]

68. Send all contributions to Mr. Rather or **me.**

69. **Whom** would you prefer to see elected president? [*Would you prefer to see him/whom elected president?*]

70. Our manager herself will give the award to **whomever** we recommend. [*We recommend him/whom.*]

71. The CEO and **I** plan to attend the morning session of the seminar.

C.L.U.E. Checkpoint 2

72. Every employee must be prepared to show **his or her** picture identification. [*Or,* Every employee must be prepared to show **a** picture identification. *Or,* All employees should be prepared to show **their** picture identifications.]

73. In creating a successful business plan, you must define your overall company goals, identify customer characteristics, and project potential sales. **These actions are** what most beginning entrepreneurs fail to do.

74. Connecticut provides tax credits, customized job training, and fast-track permitting. **These incentives explain** why many companies are moving there. [Replace the vague pronoun *which*.]

75. Our new business had cash-flow problems, partnership squabbles, and a leaky roof; however, we didn't let **these problems** get us down. [Replace the vague pronoun *it*.]

76. **People** who open new businesses are sure to have their own start-up problems. [Make the sentence plural. Or keep the sentence singular and omit *their own*.]

Super C.L.U.E. Review

77. You must send all **newly ordered** supplies to **me** or **whoever** submitted the purchase requisition.

78. Research and **development, of course, are essential if** we plan to expand into the following key markets: Pacific Rim **countries**, the European Community, and South America.

79. Exports from small **companies have increased,** but **these exports are** still **insufficient** to **affect** the balance of trade positively. [Note that *these exports* replaces the vague pronoun *it*.]

80. **Ours** is the only country with a sizable middle **class,** and **it is** hungry for consumer goods. [Note that *it* replaces *they* to agree with its antecedent, *class*.]

81. Cell Phone Depot promised **complimentary** cell phones to all new **customers,** but **this offer** attracted only **57** new accounts. [Replace the vague pronoun *it* with something more specific.]

82. Every new employee must apply to **receive a** permit to park in Lot 5-A. [The sentence could also be made plural: *All new employees must apply to receive their permits.* . . .]

83. Jeffrey and **I were** preparing a **four-**page **newsletter,** each page consisting of **three vertical columns.**

84. Poor ventilation, inadequate **lighting,** and hazardous working conditions were **cited** in the complaint. **These conditions** must be improved before negotiations may continue. [Replace the vague pronoun *This* with more specific words.]

85. We **recommend, therefore,** that a committee study our working conditions for a **three-**week period and submit a report of **its** findings.

86. The rules of business etiquette **are** based primarily on the **principles** of good **manners.** Everyone should exercise **these principles** in the workplace. [Note that the last clause may also be joined with a semicolon to the first clause.]

Career Application: Critical Thinking Questions

87. The audience for the list is Ramon, president of Prentice Consultants. However, the list will probably also be read by all the members of the proposal team.

88. Since no RFP has been submitted, this proposal is less formal than those with specific requirements. However, it makes little difference whether it is classified as formal or informal. What's important is submitting a persuasive, complete proposal.

89. These proposal parts have been mentioned:
    a.   Introduction
    b.   Background/problem
    c.   Proposal/plan/schedule
    d.   Staffing
    e.   Budget
    f.   Appendix

90. These proposal parts have not been included and perhaps should be:
    a.   Authorization section
    b.   Letter of transmittal
    c.   Abstract or executive summary
    You could ask Ramon whether these should be included. Ramon is out of the office, though, and you decide to include those sections on your list with the word "optional" after each and the name of a possible person to write that section.

91. Information about the new computer software should be included in the Staffing section.

92. The deadline should be established by Ramon or by consensus of the team. The deadline will then become part of the Budget section.

Career Application

1. Letter of transmittal—optional—Ramon?

2. Abstract or executive summary—optional—Ramon?

3. Introduction—Ramon
   Brief discussion of proposal and benefits of research

4. Background, problem—Ramon
   Description of problem and how this research can solve it

5. Proposal, plan, schedule—Sally
   Research methods (focus groups, questionnaires)
   Description of how the data will be gathered, tabulated, and interpreted
   Monitoring methods
   Timetable

6. Staffing—Amanda
   Credentials (résumés) of project leaders
   Staff description
   Discussion of new computer software

7. Budget—Tom
   Hourly or total cost figures
   Deadline for costs submitted

8. Authorization—optional—Ramon?
   Request for approval

9. Appendix—your name
   Samples of other customer satisfaction surveys
   List of satisfied customers

CHAPTER 15

Chapter Review

1. T
2. F   With an uninterested audience, speakers should be dynamic and entertaining. Being controlled works best with a neutral audience.
3. F   Often, speakers do well to put off writing the introduction until after they have organized the rest of their presentation and crystallized their ideas.
4. T
5. F   One of the easiest ways to lose an audience is to fill a talk with abstractions, generalities, and lists of dry facts.
6. T
7. F   Research shows that the use of visual aids actually shortens meetings.
8. F   Smart speakers present their key points on-screen regardless of the audience's size.
9. F   Unless the speaker is an outstanding and practiced performer, memorizing the entire presentation is not a good strategy.
10. T

Fill in the Blank

Preparing Oral Presentations and Building Rapport

11. adaptations
12. attention
13. credibility
14. problem
15. remember
16. signposts
17. appearance
18. audience
19. customize

Delivery Techniques, Cross-Cultural Presentations, and Other Media

20. notes
21. stage fright
22. static
23. discussion
24. end
25. three-point
26. storage
27. teleconferences

Short Answer

28. Four audience categories:
    a. Friendly
    b. Neutral
    c. Uninterested
    d. Hostile

29.   Questions that help speakers determine the organizational pattern, delivery style, and supporting material:
   a.   How will this topic appeal to this audience?
   b.   How can I relate this information to their needs?
   c.   How can I earn respect so that they accept my message?
   d.   What would be most effective in making my point? Facts? Statistics? Personal experiences? Expert opinion? Humor? Cartoons? Graphic illustration? Demonstrations? Case histories? Analogies?
   e.   What measures must I take to ensure that this audience remembers my main points?

30.   The ideas in an oral presentation can be organized by (a) time, (b) component, (c) importance, (d) criteria, or (e) conventional groupings.

31.   Verbal signposts are previews, summaries, and transitions that help listeners recognize the organization and main points in a presentation. They are important because the audience gets lost easily; they have no pages to flip back through.

32.   Kinds of visual aids and handouts and examples of each:
   a.   A computer and projection equipment could be used by an advertising executive to show a multimedia presentation for a new product.
   b.   An overhead projector might be used by an accountant to show transparencies of financial statements.
   c.   A flipchart might be used by an administrative assistant to show budget projections.
   d.   A whiteboard might be used to create interest or record comments during a question-and-answer period.
   e.   A video monitor could be used by a furniture designer to show a new line.
   f.   Handouts, which can include summaries, outlines, and additional material, can be used to enhance any presentation.

33.   To add interest to presentations, use multimedia elements such as sound, animation, video, photographs, charts, diagrams, and hyperlinks to Web sites. However, use only those elements that will enhance a message and engage an audience. Using too many elements will often annoy listeners or cause them to lose focus on the key points.

34.   Tips for preparing and using electronic presentation slides:
   a.   Keep all visuals simple; spotlight major points only.
   b.   Use the same font size and style for similar headings.
   c.   Apply the Rule of Seven: No more than seven words on a line, seven total lines, and 7 x 7 or 49 total words.
   d.   Be sure that everyone in the audience can see the slides.
   e.   Show a slide, allow the audience to read it, then paraphrase it. Do not read from a slide.
   f.   Rehearse by practicing talking to the audience, not to the slides.
   g.   Bring backup transparencies in case of equipment failure.

Career Track Spelling

35.	conjecture	40.	succeed
36.	consistent	41.	questionnaire
37.	complacent	42.	C
38.	surprised, grateful	43.	excellent
39.	valuable	44.	undoubtedly

Career Track Vocabulary

45.	f	56.	a
46.	d	57.	c
47.	e	58.	b
48.	c	59.	too
49.	a	60.	to
50.	b	61.	there
51.	b	62.	their, than
52.	a	63.	then
53.	c	64.	two
54.	b	65.	they're
55.	c		

C.L.U.E. Checkpoint

66. Our **recently hired** technician performed a **point-by-point** analysis of our site. [Don't hyphenate *recently hired*.]

67. Only the **four-year-old** printer was retained, and it will be inspected year by year. [Don't be tempted to hyphenate *year by year*. Notice that no noun follows it; therefore, it's not a compound modifier.]

68. Please don't take this comment **personally**.

69. We moved into the newly remodeled offices over the **three-day weekend**.

70. Ron felt that he had completed the **two-hour** aptitude test **satisfactorily**.

Super C.L.U.E. Review

71. **Were** any of the **supervisors** absent on the **Monday** following the **four-day weekend**?

72. **They're** going to visit **their** relatives in **Toledo, Ohio,** following **their coast-to-coast** trip.

73. The three *C*'s of credit **are** the following: character, **capacity,** and **capital**.

74. All **branches** except the Peachtree Plaza **office are** now using **state-of-the-art** equipment.

75. After you have checked the matter **further,** please report to the CEO and **me.**

76. Laura thought she had done **well** during the employment **interview,** but she heard nothing.

77. Some trucks **exceeded** the **5,000-pound** weight **limit;** others were under it.

78. To attract people to our convention **exhibit,** we rented a popcorn machine and hired a magician. **These attractions were** very successful. [Replace the vague pronoun *This* with specific ideas.]

79. Each of the **beautifully printed** art books **has** been priced at **$150.**

80. James Roosevelt said that his **father** gave him this **advice** on making **speeches:** "Be sincere, be **brief,** and be **seated."**

Career Application: Critical Thinking Questions

81. Kevin should know how many people will be in his audience, as well as their ages, gender, knowledge of the topic, experience, and perhaps educational levels. He must know this kind of information to be able to choose appropriate words and examples. For instance, his present talk has some jargon (*psi, dressed, cheaters,* and *bleed the hose*). Will his listeners know what he means? He could learn more about his listeners by checking their employment applications in Human Resources. He could also talk with other employees about what the audience will be like. He might also ask how former groups of new employees received this kind of talk.

82. No, Kevin's first two sections do not follow standard outlining format. However, they could easily be converted into the Roman numeral format, with main points identified by I and II.

83. Actually, his two sections are well organized. He has grouped major ideas into two headings, and items are appropriately subdivided. His wording, though, is inconsistent. Good outlines use parallel phrasing. Some of his items are commands, while others are statements in either active or passive voice. Probably the best wording uses commands. Each statement should begin with a verb ("Use tools only for their designed purposes; operate power tools only if you are trained and authorized to do so.")

84. Yes, Kevin needs a good introduction. It should gain the attention of the audience, try to get them involved, and establish his credibility. Why or how is he an expert on this topic? He also needs to preview his main points and lay the foundation for his primary goal: convincing workers that safety begins with the way they act.

85.   Kevin's talk would be much improved with visual aids. He could demonstrate many of the techniques he's discussing and show tools. He could show pictures of sloping roofs and other dangerous places requiring safety belts. He should also demonstrate how to wear a safety belt. Kevin might use a flipchart, an overhead projector, or PowerPoint slides to summarize his key safety techniques.

86.   To cover flammable and corrosive liquids, Kevin should probably briefly discuss these topics and then distribute literature about them after his talk.

87.   Good speakers move gracefully from one major topic to another with transitions, such as "Now that we've learned about safety techniques in using hand and portable power tools, I'd like to talk with you next about other kinds of equipment. First, I have some general suggestions, and then I'll speak specifically about safety belts, welding equipment, and compressed air."

88.   Kevin's talk has many general references, and these references are natural in an outline. You might encourage him to flesh out the references with specific examples. For example, he should be prepared to give several examples of "cheaters" used to force tools beyond their capacity.

89.   The conclusion should summarize the main points and provide a final focus. That focus, of course, is convincing workers that their actions are critical to safety on the job. Kevin should also encourage questions.

Career Application

Title: Using Tools and Equipment Safely

Purpose: To convince new construction workers that safety begins with them.

    I.   **Introduction**
        A.   Gain attention of audience.
        B.   Get audience involved.
        C.   Establish your credibility.
        D.   Preview the main points.

TRANSITION

    II.   **Tools**
        A.   Hand tools
            1.   Use every tool for its designed purpose only.
            2.   Keep hand tools in peak condition: sharp, clean, oiled, and dressed.
            3.   Don't use "cheaters" to force tools beyond their capacity.
            4.   Don't abuse tools, such as using a wrench as a pry bar.
        B.   Portable power tools
            1.   Don't operate unless you are trained and authorized to do so.
            2.   Use proper eye protection.
            3.   Keep all moving parts directed away from your body.
            4.   Never touch a part unless its power source is disconnected.

TRANSITION

III. Equipment

    A.   General suggestions

        1.   Inspect all equipment before using.

        2.   Know the limitations of the equipment you use; do not exceed them.

        3.   Do not interchange equipment with other contractors without permission.

    B.   Safety belts/harnesses

        1.   Wear belts when working on sloping roofs, flat roofs without handrails, any suspended platform or stage, any scaffold, ladders near edge of roofs, and all elevated work. [All the examples here could be lettered and listed vertically.]

        2.   Wear belts correctly. (Demonstrate.)

    C.   Welding and burning. Contact our supervisor before performing these tasks.

    D.   Compressed air

        1.   Check hoses and couplings daily before use.

        2.   Never crimp, couple, or uncouple a pressurized hose. Shut off valve and bleed down the hose.

        3.   Do not allow pressure to exceed 30 psi when cleaning workbenches and machinery.

        4.   Keep hoses off the ground or floor wherever they interfere with walkways, roads, and so forth.

TRANSITION

IV. Conclusion

    A.   Summarize the main points.

    B.   Provide a final focus.

    C.   Encourage questions.

CHAPTER 16

Chapter Review

1.	F	The employment process begins with introspection.
2.	T	
3.	F	The goal of a persuasive résumé is getting an interview.
4.	F	Résumés vary according to the situation; the most effective one is the one that presents an applicant's qualifications in the most persuasive manner.
5.	F	Résumés do have standard parts, but applicants should arrange these parts to most effectively present their qualifications.
6.	T	
7.	F	When preparing an inline résumé for e-mailing, include it in the body of an e-mail as plain text.
8.	F	The cover letter, while often overlooked, may be critical to the job search process.
9.	T	
10.	F	Don't be afraid to offer your hand first.

Fill in the Blank

Writing a Résumé

11. employment
12. qualifications
13. 12–15
14. networking
15. functional
16. objective
17. proficiencies
18. computer
19. graphic

Writing Letters of Application and Other Employment Messages

20. introduce
21. direct
22. source
23. qualifications
24. needs
25. contact
26. traditional
27. follow-up
28. success

Short Answer

29. Questions that will help you find a satisfying field:
    a. Do I enjoy working with people, data, or things?
    b. How important is it to be my own boss?
    c. How important are salary, benefits, technology support, and job stability?
    d. How important are working environment, colleagues, and job stimulation?
    e. Would I rather work for a large or a small company?
    f. Must I work in a specific city, geographical area, or climate?
    g. Am I looking for security, travel opportunities, money, power, or prestige?
    h. How would I describe the perfect job, boss, and coworkers?

30. Activities to get you started in your job search:
    a. Visit your school or campus career center.
    b. Search the Web.
    c. Use your library to look up government publications.
    d. Take a summer job, internship, or part-time position in your field.
    e. Contact companies in which you're interested, even if no opening exists.
    f. Sign up for campus interviews with company representatives.
    g. Ask for advice from your professors.
    h. Interview someone in your field.
    i. Monitor the classified ads.
    j. Join professional organizations in your field.

31. Traditional job search techniques include checking classified ads in newspapers, looking at announcements in publications of professional organizations, and contacting companies in which you are interested. You should also sign up for campus interviews, ask for advice from professors, and, especially, develop your own network of contacts. Electronic job search techniques include using your computer to visit many of the special Web sites that list jobs. You can learn a great deal about the job market from these sites.

32. Advantages of chronological résumés:
    a. Recruiters expect and favor them.
    b. They quickly reveal steady career growth, if you have such growth.
    c. They're easier to write than functional résumés.

33. The standard parts of a résumé are (1) the main heading, (2) career objective, (3) education, (4) work experience or employment history, (5) capabilities and skills, (6) awards, honors, and activities, (7) personal data, and (8) references. When building a résumé, arrange these parts strategically, always beginning with the main heading. Include no more than six parts.

34. Tips for maximizing the scannability of your résumé:
    a. Focus on specific keywords.
    b. Incorporate words from the advertisement or job description.
    c. Use typical headings.
    d. Use accurate names.
    e. Be careful of abbreviation.
    f. Describe interpersonal traits and attitudes.
    g. Use more than one page if necessary.
    h. Consider adding a keyword summary.

35. An *e-portfolio* is a collection of digitized materials that provides viewers with a snapshot of a candidate's performance, talents, and accomplishments. Generally presented on the Web, where they are available 24/7, e-portfolios have many advantages, such as being able to be viewed by potential employers whenever convenient and by many individuals in an organization simultaneously. More important, they offer an opportunity to show off talents, skills, and examples of a candidate's work.

36. Three strategies for presenting information in the body of a cover letter are (1) describe what you can do for the reader, (2) highlight your strengths, and (3) refer to your résumé.

Career Track Spelling

37. luxury
38. efficient
39. automatically
40. C
41. independent

42. circumspect
43. immediate, column
44. facsimile
45. representative
46. separate

Career Track Vocabulary

47. b
48. d
49. f
50. e
51. c
52. a
53. c
54. b
55. a
56. b

57. a
58. c
59. b
60. c
61. whether
62. weather
63. vary
64. very
65. waiver
66. waver

Super C.L.U.E. Review 1

67. Nokia provides **overnight** or **two-day** delivery on **its cell phones** for only **$12.50,** but it won't ship online orders to P.O. boxes.

68. City officials begged the two **companies' boards** of directors not to **desert their locations** and not to abandon local employees.

69. **China,** the **world's fastest-growing economy,** will be snapping up personal computers at a **30 percent** rate by **2010.** [Note the lack of comma in *2010.*]

70. The registration of **employees'** cars for parking permits had **gone smoothly** until we **ran** out of stickers.

71. If we are to remain **friends,** this **personal** information must be kept strictly between you and **me.**

72. The quality of e-mail messages, memos, and **reports** in this organization **needs** to be improved.

73. Although **it's** usually difficult to **elicit contributions,** I think you will find this charity drive **incredibly** fruitful.

74. Jeff **Orenstein,** who was recently appointed **marketing manager, submitted six** different suggestions for boosting sales. **Everyone** hopes **that his suggestions** will turn around this **company's** sales decline. [The best way to remedy the vague pronoun *which* is to start a new sentence without a pronoun.]

75. Stored on open shelves in **Room** 15 **are** office supplies and at least **seven** reams of old **stationery**.

76. The additional premium you were **charged,** which amounted to **$55.40,** was issued because of **your** recent accident.

Super C.L.U.E. Review 2

77. Several **copies** of the **sales** report **were** sent to the **manager** and **me immediately** after we requested it.

78. Any letter sent to a **customer** [delete comma] must have a professional **appearance; otherwise, its** message may be disregarded.

79. Here **is** a group of participating **manufacturers** [omit comma] **whom** you may wish to contact regarding **their** products.

80. As soon as the merger is **completed,** we will inform the entire **staff;** until **then, it's** business as usual.

81. The entire team of **35** managers **was** willing to **proceed** with the proposal for **Asian** expansion.

82. The **Miami River** is such a narrow and congested waterway [delete comma] that tugboat captains joke about needing **Vaseline** to slip freighters through.

83. **Companies** such as Amway and Avon [delete comma] discovered that **their** unique **door-to-door** selling method was successful in **Japan** and other **Asian countries.**

84. Locating **foreign** markets and developing **them require** aggressive **efforts; however,** many companies **don't** know where to begin.

85. Some companies sell better at home **than** abroad [omit semicolon] because they lack experience.

86. Smart organizations can boost profits almost **100** percent by retaining just 5 **percent** more of **their** current customers.

Career Application: Critical Thinking Questions

87. Yes, more information would be helpful. Specifically, you need some of the following data: age and gender makeup of the audience, approximate size of the audience, major areas of study, and employment goals. You could obtain most of this information by speaking to the program chair for the campus organization.

88. Showing real résumés presents ethical and perhaps legal complications. These résumés have been submitted in confidence; their writers might charge invasion of privacy if their résumés were used as examples. However, by removing the names and addresses, you could eliminate this barrier. It would still be a good idea, though, to discuss your concerns with your supervisor. [When you do this, she thinks it's a good idea to use the real résumés, *if* the identity of the writer can be totally concealed.]

89. If you distribute these résumés as handouts, you will lose the audience. As they study the résumés, you will no longer have their attention. A better plan is to enlarge the résumés and show them as transparencies. If you do use them as handouts, pass them out after you finish.

90. The audience will be less bewildered if you talk about one résumé first and then talk about the other. Switching back and forth between them would be confusing and frustrating for the audience.

91. Weaknesses of résumé No. 1:
    a. Fails to specify a specific career objective. Either target the objective for a specific job or omit it.
    b. Uses personal pronoun *I*. Rephrase to avoid.
    c. Lists college courses. Makes boring reading.
    d. Fails to keep items in Experience section consistent.
    e. Makes Experience section difficult to read. Skills do not stand out. Fails to give details on what he can do for future employer.
    f. Must reorganize and rename Activities and Other section.
    g. Fails to give enough details. No effort to sell or promote his talents.
    h. Makes résumé look skimpy. Seems that the candidate has little to offer, but in reality, he has considerable experience. But it is poorly described and presented.

92. Strengths of résumé No. 2:
    a. Targets specific job in objective. Reader becomes interested immediately.
    b. Develops each item in Experience section consistently. Promotes readability and comprehension by underscoring job titles and dates of employment.
    c. Uses action words to highlight transferable skills achieved.
    d. Describes specific skills from each job that might be transferable to the position for which he is applying.
    e. Organizes Education section for instant recognition of important facts.
    f. Emphasizes computer skills with special section.
    g. Overall, this résumé sells the candidate.
    h. Fills only one page!

Although this résumé is good, it's not perfect. Some of the writer's statements sound a little inflated, such as the description of his duties as a courier.

Career Application

Possible Conclusions to Be Drawn From Analysis of Two Résumés

1. Résumés of recent graduates should fill one page and be arranged attractively.

2. Consistency in headings and graphic highlighting—bullets, underlines, indenting, capital letters, white space—will enhance readability and comprehension.

3. Some résumé formats look more professional than others. Look at many model résumés. Experiment with different designs.

4. First-person pronouns are not used. Use concise wording that avoids "I."

5. The best résumés sell candidates' talents; they don't just list job duties. Use action verbs in specific statements to describe achievements.

6. Recruiters are most interested in seeing job skills that relate to the jobs they have to fill. Candidates should emphasize the skills and traits that will be useful for a targeted job.